ABORIGINES AND COLONISTS

Aborigines and Colonists

ABORIGINES AND COLONIAL SOCIETY IN
NEW SOUTH WALES IN THE 1830s AND 1840s

R. H. W. REECE

SYDNEY UNIVERSITY PRESS

SYDNEY UNIVERSITY PRESS
Press Building, University of Sydney

UNITED KINGDOM, EUROPE, MIDDLE EAST, AFRICA, CARIBBEAN
Prentice/Hall International, International Book Distributors Ltd
Hemel Hempstead, England

NORTH AND SOUTH AMERICA
International Scholarly Book Services, Inc., Portland, Oregon

To my parents and grandparents
who believed in me

First published 1974
© R. H. W. Reece 1974
Library of Congress Catalog Card Number 75-145646
National Library of Australia card number and
ISBN 0 424 06350 6

This book is supported by money from
THE ELEANOR SOPHIA WOOD BEQUEST

Printed in Australia by John Sands Pty Ltd, Artarmon, N.S.W.

CONTENTS

LIST OF ILLUSTRATIONS   vi

PREFACE   vii

ABBREVIATIONS   ix

Introduction   1

1   Blacks and Whites   4
2   Christianization and Civilization   62
3   The Background of Official Policy   104
4   The Myall Creek Trials   140
5   Gipps and the Aborigines   175

APPENDIXES

I   Conflicts Between Aborigines and Whites 1832-45   217
II   Trials of All Aborigines 1824-43   225
III   Statistics Showing Aboriginal Depopulation 1835-7   229
IV   Government Expenditure on Aborigines 1821-42   230

SELECT BIBLIOGRAPHY   232

INDEX   247

ILLUSTRATIONS

PLATES

between pages 110 *and* 111

I	'Natives of N. S. Wales. As seen in the Streets of Sydney'
II	'Annual Meeting of the Native Tribes at Parramatta, N.S.W.'
III	'A Native Family of N. S. Wales Sitting down on an English Settler's Farm'
IV	'A Native Camp of Australian Savages near Port Stevens, N.S.W.'
V	'Bushman's Hut'
VI	Aborigines attacking a shepherd's hut
VII	'Danger's Station, Mayal Creek'
VIII	'Natives spearing the overlanders' cattle. 1846'
IX	'Mrs. Fraser and the crew of the *Stirling Castle* assaulted by aborigines'
X	'Mrs. Frazer's Escape From The Savages'
XI	John Hubert Plunkett
XII	William Westbrooke Burton
XIII	Henry Dangar
XIV	Sir George Gipps
XV	'Distribution of flour at Moorunde'
XVI	'Hawker at an Aboriginal Station, Australia'
XVII	'45 Natives driven to Police Court by the Police for trespassing 1845'
XVIII	Native police, Queensland

FIGURES

1	The Nineteen Counties and Squatting Districts of New South Wales based on an official map of 1844	18
2	Massacres 1837-8 in the Liverpool Plains District	22

PREFACE

My interest in the history of Aboriginal-white relations was first aroused when looking through bundles of Native Police records in Brisbane's Oxley Library. This led me to examine the origins of that particular solution to the 'Aboriginal problem' and in turn the events of the 1830s and 1840s when the Colonial Office's concern for the Aborigines coincided with the worst racial clashes in the history of New South Wales.

My basic concern has been with the controversy which these events produced—a controversy which I believe was the most important and revealing discussion about the Aborigines during the entire century. This book is an account of the 'Aboriginal problem' as it really was and as it was seen by philanthropists, squatters, and colonial administrators. It is not intended as a history of official policy towards the Aborigines in the 1830s and 1840s, nor as an exhaustive description of Aboriginal-white relations during the period.

Although the significance of the Myall Creek massacre should not be underestimated, I have attempted to place it within the context of racial conflicts accompanying settlement of the Liverpool Plains and of Gipps' insistence on the enforcement of law in the squatting districts. Consequently the massacre and the trials are dealt with separately.

Since they have been arranged in thematic rather than chronological sequence, it will be useful to say something about the chapters. A description of the nature of contact between Aborigines and whites and the consequent problems (Chapter 1) is followed by an examination of various philanthropic schemes, the arguments of those who believed that all such efforts were a waste of time and the body of popular beliefs about the Aborigines (Chapter 2). An outline of official policy towards the Aborigines from first settlement (Chapter 3) serves as background for a description of the Myall Creek trials and the controversy which they aroused (Chapter 4) and the final chapter deals with Gipps' efforts to provide a legal solution to the 'Aboriginal problem' (Chapter 5).

My approach to the subject has naturally been influenced by the fact that all the documentary material available is from white sources and the book consequently centres on white perceptions of the Aborigines and the problems which culture contact produced. I wish that it had been possible to say more about the Aborigines' perceptions of the whites but this must be someone else's task.

The book is based on a Master's thesis submitted to the University of Queensland in January 1969 and I would like to take this opportunity to thank Professors G. G. Greenwood and R. G. Neale and Mr Roger Joyce for their assistance during my time in Brisbane. Dr Malcolm Calley and Dr Romola McSwain of the University of Queensland gave me encouragement, as did Dr Niel Gunson of the Australian National University. The staff of the Mitchell Library and the Archives Office of New South Wales were most helpful and I owe a special debt to Mr Len Payne of Bingara who has assiduously collected oral traditions of the Myall Creek and other massacres and the early settlement of the Liverpool Plains. Dr Peter Corris and Mr D. W. A. Baker of the Australian National University read the manuscript which was typed in the Department of Pacific and South-East Asian History, ANU, by Mrs Rosamund Walsh and by Mrs Candy Stancliffe of Sydney University Press.

The maps were prepared in the Department of Human Geography at the Australian National University and the plates, from the Rex Nan Kivell Collection of the National Library of Australia, the National Library's own collection and from the Mitchell Library, Sydney, are reproduced by permission.

Australian National University   R. H. W. REECE
December 1973

ABBREVIATIONS

ADB	*Australian Dictionary of Biography*
BP	Miscellaneous papers relating to the Aborigines 1796-1839, collected by Judge W. W. Burton, Archives Office of New South Wales
BT, Miss	Bonwick Transcripts from Documents in London, Missionary Section, Mitchell Library
CO	Microfilm of Colonial Office Records in the Public Record Office, London
CSIL	New South Wales Colonial Secretary's Correspondence: In-Letters, Archives Office of New South Wales
DNB	*Dictionary of National Biography*
GD	New South Wales Governors' Despatches and Replies, Mitchell Library
GG	*New South Wales Government Gazette*
GL Corr	Gipps-La Trobe Correspondence, La Trobe Library
HRA	*Historical Records of Australia*, Series I
JRAHS	*Journal of the Royal Australian Historical Society*
ML	Mitchell Library, Sydney
NSWA	Archives Office of New South Wales
PD	British House of Commons Debates
PP	British House of Commons Sessional Papers
V&P	New South Wales Legislative Council *Votes and Proceedings*

Not so very long ago, the earth numbered two thousand million inhabitants: five hundred million men, and one thousand five hundred million natives.

JEAN-PAUL SARTRE

Introduction

Overseas expansion commencing in the late fifteenth century brought Europeans into contact with the indigenous peoples of the Americas, Africa, India, Southeast Asia, Australia, New Zealand and the Pacific Islands. In each case, contact developed into what can be described as a 'colonial situation', characterized by the invaders' more or less successful subjugation of the indigenous peoples and their culture. This usually involved physical conflict, dispossession, political subjection and sometimes even a form of enslavement.

Once the invaders had established themselves, there were still linguistic difficulties, problems of administration and justice, and lingering resistance of different kinds. At some stage the invaders were also faced with perhaps the most difficult problem of all—the 'civilizing' and 'christianizing' of the indigenous people and the moral justification of colonization itself.

The British settlement of New South Wales[1] created a colonial situation in some ways different from those brought about in North America, India, South Africa and New Zealand. Its characteristics could be summarized as follows:

1. this was one of the few instances of Europeans in contact with a hunting and food-gathering people possessing a Stone-age technology;
2. the Aborigines[2] did not have anything which was valued by the whites in trade, nor were they of any significance as a labour force as long as the convict system continued;

---

[1] Throughout this work, 'New South Wales' will be taken to refer to the area proclaimed a Crown possession by Governor Sir Richard Bourke in 1835, including what is now Victoria and southern Queensland; 'Port Phillip District' refers specifically to what is now Victoria. This account does not deal with the military settlement established at Port Essington in 1838.
[2] Until the Aborigines of Australia find another name for themselves, they will remain 'Aborigines' or, for some authors, 'aborigines'. I have preferred the

3. the superiority of the invaders' arms and organization and the Aborigines' small population and lack of political unity meant that such resistance as there was to white settlement took the form of 'guerilla' activity rather than open confrontation;
4. there were no official treaties or agreements with the Aborigines and no recognition that they possessed any rights to the land which they regarded as theirs from time immemorial;
5. with the loss of their land and their appendage to white society, the Aborigines' social system quickly disintegrated and the rapid rate of population decline gave rise to a common belief that they were doomed to extinction.

These features were largely due to the unique nature of Aboriginal culture which had developed during more than 30,000 years of isolation from the rest of the human race. Their hunting and food-gathering economy involved the use of large areas of land and a nomadic life which did not permit the accumulation of material goods or the emergence of political organization. However, their religion and totem system meant a strong spiritual identification with tribal territory.

The white invaders brought with them the technology of the Industrial Revolution and a social ethic which identified personal and national achievement with the accumulation of material possessions. This was a culture with an unquestioning faith in its superiority and in its civilizing role. The whites expected Aborigines to recognize this superiority and adopt an appropriately subordinate and imitative role.

Although contact between Aborigines and whites was limited during the first three decades of settlement, the discovery of vast grasslands of the interior eminently suitable for grazing cattle and

---

former usage. There is some weight in the argument put forward by Marie Reay in *Aborigines Now: New Perspective in the Study of Aboriginal Communities* (Sydney 1964, pp. 167-8) that 'aborigines' is a term of general applicability to indigenous peoples and that the addition of a capital 'A' is 'parochial'. However, 'Aborigines' or 'Aboriginals' is becoming increasingly common in academic journals and the press where it is accepted as an abbreviation for 'Australian Aborigines'. It is also in line with the capitalizing of 'Maoris', 'Indians', or 'Amerindians' and 'Papuans' and is accepted by the Aborigines themselves. 'Aborigines' was also the official usage in Britain and N.S.W. during the period of this study. 'Blackfellows' and 'whitefellows' were used by Aborigines and whites in contemporary pidgin but are disappearing from common usage. I have used 'whites' in preference to 'Europeans' since the former term is the less awkward and ambiguous of the two.

sheep led to one of the most rapid advances of any colonial frontier. Coinciding with this movement and the bitter racial clashes which it brought about was the British government's first serious interest in the welfare of the Aborigines.

Racial conflicts arose primarily from the rapid expropriation of the Aborigines' land—a process which had been going on steadily since first settlement. In this the white settlers had been assisted by soldiers and police and there was little reason for anyone to think that killing Aborigines was a crime, especially when it was done to protect sheep and cattle, and settlers' lives.

The interests of the squatters and the new policy towards the Aborigines were most clearly contrasted in the controversy surrounding the trial and execution in 1838 of seven white stockmen for the massacre of twenty-eight or more Aborigines in the Liverpool Plains district. At this unpropitious time the British government established an Aboriginal Protectorate in the Port Phillip District.

The 'Aboriginal problem' became one of the burning issues of Governor Sir George Gipps' administration, although there were widely varying notions of what the problem was. British and colonial philanthropists and the squatters of New South Wales possessed radically different viewpoints which were sharply contrasted when Gipps attempted to carry out the wishes of a Colonial Office whose intentions were humane but whose knowledge of the actual situation in the colony was limited.

CHAPTER ONE

Blacks and Whites

To understand race conflict we need fundamentally to understand *conflict* and not *race*.

RUTH BENEDICT 1943

In its beginnings, colonization is but an enterprise of personal, one-sided and selfish interest, something that the stronger imposes on the weaker. Such are the facts of history.

ALBERT SARRAULT 1923

A pattern of contact has been repeated monotonously but nonetheless tragically in every part of Australia where white settlers have taken the Aborigines' land. Each time whites have encroached on traditional tribal territory, Aborigines have been faced with three alternatives: to resist the newcomers by whatever means found to be most successful; to abandon their territory to the whites and retreat to another part of the country, sometimes trespassing on another tribe's territory; or to accept an economically dependent and socially subservient position wherever they were allowed by the whites to remain. It is difficult to say how often they resorted to the second alternative, although the bloody inter-tribal warfare noted by white observers during the period of this study may indicate that it was very common. Wherever the Aborigines offered resistance, they usually tried to hit the newcomer at his weakest point—to drive off and destroy his sheep and cattle, to burn his huts, destroy his supplies and even kill his horses and servants. These guerilla methods were most successful where the nature of the terrain made it easy for the Aborigines to avoid reprisals and in some areas they managed to halt pastoral expansion, although the superior arms and mobility of the whites eventually prevailed. The remnants of tribes 'dispersed' by punitive expeditions eventually came into the stations formed on their tribal territory to seek an alternative source of livelihood now that sheep and cattle were replacing native game and destroying native vegetation and water-holes.

During the 1830s and 1840s the white population of New South Wales encountered the Aborigines in three significantly different situations: in Sydney, Melbourne and the larger towns where they appeared as wretched, degenerate parasites; in the older and more closely settled districts of the Nineteen Counties where they were loosely attached to sheep and cattle stations; and in the squatting districts where pastoral expansion resulted in fierce conflicts between 1837 and 1844.

THE TOWNS

Sydney

By 1845 a combination of violence, alcohol and disease had extinguished the original Sydney tribe[1] and reduced the Botany Bay tribe to one man and three women.[2] The fifty or so Aborigines living at Botany heads, the biggest camp in the Sydney area, comprised the remnants of the tribes of the Sydney district, as well as Aborigines from various parts of the colony. Seventeen years earlier, the average size of the tribes in the Sydney area had been estimated at less than thirty and before Governor Sir Richard Bourke's abolition of the annual Parramatta 'feast' in 1835,[3] attendance had dwindled from 300 in December 1821 to 160 in 1827. According to Dr Roger Oldfield in 1828, this was 'most probably as many as there

---

[1] Since contemporaries had different ideas as to what constituted a 'tribe', this description was often inaccurate. However, the task of establishing the different tribal groups in eastern Australia during early contact is beyond the scope of this study. I have retained contemporary usage in the hope that one day an historically-minded anthropologist will clear up the confusion.

[2] Evidence of the Aborigine 'Mahroot' in the 1845 'Report from the Select Committee on the Condition of the Aborigines', *V&P*, 1845, p. 944. Mahroot died in 1849.

[3] In December 1814 Governor Lachlan Macquarie invited the Aborigines of the colony to a meeting in the Parramatta market place, where, after distributing food, drink, tobacco and clothing, he told them of his plans for their Christianization and civilization. For a history of the 'feast' or 'congress' until its abolition by Sir Richard Bourke in 1835, see R. H. W. Reece, 'Feasts and Blankets: The History of Some Early Attempts to Establish Relations with the Aborigines of New South Wales, 1814-1846', *Archaeology and Physical Anthropology in Oceania*, II, No. 3, October 1967, pp. 190-206.

are, on this side of the mountains, between Broken Bay and the Five Islands'.[4]

Those who spent most of their time in or near the town of Sydney gained a subsistence from begging, carrying messages and small parcels, or from the occasional sale of fish and oysters. Barron Field, Chief Justice of New South Wales, described them in 1825 as 'not common beggars' but 'the Will Wimbles of the colony; the carriers of news and fish; the gossips of the town; the loungers on the quay'.[5] They were not regularly employed, even the pilot boat being manned by Maoris, but some of the Botany Bay Aborigines shipped on whaling voyages. Generally, they held physical labour in high disdain, perfecting begging to such a degree that they would 'even prescribe the actual sum they expect to receive which is allways proportioned to the appearence or their knowledge of the person solicited'.[6] In his 'Walk through Sydney in 1828' Oldfield described an encounter with a 'troop of blacks' marching to the music of a military band:

Bungaree[7] is at their head, with his military cocked hat on, tipped with invariable politeness to every gentleman—Good morning, Sir, how are you? 'Quite well Bungaree, thank you'. Can you lend me one dump,[8] Sir?—Master I tay Sir, you know me? have you got any coppers? 'What's your name?' Dismal, Sir. I come from the Coal Ribber you know. 'Aye, Aye, Sydney's a finer place than Newcastle?' O yes Sir, finer, murry [very] finer, Tausend houses, murry tausend houses. Have you seben-pence hapenny Sir? lend me one dump—

---

4 *The South-Asian Register*, No. 2, January 1828, p. 105.
5 'Narrative of a Voyage to New South Wales' in Barron Field (ed.), *Geographical Memoirs on New South Wales*, London 1825, p. 435.
6 J. Dunlop, 'Incomplete account of the psychology and some of the customs of the aborigines of N.S.W.', ML, MS. Document 468, n.p.
7 'King' Bungaree, as he was also styled, was the best known Aborigine in Sydney and possibly the colony until his death in 1830. Originally from the Broken Bay tribe, he picked up English quickly and accompanied Matthew Flinders and P. P. King on their voyages, making himself useful during contacts with strange tribes. Settled in Sydney with the remnants of his own people, he became a celebrated mimic of prominent personalities and was always easily recognizable in the cocked hat and military uniform given to him by various governors. In 1815 Governor Lachlan Macquarie made a vain attempt to settle Bungaree and his people on a farm at George's Head, at the same time installing him as 'Bungaree: King of the Blacks'. Macquarie and his successors became reconciled to Bungaree as one of the institutions of Sydney town. *Sydney Gazette*, 27 November 1830; *ADB*, Vol. I, p. 177.
8 Coin punched from the centre of a Spanish dollar and worth 1s. 3d.

coppers master—buy a loaf, you know—look at my belly—murry hungry Sir.[9]

Another anecdote related by the surgeon Peter Cunningham described the 'cheekiness' and ingenuity of the Aborigines whose success in begging did not depend on adopting the servile demeanour of their London and Dublin counterparts:

When walking out one morning, I accidentally met a young scion of our black tribes, . . . who saluted me with 'Good morning, sir, good morning', to which I in like manner responded, and was proceeding onwards when my dingy acquaintance arrested my attention by his loud vociferation of 'Top, sir, I want to speak with you'. 'Well, what is it?', said I. 'Why, you know, I am your *servant*, and you have not paid me yet.' 'The devil you are!' responded I; 'It is the first time I knew of it, for I do not recollect ever seeing your face before'. 'Oh yes I *am* your servant', replied he very resolutely; 'dont I top about Massa ———'s, and boil the kettle for you sometimes in the morning?' I forthwith put my hand in my pocket, and gave him all the halfpence I had, which I left him carefully counting, and proceeded on my walk; but before advancing a quarter of a mile, my ears were again assailed with loud shouts of 'Hallo! top, top!' I turned around, and observed my friend in 'the dark suit' beckoning with his hand, and walking very leisurely toward me. Thinking that he was despatched with some message, I halted, but as he walked on as slowly as if deeming I ought rather to go to him than he come to me, I forthwith returned to meet him; but on reaching close enough, what was my astonishment on his holding out the halfpence in his open hand, and addressing me in a loud, grumbling, demanding tone with—'Why this is not enough to buy a loaf! you must give me more'. 'Then buy *half* a loaf', said I, wheeling about and resuming my walk, not without a good many hard epithets in return from the kettle-boiler.[10]

The 'Sydney blacks' were notorious for their apparent physical and moral degeneracy, Oldfield describing them as

mere lumps of misery; their legs and arms shrunk like anatomical preparations; their eyes fixed in a state of insensibility, and looking altogether as if they were waiting to give up the ghost.[11]

When they could not buy or beg spirits, they manufactured 'bull' from sugar bags or molasses and the sediment of rum barrels mixed with water. Under its potent influence they would frequently quarrel and fight in the streets, sometimes using waddies and spears

[9] *The South-Asian Register*, No. 4, December 1828, p. 322.
[10] *Two Years in New South Wales*, 2 vols, London 1827, Vol. II, pp. 24-5.
[11] *The South-Asian Register*, No. 2, January 1828, p. 102.

and threatening or roundly abusing any pedestrian who refused them drink or money or attempted to mediate in their disputes. More often, however, they were given rum and encouraged to fight each other.

They were required by a government order to wear clothing within the 'Metropolis' but the result was a caricature of European dress.

> In the same group, we sometimes see a man with only a pair of trousers, another with a shirt, another a jacket without any other sub-tegument; or a female wearing only a skirt with a frilled cap stuck in her hair obliquely; another has perhaps a red or yellow jacket over a skirt; everyone in short wearing what the humour of individuals has bestowed, no matter how motley and fantastic.[12]

The nature of their food, their scorn of washing and their habit of rubbing themselves with fish-oil or marsupial fat endowed them with a smell which, like that of Swift's Houhyhnhnms was 'not so sweet as a cow'. According to Oldfield, their dirtiness also resulted in a 'cutaneous eruption in the form of erysipelas' which the Aborigines called *djeebal*. Outbreaks of epidemic diseases such as influenza and measles killed many, although there was no report of 'smallpox' in the Sydney area from the first epidemic in 1789 until the arrival of the *Canton* in 1835.

It is likely that many of the Aboriginal women were prostitutes although Barron Field claimed that there had never been a case of a white man cohabiting with an Aboriginal woman.[13] In 1845 there were seven half-castes at Botany and one or two whites were described as living with Aboriginal women there.[14]

When the Quaker missionary Daniel Wheeler landed at Sydney in 1834, he was 'saluted by a most appalling volley of dreadful oaths and imprecations, from some of the poor intoxicated creatures, in the garb of sailors, that were standing about the stairs'.[15] Other groups were 'rolling about the streets . . . altogether intoxicated', their 'emaciated frames' convincing him of their imminent disappearance from the face of the earth. After a visit to one of the

---

[12] Ibid., p. 103.
[13] 'Narrative' in *Geographical Memoirs*, p. 436n.
[14] 'Report from the Select Committee on the Condition of the Aborigines', *V&P*, 1845, p. 946.
[15] *Effects of the Introduction of Ardent Spirits and Implements of War amongst the Natives of some of the South Sea Islands and New South Wales*, London 1839, p. 5.

small coves on the northern side of the harbour where he found an Aboriginal woman and her children in a lamentable state of disease, Wheeler concluded that the Aborigines were beyond assistance:

> Their debased condition is greater than can well be conceived, and such as to render every attempt to assist them fruitless; if the money is handed to them, it is immediately exchanged for rum; or if clothes, they are forthwith sold or exchanged for whatever will procure strong drink.[16]

At night the Aborigines did not camp in the town but retired with fire-sticks into the thick bush or to sandstone rock shelters with which the coves of the harbour abounded. A favourite haunt was the Serpentine rock in the Domain where their revels were within earshot of Government House. A reserve of land at Elizabeth Bay set aside for them by Governor Lachlan Macquarie in 1821 had been abandoned by 1826 and the material of the huts used for fuel or exchanged for food and drink. However, the reserve at George's Head which had been established in 1815 for Bungaree and his people and revived in 1821 was probably still being used during the 1830s because there were many contemporary references to a large camp on the northern side of the harbour. By 1845 most of the Aborigines on the southern side were more or less permanently camped near the heads at Botany.

Between 1837 and 1839 the Sydney newspapers carried frequent complaints about the riotous behaviour of Aborigines in the streets. On 9 March 1837 the *Sydney Gazette* reported that

> On Tuesday, between three and four o'clock, the largest mob we have ever witnessed, assembled at the junction of George and Bridge—streets, and . . . exhibited their beastly antics, and brutal contests, in a state of semi-nudity, and complete drunkenness, in that character of ferocity which savages only can assume.

Two similar incidents took place in George and King Streets later in the same month. When Aborigines resorted to weapons on the former occasion, the police and passers-by intervened; but on the latter, 'a party of constables stood by laughing and joking at their freaks, instead of taking them into custody',[17] and a number of Aborigines were wounded. Disturbances of this kind led one of the witnesses before the Legislative Council's Committee on the Abori-

---

[16] Ibid., p. 4.
[17] *Sydney Gazette*, 30 March 1837.

gines Question in 1838 to recommend that the 'most vicious characters' should be prosecuted under the Vagrants Act and all others
removed from the town in order to rescue them from destruction.[18]
Subsequently *The Australian* of 15 January 1839 reported that five
Aborigines with 'euphonious names' had been charged with drunkenness and fighting in the streets after a 'most disgusting scene' the
previous Sunday afternoon opposite the main gate of the Macquarie
Street Barracks:

> five or six black men and the same number of women, beastly drunk,
> were exposing themselves to the passengers, dancing their native
> dances and disturbing the whole neighbourhood.

Their observations of the 'Sydney blacks' caused most whites to
think that the culture of the Aborigines was of no more interest or
significance than the antics of animals. Nor was there much of their
traditional culture to be seen by the time Gipps arrived in the
colony. Corroborees which had been common entertainments
during the early days of settlement were reported as rare events by
1830. Five years earlier Barron Field had given a detailed description of one 'because in a few years, perhaps, even the corrobory
will be no more'.[19] Already the custom of adult tooth incision, so
carefully described by Colonel David Collins,[20] was 'obsolete in the
neighbourhood of our settlements'.[21] Oldfield, too, noticed that by
1828 the regular 'assemblies', ceremonies, dances, and 'mock battles'
noted by Collins had been abandoned. Instead of corroborees:

> While they are reeling in the streets, and quarrelling, an individual or
> two will frequently begin dancing, from the heartless excitement of
> bad liquor on an empty stomach.[22]

By 1830 it was also well known that the Aborigines in the Sydney
area had lost many of their traditional skills. When recommending
to Lieutenant-Governor Sir George Arthur that Aborigines from
New South Wales could be useful in 'collecting' the Aborigines of
Van Diemen's Land, John Batman, later of Port Phillip fame, emphasized that they should be obtained from the Cowpastures or

---

[18] 'Report of the Committee on the Aborigines Question', *V&P*, 1838, p. 32.
[19] 'Narrative' in *Geographical Memoirs*, pp. 433-4.
[20] *Account of the English Colony in New South Wales*, 2 vols, London 1798-
1802, Vol. I, pp. 575-83.
[21] Field, 'Narrative' in *Geographical Memoirs*, p. 433.
[22] *The South-Asian Register*, No. 2, January 1828, p. 101.

Liverpool, 'as those brought from the Town of Sydney are all accustomed to the *drinking* of *Spirits* and have also lost in a great measure their Native gift of tracking through the Bush'.[23]

Perhaps the most important point about the Sydney Aborigines is that they did not accept an inferior status in colonial society. Oldfield remarked that in their intercourse with whites the 'familiarity of their address is sometimes taken to be impudence'[24] while Barron Field wrote at length of their confident manner:

> They bear themselves erect, and address you with confidence, always with good-humour, and often with grace . . . They have a bowing acquaintance with everybody, and scatter their How-d'ye-do's with an air of friendliness and equality, and with a perfect English accent, undebased by the *Massa's*, and *Missies*, and *me-no's* of West Indian slavery . . . [The Aborigine] has no notion of that inferiority to us, the oppression of which feeling reduces the New Zealanders and South Sea Islanders almost to despair; and he despises the comforts of civilization, although he has nothing of his own but his 'hollow tree and liberty' without even the 'crust of bread'. What then must be his opinion of our servants? men and women, who sacrifice their liberty and independence for the second-rate comforts of civilization, which they earn by submitting to perform menial offices for those who enjoy the first-rate, and by ministering to their artificial wants; for which even first-rate comforts the naked native has a contempt. With us masters, all he contends for nevertheless is equality.[25]

Aboriginal parents were happy enough for their children to be clothed, fed and taught by the whites but could not accept the idea of their becoming domestic servants, a lot which was almost inevitable for those brought up in white households. According to Field, some Aborigines (or 'Indians' as he preferred to call them) had even applied to Macquarie for convicts to be assigned to them as servants.[26]

By 1845, however, the numbers and morale of the 'Sydney blacks' had suffered considerably. 'Mahroot' or 'The Boatswain', last male member of the once 400-strong Botany tribe, had been brought up in a white household during part of his youth and had

---

[23] Batman to P. A. Mulgrave, Chief Police Magistrate at Hobart, 15 March 1830, ML, MS. Ab113/3. The Aborigines who were taken to Van Diemen's Land were referred to as the 'Sydney Blacks', but in fact they came from Jervis Bay.

[24] *The South-Asian Register*, No. 2, January 1828, p. 103.

[25] 'Narrative' in *Geographical Memoirs*, pp. 435-7.

[26] Ibid., p. 437.

only a dim memory of tribal life. Looking back over fifty years he reminisced in 'a half-musing tone' to an English visitor:

> Well Mitter (Mr.) . . . all black-fellow gone! all this my country! pretty place Botany! Little pickaninny, I run about here. Plenty black-fellow then; corrobbory; great fight; all canoe about. Only me left now, Mitter —Poor gin mine tumble down, (die.) All gone! Bury her like a lady, Mitter —; all put in coffin, English fashion. I feel lump in throat when I talk about her; but,—I buried her all very genteel, Mitter —.[27]

Melbourne

During 1840 there were sometimes as many as 400 Aborigines from all parts of the Port Phillip district living on the outskirts of Melbourne. Already their 'non-conformity in attire . . . their temptations from offers of drink by thoughtless colonists, and their inveterate begging' had made them a 'public nuisance'.[28] Edmund Finn's description indicates how the Aborigines must have appeared to many of the townsfolk.

> At almost every turn one met with the Aborigines, in twos and threes, and half dozen—coolies,[29] lubras, gins, and picaninnies—the most wretched-looking and repulsive specimens of humanity that could be well found. The men half-naked, with a tattered 'possum rug, or dirty blanket, thrown over them, as far as it would go; and the women just as nude, except when an odd one decked herself out in some cast-away petticoat, or ragged old gown. The young 'gin' had usually stowed in some mysterious receptacle on her back, a sooty-faced, curly-haired baby, whilst the younger members of the 'unfair sex' dandled mangey-looking cur-dogs as playthings in their arms. Their eternal 'yabbering whine' was for 'backsheesh' in the form of white silver money, a 'thik-pence' or so, to invest in tobacco or rum, for they soon grew inordinately addicted to both.[30]

Their changing way of life was reflected most clearly in physical decline. The journalist Thomas McCombie noted that

---

[27] Quoted by J. P. Townsend, *Rambles and Observations in New South Wales* . . . , London 1849, p. 120.

[28] W. Westgarth, *Personal Recollections of Early Melbourne and Victoria*, Melbourne 1888, p. 14.

[29] This was a common term for unmarried male Aborigines before the arrival of the Chinese. See Alfred Joyce, *A Homestead History* . . . , G. F. James (ed.), Melbourne 1942, p. 84.

[30] *The Chronicles of Early Melbourne 1835 to 1852*, 2 vols, Melbourne 1888, K, 110. See also, R. Howitt, *Australia: Historical, Descriptive and Statistic;* . . . , London 1845, p. 185.

the blacks, especially the half civilised or mongrel tribes in the neighbourhood of towns, when past thirty or thirty-five, lose their free,
elastic tread, the hair on the head and chin, once jet black, becomes
mixed and stunted; the face loses the soft, graceful outline, and
becomes sinister, wrinkled and haggard; the lines of the countenance
speak of mean cunning: the whole air is equivocal.[31]

Camping in small parties along the Yarra River from Hawthorn to
Heidelberg, they made expeditions to bakeries and slaughter-yards
where they could usually obtain stale bread and offal. Otherwise
they roamed the streets of the township selling small articles, begging, and occasionally thieving. A number even obtained firearms
and took up position on the main roads where they demanded six-
pences of travellers 'with a saucy and sometimes a menacing air,
which made them practically robbers'.[32]

As early as 1839 the *Port Phillip Gazette* urged the Chief Protector of Aborigines, Robinson,[33] to exclude them from the town
where their 'vagrant and pilfering habits' were fast becoming 'a
perfect nuisance'.[34] In September 1840, a small boy on an errand
for his mother was attacked by three Aborigines, beaten, and robbed
of his money. Remarking on this, the *Gazette* repeated its earlier
suggestion that a reserve should be set aside for their visits to the

---

[31] *Australian Sketches*, Melbourne 1847, p. 116.

[32] Alexander Sutherland, *Victoria and Its Metropolis*, 2 vols, Melbourne 1888,
Vol. I, p. 241.

[33] George Augustus Robinson (1788-1866), son of a Lincolnshire builder,
emigrated to Hobart in 1824 where he set up business as a builder. In 1829
he was appointed by the government to conciliate the Aborigines of Bruny
Island but his desire for more knowledge of Aboriginal language and customs
soon took him to the wild southwest coast. He spent most of the time between
1830 and 1834 travelling around the island in search of the Aborigines who
had survived the combined onslaught of settlers and soldiers and would
accept his promises of government protection and assistance. Those who did
were taken to islands in Bass Strait and finally a permanent settlement was
established at Flinders Island. Robinson took charge in 1835 and achieved
some success in teaching them English, but mortality from introduced
diseases, including what was probably tuberculosis, rapidly reduced their
numbers. In 1836 he refused the appointment of Protector of Aborigines in
South Australia but accepted a similar position at a higher salary in 1838
when he became Chief Protector in charge of the Port Phillip Aboriginal
Protectorate. See *ADB*, Vol. II, pp. 385-7; Clive Turnbull, *Black War: The
Extermination of the Tasmanian Aborigines*, Melbourne 1948; N. J. B.
Plomley (ed.), *Friendly Mission: The Tasmanian Journals of George Augustus
Robinson*, Hobart 1966.

[34] 17 April 1839.

neighbourhood of Melbourne, so that they could be effectively prevented by the Protectors from entering the township:

> Their system of begging, thieving, their indecent exposure of person, their fulsome appearance and savour, all demand some wholesome restrictions on their actions.[35]

Equally offensive were the 'mangy curs' which accompanied the Aboriginal women and children everywhere in large numbers.[36] It was claimed that these dogs contaminated many of the town dogs and public indignation was heightened by the women's habit of washing them near the Yarra pumps which provided the town's water supply.[37]

Another reason given for excluding the Aborigines from the vicinity of Melbourne was the prevalence of epidemic diseases in their camps. In 1839 the *Gazette* reported that several Aborigines had died of dysentery and influenza and many others were extremely ill and enfeebled. Mothers were advised not to take their children near the camps and Robinson, whose 'obtuseness requires us so constantly to point out a line of duty'[38] was urged to remove them as quickly as possible. It was also feared that the whites' habit of providing Aborigines with spirits would ultimately precipitate conflicts between the wilder natives and white drunkards. Already there had been a number of frays between the Goulburn and Yarra tribes and Robinson was criticized for allowing the former to go beyond their own territory:

> we know that in their natural habitats the most deadly feuds are constantly arising from trespasses committed by one tribe on the hunting grounds of another.[39]

It was the rumour of an imminent battle between Aborigines already gathered near Melbourne and some newly-arrived 'wild blacks' from Gippsland which caused Major Samuel Lettsom to bring his troopers to Melbourne in late 1840. He had originally been sent to the Ovens River with four men to investigate an armed attack on Dr Mackay's station and, although it was outside his in-

---

[35] 30 September 1840.
[36] The *Port Phillip Gazette* of 19 November 1842 reported that on the previous Thursday three 'lubras' had come into town accompanied by no less than seventeen dogs. See also, the report by Protector William Thomas, *V&P*, 1843, p. 507.
[37] *Port Phillip Gazette*, 15 February 1843.
[38] 8 May 1839.
[39] *Port Phillip Gazette*, 24 April 1839.

structions, he decided with Port Phillip Superintendent Charles La Trobe's approval to disperse the large encampments along the Yarra. Provided with twelve more troopers and a further twenty-seven men from the 28th Regiment, Lettsom marched north along the river, only to find the first camp deserted. At the second, most of the Aborigines escaped into the river or the tea-tree scrubs but some old men, women and children were captured, together with three muskets and pistol. Lettsom claimed this to be the tribe which had fired on the police some time previously.

A few days later, Lettsom was informed that the Aborigines had re-assembled at camps on the Eltham road between Darebin Creek and the River Plenty. This time he proceeded with more caution and a dawn attack resulted in the capture of 400 Aborigines and the death of one man who was allegedly shot in the act of waddying an officer. The miscreants were marched to Melbourne and the townspeople turned out in force to see the motley procession wending down Bourke Street, and up Batman's Hill.

La Trobe was at a loss what to do with the Aborigines, but decided to release all the old men, women and children and to imprison thirty-three of the most 'desperate' men. Some were locked up overnight in a brick warehouse owned by the Commissariat on the corner of Bourke and King Streets, however a search next morning revealed that all had escaped by tunnelling beneath the floor and La Trobe released the others from gaol some days later. The exercise had some temporary effect. According to one contemporary, 'the blacks congregated in fewer numbers around Melbourne, and were much less aggressive in their conduct'.[40] But the problem of Aboriginal 'vagrancy' remained unsolved. In 1845 Henry Moor, Mayor of Melbourne, complained to La Trobe in the same terms as the *Gazette*, recommending that they should be permanently removed from the precincts of the town.[41] In reply, La Trobe emphasized that efforts during former years had been directed toward their exclusion, but that the Protectors and the foot police had been unsuccessful in this task.[42] While promising further assistance, he wrote to Colonial Secretary Deas Thomson for advice, only to be told rather unhelpfully that he was to use every possible

[40] Sutherland, *Victoria*, Vol. I, p. 241. For Lettsom's report to Gipps, see *GD*, ML, MS.A1224, pp. 321-34.
[41] *Victorian Chief Secretary's Records*, Inwards Correspondence No. 45/1325.
[42] *Victorian Chief Secretary's Records*, Outwards Letter book 'Q', pp. 131-2.

means 'consistent with the law' to discourage them from entering the town.[43] But it was impossible for the Protectors to keep the Aborigines away from Melbourne, which could offer much more food than the impoverished Protectorate establishments, together with tobacco and alcohol. In 1843 Protector William Thomas described the difficulty of keeping Aborigines on the reserve at Narre Narre Warren, forty miles from Melbourne:

> On one day this month, between the Yarra and the Northumberland Hotel in the public road, I went up to four groups who had fires at midday enjoying themselves; I counted their mendicant fare thus early in the day; there were 21 good white loaves, besides abundance of meat from the shambles [slaughter yards]; one of them holding up two loaves exclaimed, 'no like this at Nerre Nerre Warren, no good Nerre Nerre Warren, Marnameek (very good) Melbourne'.[44]

The Aborigines, he said, had 'strong motives for becoming mendicants'.

Depopulation is comparatively well documented for the Port Phillip district where within the experience of one generation of settlers the Aborigines were reduced to a pathetic remnant. Most contemporaries agreed that the Aboriginal population in 1835 had been in the vicinity of 7,000 but by 1877 the first detailed Victorian census showed that only 1,067, including part-Aborigines, remained.[45] E. M. Curr noted that the Bangerang tribe declined within ten years from 200 to less than 80,[46] and Captain Foster Fyans who had 'mustered' 275 on his arrival at Portland Bay as Crown Lands Commissioner could only account for 20 in 1853.[47] In the same year a squatter counted nine women, seven men and one sickly child as the remnants of the Barrabool Hill tribe which had formerly numbered 'upwards of 300',[48] and he could recollect no more than seventeen births over twenty-four years. Protector Edward Parker recorded in 1841 that during the previous two years,

---

[43] *Victorian Chief Secretary's Records*, Inwards Correspondence No. 45/1325.

[44] *V&P*, 1843, p. 542.

[45] Victorian Legislative Assembly, *Votes and Proceedings*, 1877-8, III, 'Fourteenth Report', Appendix X, p. 12.

[46] *Recollections of Squatting in Victoria* . . . , Melbourne 1883, p. 235.

[47] T. F. Bride (ed.), *Letters from Victorian Pioneers* . . . , Melbourne 1895, p. 121.

[48] G. T. Lloyd, *Thirty-Three Years in Tasmania and Victoria* . . . , London 1862, p. 456.

twenty-four of the Jajourong men had been killed by hostile tribes.[49]

Whatever the reasons given by contemporaries for the decrease, it inevitably created the very strong impression that the Aborigines would be extinct by the end of the century. Since the decline was most pronounced in the Port Phillip District during the first ten years of settlement, it is not surprising that the settlers there should have been the strongest exponents of this belief.

THE NINETEEN COUNTIES

The number of Aborigines living within the boundaries of the Nineteen Counties[50] had declined noticeably during the first fifty years of settlement. The most commonly accepted estimate during the 1830s was 500,[51] yet Governor Sir Arthur Phillip in 1788 had estimated the population in the area between Botany Bay and Broken Bay alone at 1,500.[52] As early as 1824 the Parramatta 'feast', which attracted seven or eight tribes from as far as Broken Bay, Jervis Bay, the Monaro and possibly Port Macquarie, could only muster 400[53] and there is reason to believe that every Aborigine who was physically capable of making the journey would have been present. In 1835 Major Sir Thomas Mitchell, the colony's Surveyor-General, noted that the Aborigines had almost disappeared from the Hunter River valley[54] and in his 1837 report on the Lake Macquarie Aboriginal mission the Rev. L. E. Threlkeld[55] pointed out that there were only three individuals remaining of one tribe

---

[49] Cited by H. G. Turner, *Victoria: The First Century* . . . , Melbourne 1934, p. 235.
[50] See Figure 1.
[51] J. C. Byrne, *Twelve Years' Wanderings in the British Colonies* . . . , 2 vols, London 1848, Vol. I, p. 279.
[52] *HRA*, I, p. 29.
[53] *Sydney Gazette*, 30 December 1824.
[54] *Three Expeditions into the Interior of Eastern Australia* . . . , 2 vols, London 1838, Vol. I, p. 10.
[55] Lancelot Edward Threlkeld (1788-1859) went to the Society Islands in 1817 where he served the London Missionary Society. In 1824 he accompanied the Rev. Daniel Tyerman and George Bennet to Sydney and was placed in charge of a new mission to the Aborigines on the shores of Lake Macquarie where Tyerman and Bennet had persuaded Brisbane to set aside 10,000 acres. A quarrel with the Society and with Samuel Marsden, its representative in the colony, led to his dismissal in 1828 but Archdeacon W. G. Broughton persuaded the Executive Council to pay his salary. This arrangement was maintained until 1841 when his latest annual report indicated that there were no longer sufficient numbers of Aborigines in the district to warrant

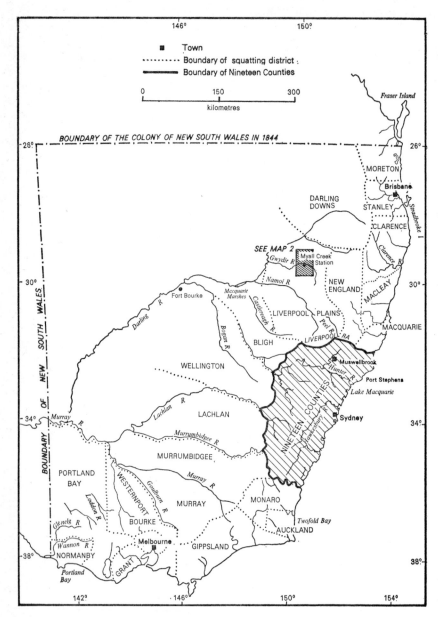

FIGURE 1 The Nineteen Counties and Squatting Districts
of New South Wales based on an official map of 1844

which four years previously had numbered 164.[56] During the 1840s the rate of depopulation increased markedly, one observer concluding from the declining ratio of children to parents that the Aborigines' extinction was mathematically inevitable.[57]

By 1838 the remnants of tribes whose territories lay within the Nineteen Counties had drifted in to the towns or were wandering from station to station begging for food. Sometimes, especially in winter, they remained on one station and in 1835 Mitchell remarked that those surviving in the Hunter Valley had collected at such places as Segenhoe.[58] A large number were also semi-permanently camped near the huts of the Australian Agricultural Company's establishment at Port Stephens where some of the men were employed[59] and where the Company's convict servants visited women in the camps.

On those stations where settlers allowed them to collect, the Aborigines subsisted on skim milk, offal and bran in return for casual labour as bark-cutters, sheep-washers and reapers; women

---

continuing the mission. Threlkeld was the first man to study Aboriginal language systematically. With the assistance of the Aborigine McGill he translated parts of the New Testament into the Awabakal or Lake Macquarie dialect and published a grammar. He was also frequently employed by the government as a court interpreter. Threlkeld was an outspoken defender of the Aborigines and in addition to an influential correspondence with Judge W. W. Burton and others he was one of the founders of the N.S.W. Aborigines Protection Society in 1838. An important collection of Threlkeld's writings, together with a valuable biographical essay, are now available in Niel Gunson (ed.), *Australian Reminiscences of L. E. Threlkeld, Missionary to the Aborigines, 1824-1859*, Australian Aboriginal Studies No. 40, Australian Institute of Aboriginal Studies, 2 vols, Canberra 1974. Wherever possible, references have been made to Gunson's collection which includes: a section of Threlkeld's 'Reminiscences' first published in *The Christian Herald*, and *Record of Missionary and Religious Intelligence*, Sydney, 26 February 1853-28 April 1855; 'Memoranda Selected from Twenty Four Years of Missionary Engagements in the South Sea Islands and Australia . . . 1838' compiled for Judge Burton in 1838 and now located in Supreme Court Papers, NSWA, No. 1123; Lake Macquarie Mission reports 1838-41; and selected correspondence 1824-59. See also, *ADB*, Vol. II, pp. 528-30; B. W. Champion, 'Lancelot Edward Threlkeld', *JRAHS*, Vol. XXV, 1939, pp. 279-329, 341-411; and K. H. Clouten, *Reid's Mistake: The Story of Lake Macquarie from its Discovery until 1890*, Sydney 1967, pp. 21-35.

56 'Report from the Committee on Immigration', *V&P*, 1841, pp. 43-5.
57 'A Few Words on the Aborigines of Australia', *The New South Wales Magazine*, I, No. 2, February 1843, p. 52.
58 *Three Expeditions*, Vol. I, p. 20.
59 'Report from the Committee on Immigration', *V&P*, 1841, pp. 43-5.

were occasionally employed as shepherds and domestic servants. However, many settlers were content to provide food as a peace-offering to ensure the safety of their sheep and cattle. During the summer months the men returned to hunting and fishing and Charles Darwin encountered such a party on his journey from Sydney to Bathurst in 1835.[60] Collection of the remaining Aboriginal population in the Nineteen Counties was encouraged and assisted by Governor Sir Richard Bourke who from 1832 authorized the distribution of government-supplied blankets by settlers at the beginning of winter in the hope that this would cause the Aborigines to find regular employment and develop settled habits.[61] Numbers also collected on the missions at Lake Macquarie and Wellington Valley where food and shelter were available, but the limited financial resources of missionaries and the rapid encroachment of white settlement caused them to drift towards the stations and the towns where alcohol and tobacco as well as food could more easily be obtained. By 1838 Threlkeld's mission had lost most of its Aborigines to the growing town of Newcastle and sixty had died at the mission of drink and disease since its foundation in 1826. In his 1881 mission report he remarked despairingly that McGill,[62] his early protégé, 'displays his knowledge of Christianity at Newcastle Town where drink has attractions far more strong than my study possesses at the Lake'.[63]

Camps on the stations and near the towns were probably highly unsanitary and epidemics such as the 'variolous' disease which killed off half the Aborigines of the Scone and Dungog district about 1835[64] were not uncommon. Epidemics of measles were reported near Sydney in 1835,[65] 'smallpox' at Wellington Valley in 1832[66]

[60] *Journal of Researches into the Natural History and Geology of the Countries Visited during the Voyage of H.M.S. Beagle Round the World*, 7th edn, London 1890, p. 528.

[61] *GG*, 17 October 1832, p. 339. For the history of blanket distribution, see Reece, 'Feasts and Blankets'.

[62] For an account of McGill or Biraban, see Gunson, *Australian Reminiscences and Papers of L. E. Threlkeld*, Vol. I, pp. 6-7 and *ADB*, Vol. I, pp. 102-4.

[63] Ibid., Vol. I, p. 133.

[64] Letters from Dr E. M. McKinlay, J.P. (Dungog) and Joseph Docker, J.P. (Scone), 'Replies to a Circular Letter from the Select Committee on the Condition of the Aborigines', *V&P*, 1845, p. 969.

[65] Rev. John Saunders, *Letterbook 1834-5*, ML, MS.B1106, p. 77.

[66] G. Bennet, *Wanderings in New South Wales* . . . , 2 vols, London 1834, Vol. I, pp. 148-61.

and influenza in the Monaro in 1839,[67] as well as venereal and respiratory diseases more difficult to determine. Addiction to rum must also have had a generally destructive effect on health and probably increased the Aborigines' susceptibility to disease.

By 1830, relations between the two races in the Nineteen Counties had fallen into a fairly settled and peaceful pattern and apart from occasional sheep and cattle stealing and petty thefts, there were very few disturbances. However, any thought of making provision for the material welfare of the Aborigines by erecting huts and paying fixed wages was inhibited by the belief that they would soon be extinct.

THE SQUATTING DISTRICTS

In some of the oldest settled parts of the squatting districts,[68] such as the Monaro, Yass Plains and the southern end of the Liverpool Plains, the relationship of Aborigines to whites was similar to that in the Nineteen Counties.[69] Apart from occasional attacks on sheep and cattle and thefts of corn, potatoes and provisions, it was peaceful enough. After initial resistance, the Aborigines had collected on those stations where they were tolerated and some were employed in seasonal tasks, receiving in return food, tobacco and clothing which they shared with their dependants. At Twofold Bay in 1844, the Imlay brothers were employing eighteen Aborigines (and Benjamin Boyd a similar number) at their bay-whaling establishments during the catching season.[70]

As in the Nineteen Counties, the rapid decline of Aboriginal population was noted by white observers. In 1846 Mitchell retraced his 1832 journey along the Bogan River, meeting the remnants of a tribe which had greeted him in large numbers only a few years earlier:

> The chief who formerly guided us so kindly had fallen into a hopeless struggle for the existence of his tribe with the natives of the river Macquarie, allied with the border police on one side; and the wild

[67] *The Australian*, 16 February 1839.
[68] See Figure 1.
[69] On W. E. Riley's station at Yass Plains the Aborigines remained each winter, subsisting on skim milk and bran which he gave to them. W. E. Riley, 'The "Corobberie" or Dance of a Tribe of Natives in the Southern Interior of New South Wales', *Riley Papers*, ML, MS.A109, p. 65.
[70] H. P. Wellings, *Benjamin Boyd in Australia*, Sydney 1936, pp. 44-5.

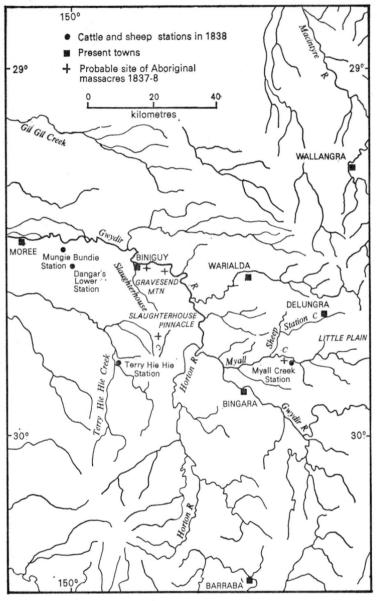

FIGURE 2   Massacres 1837-8 in the Liverpool Plains District

natives of the Barwon on the other. All I could learn of the rest of the tribe was, that the men were almost all dead, and that their wives were chiefly servants at stock stations along the Macquarie.[71]

On the frontiers of pastoral settlement, expansion was almost invariably accompanied by some degree of conflict. Since very few statistics and reports were compiled, it is difficult to obtain an overall view of the problem but such records as there are indicate that between 1837 and 1846 the colony experienced the worst racial clashes in its history, the squatting districts of Portland Bay and Liverpool Plains being most severely affected. The spate of attacks on property and life in these two areas, reaching a climax in 1842-3, was even referred to by some contemporaries as an Aboriginal 'rising' in the colony.[72]

In the Portland Bay district, especially along the Eumeralla, Glenelg and Wannon rivers, the rapid taking up of land by squatters and the subsequent collection of large numbers of dislocated Aborigines on the Mount Rouse Protectorate station without adequate provision for their sustenance and control, made attacks on neighbouring stations inevitable. The extent of this problem was indicated in a number of petitions from squatters describing the destruction and murders which had led to the abandonment of some stations.[73]

In 1844 an analysis of all officially recorded conflicts in the entire Port Phillip district revealed that since 1836, 40 whites and 113 Aborigines had been killed,[74] most of them in the Portland Bay area. However, La Trobe observed that these figures were unreliable because the deaths of Aborigines were frequently not reported to the authorities.[75] In the words of one Police Magistrate:

A murder committed by the blacks is paraded in the papers, and everybody is shocked; but there have been hundreds of cold-blooded

[71] *Journal of an Expedition into the Interior of Tropical Australia* . . . , London 1848, p. 30. This was the tribe which was severely 'punished' after the William Lee incident. See page 51.
[72] Roderick Flanagan, *The Australian Aborigines*, Melbourne 1881, pp. 130-40; Alexander Harris, *Settlers and Convicts* . . . , Melbourne 1953, pp. 212-13.
[73] For one of these petitions, see Appendix I.
[74] *V&P*, 1844, Vol. I, pp. 718-19. Dr Peter Corris has estimated that the number of Aborigines 'more or less known to have been killed' in Western Victoria alone at 146. *Aborigines and Europeans in Western Victoria*, Occasional Paper in Aboriginal Studies No. 12, Australian Institute of Aboriginal Studies, Canberra, 1968, p. 228.
[75] *V&P*, 1844, Vol. I, p. 720.

murders, perpetrated by the whites on the outskirts of the Colony, which we have never heard of.[76]

Other contemporaries claimed that for every white reported killed in the Port Phillip district, there were from 50 to 100 Aborigines who had lost their lives.[77]

Conflicts on the Liverpool Plains were more extensive and although the statistics are less satisfactory than for Port Phillip where there were at least Protectors whose business it was to inquire into the deaths of Aborigines, the area will be treated separately and in greater detail at a later point in this chapter.

Many of the clashes reported after 1837 were the result of increased use of overland routes from the Sydney district to Port Phillip and Adelaide and the formation of new stations along the tributaries of the Darling and Murray rivers. Aborigines from distant parts were attracted by news of large numbers of sheep and cattle and drayloads of flour, sugar, tea, tobacco and other commodities which, to their annoyance, the whites were usually unwilling to share. In April 1838 a large mob of sheep and cattle and a drayload of supplies belonging to William Pitt Faithfull were being driven from his Goulburn station to the Port Phillip district where he planned to take up some new stations. The eighteen men, most of them assigned servants, who comprised the party were accompanied for some distance by a large number of Aborigines who assisted with the droving. But on the morning of 11 April when they were camped at the Broken River, near the present town of Benalla, they were attacked by a party of 150 or more warriors and eight of the whites were killed.[78] The tribe said to have been involved was later caught and 'punished' by a private expedition led by Lieutenant-Colonel H. White, a squatter living in the Broken River area.[79] By contrast, a party of Mounted Police sent out from Sydney was unable to make contact.

Lack of evidence makes it impossible to give a reliable explanation of the incident, but according to the historian Thomas Rusden,

---

[76] 'Report of the Committee on Police and Gaols', *V&P*, 1839, Vol. II, p. 75.

[77] Byrne, *Twelve Years' Wanderings*, Vol. I, p. 276.

[78] For a report of this incident, see *Letters from Government Offices*, ML, MS.A664, pp. 155-69, *The Sydney Herald*, 21 May 1838, and S. Uren, comp., *The Massacre of the Faithfull Party*, typescript, ML, n.d. The massacre held up further settlement of the district for the remainder of 1838.

[79] White to Deas Thomson, 15 April 1838, ML, MS.A664, pp. 160 ff.

who later employed one of the survivors, the trouble arose when the whites refused to supply the tea, sugar and other items which they had promised to the Aborigines in return for their women.[80] Faithfull himself could find no reason for the attack when questioned by a Committee of the Legislative Council in the following year but he did point out that the country was extremely dry at the time and that there was very little game.[81] Attacks on surveying parties at the Gwydir River in 1832[82] and at New England in January 1838 had also been motivated by the desire for rations.

The 'Faithfull massacre' was the first and last of such incidents on the route from the Murray to Port Phillip where the country was fairly open,[83] but there was more difficulty along the lower Murray. The Aborigines of the Maraura tribe systematically attacked and plundered overlanding parties, especially at the narrow neck of land separating Lake Victoria from the river—the area where Major Mitchell's party had fired on and killed a number of Aborigines in May 1836. There were a number of pitched battles and four successive parties of police and soldiers had to be sent from Adelaide before the Aborigines could be caught and 'pacified'.[84] Parties of squatters are said to have finished off the troopers' work at a notorious massacre where the blood of dead and dying Aborigines gave *Rufus Creek* its name.[85]

The guerilla tactics of the Aborigines had been facilitated in this area by the thick scrubs which armed horsemen could not penetrate. Similarly, the terrain of parts of the Glenelg and Eumeralla Rivers in the Portland Bay district offered useful shelter, as did the Macquarie Marshes, the Kunderang ravines at New England and the thick scrubs along the Clarence and other coastal rivers. Constant depredations and the absence of police caused squatters and their servants in the remote districts to band together in armed

---

[80] *History of Australia*, 2nd edn, 3 vols, Melbourne 1897, Vol. II, p. 163.
[81] 'Report from the Committee on the Crown Lands Bill', *V&P*, 1839, Vol. I, p. 15.
[82] Mitchell, *Three Expeditions*, Vol. I, p. 110.
[83] White to Deas Thomson, 15 April 1838, ML, MS.A664, pp. 160 ff. See also Uren, *The Massacre*, pp. 8-9.
[84] See K. Hassell, *The Relations between the Settlers and Aborigines in South Australia, 1836-1860*, Adelaide 1966, pp. 62-70 and C. Richards, 'The "Marraa' Warree" Tribes or Nation and their Language', *Science of Man*, VI, No. 8, September 1903, pp. 119-26.
[85] E. Morey Papers, ML, MS.A833, pp. 199-201.

expeditions to punish thefts and murders and to prevent Aborigines
from coming near the stations by 'dispersing' their camps.

The novelist Rolf Boldrewood,[86] who established 'Squattlesea
Mere' station on the Eumeralla River near Port Fairy in 1844, took
part in a punitive expedition against the Mount Eeles tribe which
was organized after the theft of a flock of ewes. For John Cox,[87]
one of the squatters involved,

> It was the first time I had ever levelled a gun at my fellow-man . . . I
> did so without regret or hesitation in this instance. I never remember
> having the feeling I could not miss so strong in me—except in snipe-
> shooting. I distinctly remember knocking over *three* blacks, two men
> and a boy, with one discharge of my double barrel.[88]

But the most active member of the party was a 'tame' Aborigine
employed on Cox's 'Mount Napier' station further up the river:

> Sou'wester had a good innings that day. He fired right and left, raging
> like a demoniac. One huge black, wounded to death, hastened his own
> death by dragging out his entrails, meanwhile praising up the weapons
> of the white man as opposed to those of the blacks. Sou'wester cut
> short his death-song by blowing out his brains.[89]

If these accounts seem sensational, numerous descriptions of similar
incidents, some involving Mounted, Border and Native Police, can
be found in the memoirs of squatters from many areas, as well as
in official records.[90]

Another squatter, James Coutts Crawford, outlined what he regarded as the typical pattern of events leading up to these conflicts:

---

[86] The *nom de plume* of the novelist Thomas Alexander Browne (1826-1915).

[87] Two years earlier, part of Cox's 'Mount Rouse' station had been requisitioned
as an agricultural reserve for the Protectorate's southwestern district
establishment.

[88] R. Boldrewood, *Old Melbourne Memories*, Melbourne 1884, p. 52.

[89] Ibid., pp. 52-3.

[90] Port Macquarie: R. Brough Smyth, *The Aborigines of Victoria*, 2 vols,
Melbourne 1878, Vol. II, pp. 336-9; J. Henderson, *Excursions and Adventures
in New South Wales*, 2 vols, London 1851, Vol. II, pp. 4, 6, 116. New
England: E. and L. Irby, *Memoirs of Edward and Leonard Irby*, Sydney
1908, pp. 59-61, 89-90. Murray: Byrne, *Twelve Years' Wanderings*, pp. 230-2,
250-2; J. Kirby, *Old Times in the Bush of Australia . . .*, Melbourne 1895, pp.
80, 89-101. Wannon: GD, ML, MS.A1226, pp. 229-91. Ovens River: Bride,
Letters, p. 152. Gippsland: T. W. H. Leavitt and W. D. Lilburn, *The Jubilee
History of Victoria and Melbourne*, 2 vols, Melbourne 1888, Vol. II, Pt IV,
p. 91, entry for William Lucas; F. J. Meyrick (ed.), *Life in the Bush (1840-
1847): A Memoir of Henry Howard Meyrick*, London 1939, pp. 136-7.

A stockholder is in want of a fresh run for his stock and therefore proceeds with them outside his neighbours and therefore in contact with an uncivilized tribe of blacks. He erects his hut and stockyard and takes up his residence. A day or two after his first arrival one or two blacks drop in. They are well received and entertained, get some meat and damper fare offered, a little tobacco, which never having used they look at with disgust. The next day a few more of their friends drop in and in a week or so the whole tribe is domesticated with the squatter and they are great friends. Soon however, they see an ox killed, cut up, and prepared for eating and they eat part of him themselves. That evening, out of curiosity, they kill one for themselves and eat him, then hide and other remains are found the next morning. The blacks are remonstrated with, they then proceed to spear some every day. The squatter at length takes up arms, they spear him or any of his stockmen when they find them with their backs turned and war commences and often continues for months and years.[91]

From the Murrumbidgee River, Alexander Harris[92] described the dilemma facing shepherds, stockmen and hut keepers whose responsibility it was to protect their masters' stock and property against Aboriginal attacks:

On the one hand there were the stock owners saying 'If you lose your sheep, if you cannot muster your cattle, we will make such of you as are free pay for them out of your wages, and such of you as are bond, we shall flog'. On another part there were the Protectors saying, 'Use firearms against the aborigines and you die by the halter'. On the third part, the aborigines were ready with the tomahawk and spear to murder them if they did not resist.[93]

It was in the vital interests of the squatters to make the country safe for their stock and their servants, and the desire to protect their property prompted feelings and actions which Christian gentlemen might otherwise have found inconceivable. Henry Meyrick, for example, could

91 D. H. Pike (ed.), 'The Diary of James Coutts Crawford: Extracts on Aborigines and Adelaide, 1839 and 1851', *South Australiana*, IV, No. 1, March 1965, pp. 4-5.
92 Alexander Harris (1805-74) migrated from Scotland to N.S.W. in 1825 and worked as a cedar-cutter on the south coast before taking up a small station somewhere south of Goulburn. In a number of books, the most important of which was *Settlers and Convicts* . . . , London 1847, he gave cogent expression to the views of the squatting interest on the Aborigines, especially on the Myall Creek case. He was one of the signatories to a petition calling for the commutation of the sentence on the convicted murderers.
93 'Religio Christi' in A. A. Chisholm (ed.), *The Secrets of Alexander Harris*, Sydney 1961, p. 207.

remember the time when my blood would have run cold at the mention of these things, but now I am become so familiarized with scenes of horror from having murder made a topic of everyday conversation.[94]

Although unwilling to ride up to Aboriginal camps and fire indiscriminately, as was the practice in parts of Gippsland, Meyrick confessed that he would shoot an Aborigine caught in the act of killing his sheep 'with as little remorse as I would a wild dog'.[95] Others in later years when there was no longer any chance of prosecution boasted of having taken part in pitched battles where 'many of the bravest warriors bit the dust'.[96] Indeed, there was some truth in contemporary allegations that the life of an Aborigine was as nothing against the safety of stock and property.[97]

Although most of the punitive expeditions were designed to 'teach the blacks a lesson' by showing them the high price to be paid for stealing stock and attacking whites, there was at least one instance of stockmen deliberately setting out to exterminate all the Aborigines in their district.

The Liverpool Plains, or *Corborn Comleroy*[98] (land of the Kamilaroi people)[99] as they were known by the Aborigines, were discovered by John Oxley in 1827 and were first settled in the early 1830s[100] by Hunter River landholders who needed more pasture for their rapidly increasing sheep and cattle, especially with the onset of the long drought of 1837-45. From the very beginning the tribes of the Kamilaroi people appear to have resisted the whites.

[94] *Life in the Bush*, p. 137.
[95] Ibid., pp. 136-7.
[96] Bride, *Letters*, p. 152.
[97] *The Sydney Herald*, 24 August 1842.
[98] This name was recorded by Lieutenant W. H. Breton, *Excursions in New South Wales, Western Australia and Van Diemen's Land* . . . , London 1833, p. 101.
[99] According to N. B. Tindale, 'Distribution of Australian Aboriginal Tribes: A Field Survey', *Transactions of the Royal Society of South Australia*, LXI, Pt I, 1940, p. 191, the territory of the Kamilaroi extended from Walgett to Nindigully, Talwood, Garah, Moree, Bingara, Tamworth, Quirindi, Bundella, Gwabegar and Come-by-Chance. See Map 2.
[100] When Mitchell crossed the Liverpool Range in late 1831 he visited Loder's on Quirindi Creek which was evidently the northernmost station at that time, although James Baldwin is reported to have established himself on the Namoi River in 1825 or 1826. By 1832, when the Australian Agricultural Company selected a total of 500,000 acres in the Liverpool Plains and Peel River areas, it was found that 23 squatters were occupying that territory. Although 'limits of location' for the purchase and leasing of land were laid down in 1829, these were impossible to police and it was not until 1837 that

According to William Gardner, shortly after the stations were formed on the Namoi River the neighbouring tribes who had met for some ceremonial purpose issued a formal challenge to the whites to do battle on a fixed date. However, the sixteen heavily-armed stockmen refused to come out of their barricaded hut to fight the 'immense number of Blacks' and after attempting to remove the roof the latter retreated, losing numerous dead and leaving behind 'nearly a dray heap of Spears, Waddies, Boomerangs & Nulla Nullas & Hielamans'. They were then followed on horseback by the stockmen who 'taught them they knew how to fight' and the incident was commemorated by naming the area 'Waterloo Plains'. From that time the Aborigines of the Namoi were 'quiet and peaceable, never attempting to molest the whites' and were employed in grinding corn, fetching wood and water and looking after sheep.[101]

Large tracts of land were quickly taken up along the Gwydir or 'Big River'[102] and in April 1836 two of the Hall brothers' stockmen were killed while forming a new station. In September and November of the following year four more white servants were murdered on Bowman's and Cobb's stations and a petition was got up asking the government to provide protection.[103] On 28 November Robert Scott,[104] a Hunter River landholder who also had cattle runs on the

---

the government began to issue annual licences for the depasturing of stock beyond the limits. However, pre-occupancy was already an effective right as far as the squatters were concerned and there was a brisk commercial trade in stations until the slump of the early 1840s. One £10 licence could be used for a number of stations in various districts and this was one of the major anomalies which Gipps attempted to reform in his 1844 squatting regulations. During 1837-8, 26 licences were taken out for the Liverpool Plains.

[101] 'Discription of a Map of the Five Northern Districts . . .' in J. Calvert, 'Mineral & Topographic Survey of the Five Northern Districts. New South Wales . . . 1845', ML, MS.A3951, and 'Productions and Resources of the Northern and Western Districts', ML, MS.A176-1 and A176-2.

[102] 'Big River' was the original name of the Clarence River and during the 1830s it was thought that what is now the Gwydir River flowed into the Clarence, since both occupied the same latitude. To confuse the matter even further, contemporaries also referred to what are now Meehi Creek and the upper Macintyre as 'Big River'. See HRA, XIX, p. 701 for Gipps' difficulty in describing the location of the Myall Creek massacre.

[103] For a list of Aboriginal 'depredations' on the Liverpool Plains, 1832-8, included with the petition, see Appendix I.

[104] Robert Scott (1799?-1844) was educated at St Andrew's and Lincoln's Inn and was granted 2,000 acres of land on the Hunter River when he arrived in N.S.W. Appointed to the magistracy in 1824 and later a director of the Commercial Banking Co., Scott was a prominent member of the 'exclusivist'

Liverpool Plains, informed the Colonial Secretary that the Aborigines along the Gwydir had become 'extremely hostile'.[105] He enclosed a letter from James Glennie, a squatter recently returned from his station on the Plains, who said that unless something was done all the stations in the area would have to be abandoned. Referring to the murders of whites at Bowman's and Cobb's, Glennie said that he expected the same thing to happen at Crawford's since

> at these three stations, the men have endeavoured to make friends with the Blacks, and have got them to cut bark for them—and of course they have taken their gins, and the first time they have refused the Blacks something, the Blacks have killed them.[106]

Glennie, who had given strict orders that Aborigines were not allowed to come on to his stations, also told Scott that the actions of Egan, one of Scott's overseers, had not improved matters:

> Before Egan took charge of your cattle the stockmen used to be armed at the different stations but as soon as they found out that Egan was going about from station to station endeavouring to find out whether any Blacks had been killed by any of the white people, the stockmen ceased to carry arms and from that time the Blacks have been particularly troublesome. Before they were afraid to meet a stockman, now they are found killing the cattle and dare the stockman to come near them. While I was up [there] eight head of yours were killed by the Blacks. Brown met 17 of them carrying the beef of one they had just killed to the mountains, and they stopped, and told him if he did not go away they would spear him. They are keeping to your cattle because they know that Egan would not let the stockmen prevent them.[107]

Scott urged the Acting Governor, Colonel Kenneth Snodgrass, to provide protection for the whites

> lest by being driven to desparation they take up arms in their own defence, and under excited feelings, these undisciplined men proceed to lengths that would probably be found unnecessary and avoided by responsible and unprejudiced persons.[108]

---

class in the colony. His 'Glendon' estate which he enlarged to 10,000 acres was famous for its stud-horses and was visited by artists, clergy and explorers including Ludwig Leichhart. Scott corresponded with Judge Burton on the Aborigines and gave evidence before the 1838 Committee on the Aborigines Question. He was dismissed by Gipps from the magistracy in December 1838 for the part he played in the Myall Creek trials.

[105] Scott to Deas Thomson, 28 November 1837, *BP*, No. 55.
[106] Glennie to Scott, 21 November 1837, *BP*, No. 55a.
[107] Ibid.
[108] Scott to Deas Thomson, 28 November 1837, *BP*, No. 55.

Further fuel was added to the fire when Alexander Paterson, Crown Lands Commissioner for the Liverpool Plains district, wrote from Archibald Bell's station on the Manilla River in early December:

> The harassing and killing of Cattle is even greater here than on the Namoi, and seems to be getting worse every day. The remains of six bullocks have been found at one of their [Aboriginal] encampments used at one feast. On another occasion when a party went in pursuit of them after they had murdered Mr Cobb's men, they found the remains of 28 sheep at the place where they had encamped the first night after the murder . . . They found 250 fires and the boy [an Aborigine from Fleming's station who had tracked them] said there might be four at each fire.[109]

Paterson shared Glennie's views that it was most imprudent of the men to 'harbour and encourage' Aborigines on the stations, but he believed that the main cause of the outrages was white men living with the Aborigines and leading them in their depredations:

> The Black boy . . . says that there are three white men with them painted like the Blacks, and this statement is corroborated by his taking the party to a hut in the mountains constructed evidently by white men. The wall plates were morticed and pegged down, the bark put on with green hide, the door hung with hide hinges, and berths for sleeping in put up.[110]

Threlkeld reported at the end of 1837 that 'aggressions of the most irritating nature' had been committed by Aborigines in the interior, but that

> the mode of surrounding a herd, the Slautering of the beasts, the preserving of the flesh by smoke and the plaiting of whips from the hides, were the lessons of a convict Stockman, and under such tutors, so numerously scattered amongst the tribes in the interior, it is not marvellous that they should become adept pupils in such arts: upwards of eighty men were shot in retaliation for this affair.[111]

[109] Paterson to Deas Thomson, 6 December 1837, *HRA*, XX, p. 253.
[110] Ibid., p. 253.
[111] Gunson, *Australian Reminiscences and Papers of L. E. Threlkeld*, Vol. I, p. 136. George Clarke, also known as 'The Barber', a convict runaway who lived with the Aborigines of the Liverpool Plains for five years before being captured by the Mounted Police in November 1831, was almost certainly the origin of these stories. Major Mitchell's 1831-2 expedition to the Gwydir was influenced by Clarke's report of a large river called the 'Kindur' which Clarke claimed to have followed in a south-westerly direction to the sea. According to Mitchell, Clarke

Snodgrass called in Major James Winniett Nunn, Commandant of the Mounted Police, showed him Paterson's letter and gave him *carte blanche* to remedy the situation:

> You must lose no time in proceeding; you are to act according to your own judgement, and use your utmost exertion to suppress these outrages. There are a thousand Blacks there, and, if they are not stopped, we may have them presently within the boundaries.[112]

When Nunn and his party of twenty-three troopers reached Robert Fitzgerald's 'Green Hatches' station on the Namoi River in January 1838 they were told that 'wild blacks' who had killed one of Hall's men had been spearing cattle during the previous few days and were now camped in great numbers further down the river. Guided by another squatter's stockmen, the police party succeeded in surrounding the group and 'capturing' them without loss of life. According to his own account, Nunn then told the Aborigines through

had even accustomed himself to the wretched life of that unfortunate race of men; he was deeply scarified like them, and naked and painted black, he went about with a tribe, being usually attended by two aboriginal females, and having acquired some knowledge of their language and customs.

But this degenerate 'white man' was not content with the solitary freedom of the savage life, and his escape from the state of servitude. He had assumed the cloke and colour of the savage, that he might approach the dwellings of the colonists, and steal with less danger of detection. In conjunction with the simple aborigines whom he misled, he had organized a system of cattle-stealing, which was coming into extensive operation on the Liverpool Plains, when through the aid of some of the natives, who have in general assisted in the detection of bushrangers, he was at length discovered and captured by the police. (*Three Expeditions*, Vol. I, pp. 1-2).

Shortly after being captured, Clarke sawed through his irons and escaped from Bathurst Jail, causing some apprehension that he would assemble the Aborigines beyond the settled districts and drive off the colonists' cattle. However, he was recaptured and banished to Norfolk Island until 1835 when he applied to Mitchell to join his next expedition. The Surveyor-General asked for him through Colonel Snodgrass but Bourke 'appreciated his offer much more judiciously, as events proved, and sent Clarke to Van Diemen's Land, where he was soon after hanged'. Ibid., Vol. I, p. 352. Mitchell described him as a man of unusual talents 'who . . . under favourable circumstances, might have organized the scattered natives into formidable bands of marauders'. (Ibid., Vol. I, p. 352). In December 1831 Mitchell discovered Clarke's large stockyards, the remains of a hut and signs of a large Aboriginal camp on the Namoi River (near today's Boggabri) where the bones of cattle were scattered in profusion.

[112] *HRA*, XX, p. 250.

an interpreter that they were charged with murder, spearing cattle and other outrages and that they should deliver up the guilty ones. Some of the 'tame blacks' in the group then pointed out two Aborigines whom they accused of killing Hall's men, together with a number of others said to have speared cattle. The prisoners were taken back to the police camp at 'Green Hatches' but shortly after they had been handed over to the sentries two of the Aborigines slipped their handcuffs and one was shot trying to escape. Setting the others free but retaining one as a guide, Nunn then proceeded to Bell's cattle station on the Gwydir and from there to Cobb's where he found

> everything in the greatest confusion, the Shepherds and people all afraid to leave the vicinity of their huts, and the sheep all crowded about, and not a man could be induced to take them to pasture, until I had sent parties out to scour the country and ascertain that the Blacks were not in the neighbourhood.[113]

Having decided to pursue the tribe which had killed two of Cobb's men, Nunn continued westward along the Gwydir and four days after leaving Marshall's station, then the lowest on the river, came upon some Aborigines who admitted having been with the tribe. Guided by them to a nearby creek, the troopers discovered a party of Aborigines camped on the opposite bank with thick scrub behind them. In the ensuing *mêlée*, a corporal was speared in the leg and a number of the escaping Aborigines shot. A party of local squatters who visited the site later reported that sixty or seventy Aborigines had been killed, 'some of them . . . shot like crows in the trees'[114] and Threlkeld in his mission report for 1838 said that the number may have been as high as 'two or three hundred'.[115] At any rate, the slaughter was notorious and the place[116] was referred to as 'Vinegar Hill' after the New South Wales Corps' attack on convict rebels near Castle Hill in 1804 and the stream was henceforth known as 'Slaughterhouse Creek'.

113 Ibid., p. 250.
114 *The Sydney Morning Herald*, 2 July 1849. Mrs Campbell Praed, *The Australian Life: Black and White*, London 1885, p. 13, described a strikingly similar encounter.
115 Gunson, *Australian Reminiscences and Papers of L. E. Threlkeld*, Vol. I, p. 146.
116 Local tradition has it that the massacre took place at the junction of Slaughterhouse Creek and the Gwydir, a place known to the Aborigines as *Bin-e-gur* (little red hill) and now Biniguy. 'Slaughterhouse' became a

According to local tradition, before Nunn's party returned to Bell's station on the Manilla River there was at least one more large encounter. There were also persistent rumours that after Vinegar Hill, Nunn's troopers shot every Aborigine they saw. John Cobb told Threlkeld that Nunn had boasted to a large party at his station of 'popping off with his holster pistols the Blacks whenever one appeared from behind a tree'.[117] At the official inquiry eighteen months later, Nunn and one of his officers put the number of Aborigines killed on the Gwydir at 'six or seven' but by this time the Myall Creek trials and the publication of a government order upholding the rights of Aborigines as British subjects meant that there were compelling reasons to suppress the full details. In any case, the police had apparently not bothered to count all the bodies.

'Major Nunn's campaign', as it was known in the district, was hardly a solution to racial strife. In March, Aborigines killed two of Surveyor Finch's men and plundered their stores in the neighbouring district of New England; and in April one of Fitzgerald's hutkeepers on the Gwydir was killed, his hut stripped and his two companions attacked when they arrived on the scene. During the following months, stockmen on stations along the Gwydir organized themselves in armed parties which scoured the countryside in a concerted campaign to 'get rid' of all the Aborigines in the district, including the 'tame blacks' attached to the few stations where overseers allowed them to remain. This is still known in local tradition as 'The Bushwhack' or 'The Drive' and there can be no doubt that the stockmen and some of their employers believed that Nunn's methods could be employed with impunity.

In May, a group of between forty and fifty Aborigines[118] arrived

---

common appellation for places where Aborigines had been killed. Charles Daley, *The Story of Gippsland*, Melbourne 1960, p. 38, records a tradition that when sixteen Aborigines were shot and their bodies thrown into a deep hole in the Murrindal River in Gippsland, the place was 'known for years afterwards as Slaughterhouse Gully'.

117 Threlkeld to Judge W. W. Burton, 8 February 1839, in Gunson, *Australian Reminiscences and Papers of L. E. Threlkeld*, Vol. II, p. 275.

118 These Aborigines are locally believed to have belonged to the *Weraerai* whose territory, according to N. B. Tindale, extended along the Gwydir west to Moree, north to Gilgil Creek and east to Inverell. William Gardner, on the other hand, described the 'Myall Creek Big River' Aborigines as speaking the 'Queenbal' language which is almost certainly Tindale's *Kwiambal*, occupying the lower Severn River, Fraser Creek and Ashford area to the east of Myall Creek station. According to local tradition, the burial

at Henry Dangar's station on Myall Creek[119] near the Gwydir River and set up camp close to the men's huts. Unlike other Aborigines in the area, the group were known to be peaceable and well-behaved and had been living for some time on McIntyre's and Wiseman's stations nearby where they were occasionally employed in cutting sheets of bark and other small tasks. They had come earlier to Myall Creek with Andrew Eaton, the convict hutkeeper on Peter McIntyre's station 'for the purpose of making them friends with Mr. Dangar's men'. They had been on such good terms with Eaton that he allowed them to sleep in his hut.

Charles Kilmaister, a prisoner for life assigned to Dangar and

grounds of the *Weraerai* were half a mile from the Myall Creek station huts and these were located in 1964 by Mr Cecil Wall (now deceased) and Mr Len Payne of Bingara and later inspected by Professor Isabel McBryde of the University of New England. A few miles to the north is a small plain with sandstone outcrops where they fashioned spears and other implements from the *myall* scrub (see below). However, contemporary evidence indicates that it was the first time this particular group had visited the station since the huts were built. There is a strong possibility that they were *Kwiambal* who had moved out of their traditional territory, with the encouragement of white protection, to become 'station blacks'. I am indebted to Professor Tindale for this suggestion.

119 Named after the *myall*, a species of acacia which grew in profusion along the banks of a creek flowing into the Gwydir, the station was situated about half way between the present towns of Bingara and Delungra. Dangar (1796-1861) arrived in N.S.W. from England in 1821 and joined the Survey Department. During 1822-3 he surveyed the Hunter Valley for settlement and in 1824 crossed the Liverpool Range. Dismissed by Darling after a board of inquiry had shown that he had used his position for financial gain, he was employed by the Australian Agricultural Company and surveyed land on the Liverpool Plains in preparation for its claim there. It was no doubt during this visit that he chose locations for three stations of his own which he developed after leaving the Company's service in 1833, together with 'Gostwyck' and possibly other stations in the New England district. Dangar was listed in the *Government Gazette* as having a licence for ' "Gostwyck" etc.' in 1840 but it was not until 1848 that he was listed for 'Myall Creek' (48,000 acres), 'Moonbi' (25,600 acres), 'Buleori' (64,000 acres) and 'Karee' or 'Far West' (64,000 acres). 'Myall Creek' is believed to have originally extended over 300,000 acres although there is no way of checking this. The station huts were probably built in 1835 or 1836 and the stockyards were completed in 1837. Dangar opposed the abolition of transportation and the assignment system and later strongly advocated the importation of coolie labour. In 1844 he bitterly opposed Gipps' squatting regulations. E. C. Rowland 'The Life and Times of Henry Dangar', *JRAHS*, XXXIX, Pt I-II, 1953, pp. 1-23, 49-76; *ADB*, Vol. I, pp. 280-2. It seems extraordinary that the *ADB* entry of more than four columns should make no mention of the Myall Creek massacre and Dangar's membership of the Hunter River Black Association.

employed as a stockman at Myall Creek, became very friendly with
the Aborigines and after work each day would join in their dancing
and singing. It was he who persuaded the station overseer, William
Hobbs, that they should be allowed to stay. Hobbs gave them whatever food was available but each morning the men of the group
went out hunting for opossums and other game unless they were
asked to cut bark or perform other small tasks. As the relationship
developed, most of the Aborigines were given European names and
the hutkeeper, George Anderson, another prisoner for life, took an
attractive young girl called 'Ipeta' as his bed-mate. There were
more than a dozen women in the group and almost as many children including 'Charley', a precocious three-year-old who quickly
picked up some English and became a general favourite. Among
the men was 'King Sandy', an old man called 'Joey' (whose proudest
possession was a Scotch cap which a white man had given to him)
and 'Daddy', a massive white-haired old man who was the 'doctor'
or *karadjee*[120] of the group. In a basket he carried some small
crystals of quartz revered by the Aborigines and used in many of
their ceremonies.[121] On 5 June Hobbs despatched two assigned
servants, Andrew Burrows and Charles Reid, with a mob of bullocks
to Dangar's lower station on the Gwydir about sixty miles to the
west and two days later he set out to follow them. On the evening
of 8 June, Burrows and Reid reached Archibald Bell's station where
John Russell, a former convict freed by servitude, was employed
as a stockman. Russell and seven or eight other stockmen from
neighbouring stations[122] now gathered at Bell's had been out looking

---

[120] In Aboriginal society the *karadjee* possessed special mythological and
religious knowledge as well as carrying out the functions of doctor and
sorcerer. See A. P. Elkin, *Aboriginal Men of High Degree*, Sydney 1945.
According to local tradition, Daddy was 6 ft 7 in. Hobbs said that he 'was
the largest man I ever saw, either white or black'. (*Sydney Gazette*, 20
November 1838.)

[121] Elkin, *Aboriginal Men of High Degree*, describes in detail the significance
and use of these talismanic crystals.

[122] Among these Burrows recognized: John ('Black') Johnston, a negro free by
servitude employed by James Cox of Moree; Charles Toulouse, assigned
servant to James Glennie ('Gineroi' station); Edward Foley, assigned servant
to Joseph Fleming ('Mungabundi' station); William Hawkins, a ticket-of-
leave men employed by Andrew Blake (Mosquito Creek); George Palliser,
free by servitude and employed by Archibald Bell ('Bengaria' station). Other
members of the party which came to Myall Creek were: Charles Lamb, a
ticket-of-leave man employed by John Cobb ('Gravesend' station); John
Blake, assigned servant to James Glennie ('Gineroi' station); James Parry,

for Aborigines who had speared some cattle and a horse down river. They were making preparations for another expedition and Russell, who normally wore a cutlass, was making a strap for it and a pouch for ammunition.

The men said they wished that Charles Lamb, an assigned servant working on John Cobb's station nearby, had come and that if they could get all the men who were expected they would have twelve or thirteen. When they asked Burrows if there were any Aborigines at Myall Creek, he told them that a group had been there for four or five weeks and some of the men then remarked that these could not have been the ones committing depredations down river. As they left next morning, Burrows and Reid noticed that the men were getting ready to set off and later in the day they met John Fleming, native-born son of Joseph Fleming, who managed his father's station next to Dangar's lower station. Fleming, armed with a fowling piece and a sword, told them that he and another man had just been out after Aborigines and that he was anxious to join the party. He only hoped that his tired mare could make Bell's station in time to catch up with them.

The same day (Saturday, 9 June) Thomas Foster, the overseer of Dr William Newton's station, came to Myall Creek looking for Aborigines to cut bark. After spending the night at the station he left the next morning with ten men from the group who were unarmed except for some 'tomahawks'. Among them was King Sandy.

Meanwhile the armed party, swelled by the addition of James Parry (assigned servant to Daniel Eaton) and John Blake (assigned servant to James Glennie) had commenced their expedition by calling at Newton's to ask if there were any Aborigines cutting bark there. They then went on to T. Simpson Hall's station where they were joined by James Oates, otherwise known as 'Hall's Jemmy'. By this time Fleming had evidently caught up with the party.

Returning to Newton's on Sunday afternoon, Foster was told that the party had come looking for 'blacks'. Knowing only too well what the men were up to, he told the ten Aborigines who had come with him to go back to Dangar's immediately by way of the mountains and tell their people to escape as quickly as possible.

---

assigned servant to Daniel Eaton ('Binegui' station); James Oates (also known as 'Hall's Jemmy'), assigned servant to T. Simpson Hall ('Bingera' station); John Fleming, son of Joseph Fleming and overseer of his father's station ('Mungabundi').

Unfortunately, they could not make the station in time. An hour
and a half before sunset the armed party galloped up to Myall
Creek brandishing their swords and guns. When they saw them
coming the terrified Aborigines crowded into the men's hut, begging
Kilmaister and Anderson to save them. But Russell and another
man went into the hut where they handcuffed most of the weeping
and protesting Aborigines and strung them to a long tethering-rope
fastened to one of the horses.[123] When Anderson asked Russell what
they were going to do with them, he said that they only wanted to
take the Aborigines to the back of the range and 'frighten' them
before letting them go. One woman was untied and given to 'Davey',
a young Peel River Aborigine who had brought cattle to Myall
Creek for Dangar and was now employed on the station. Anderson
then asked for a woman but the 'good-looking gin' he was given
was not Ipeta. Davey and Anderson managed to save King Sandy's
little boy by hiding him under a bed. They also tried to save
Charley who had been hiding all the while behind the hut but he
insisted on going with his 'mama'. Kilmaister, who had been talking
with the men since their arrival, took his pistols and went to fetch
his horse so that he could accompany the party.[124] The Aborigines,
children at their sides and babies clinging to their mothers' backs,
were then forced along by the mounted men towards a newly-
constructed set of stockyards about half a mile to the west of the
huts. With the exception of one or two women, all were slaught-

123 This method was used by squatters to slaughter the 'tame blacks' on
neighbouring stations after the murder by Aborigines of the Fraser family
at 'Hornet Bank' station on the Dawson River near Taroom in Central
Queensland in 1857 (Donald Gunn, *Links with the Past*, Brisbane 1937,
p. 37). W. H. Suttor told the N.S.W. Legislative Council in 1849 of a case
where some men who had surrounded a tribe of Aborigines containing
cattle-thieves sought his permission 'to tie the miserable blacks on a string
and shoot them all'. (*The Sydney Morning Herald*, 2 July 1849). There are
also a number of reports from northern N.S.W. and southern Queensland of
Aborigines being tied or handcuffed together and taken long distances so
that they would not come back to the stations.

124 There is no evidence to support the *Sydney Gazette*'s belief that Kilmaister
was the 'ringleader' of the group although his actions were certainly
extraordinary in view of his former close relations with the Aborigines.
Russell and Fleming appear to have played important parts but as Mr Len
Payne has pointed out to me the latter received 'undue credit simply
because he had enough fear and good fortune to escape'. Russell's more
mature age and his careful preparations for the expedition, together with
various pieces of circumstantial evidence, lend weight to Payne's belief that
he and Blake were the 'ringleaders'.

ered; according to Davey who visited the scene immediately after the massacre, Daddy was decapitated and the children slashed or decapitated with a *cobawn knife* (cutlass) and one or two shots were fired.[125] Davey, unnoticed in the gathering dusk, watched from behind a tree.

The men did not come back to the Myall Creek huts that night but some hours after nightfall the ten Aborigines returned from Newton's, only to be told by Davey and Anderson that they were too late. When they indicated that they wanted to bury the remains immediately, Davey warned them that the men were probably waiting in ambush and sent them away, together with the two women, King Sandy's little boy who was now re-united with his father, and two other boys who had escaped into the creek when they saw the men approaching.

Having camped out overnight on the creek, the party arrived after sunrise at Newton's where they learnt that the bark-cutters had already left. 'God knows where they are now', Foster told them. He would not allow one of the men, John Blake, to leave an Aboriginal woman whom he had brought with him at the station and the party then rode on to Dight's where they had breakfast. Blake left the woman there, saying that he would call for her later. That night the party returned to Myall Creek and the next morning after breakfast Russell, Fleming and Kilmaister collected firebrands and all the men, with the exception of Foley who stayed with Anderson in the hut to guard the weapons, went back to the scene of the massacre. While they were busy dragging the bodies

---

[125] Mr Cecil Wall told Mr Payne in 1964 that the story passed down in his family was of the Aborigines being killed inside the stockyards. As a boy, Wall had been shown dark stains on the stockyards fence which were said to have resulted from the massacre. Hobbs and other witnesses at the Myall Creek trials made no mention of the stockyards although the prosecution referred to them as 'a convenient place'. At any rate, the bodies would have had to be removed some distance in order to avoid setting fire to the yards. In 1964 Mr Wall took Mr Payne to what he recalled as being the site of the long-demolished yards about half-a-mile from the present Myall Creek station and they were able to discover not only some large old posts which had evidently served as fence uprights but a pair of 18 lb handwrought hinges buried in the earth which had probably been part of the main gates. Mr Payne and I examined the site once again in April 1972 and found several posts. These details are important in view of the fact that a number of people in the Bingara district continue to deny that the stockyards ever existed on Myall Creek station and that the massacre ever occurred.

D

to the nearby ridge and building a huge bonfire around them, Foley pulled one of the men's swords out of its case and showed Anderson that it was covered with blood.

When the men returned, Fleming told Kilmaister to 'go up by and by and put the logs together, and to be sure that all was consumed'. Before the party left, they threatened Billy, Davey's younger brother, that they would kill him unless he showed them where there were more Aborigines to be found. They then went to McIntyre's station where they killed an unknown number of Aborigines, and to a nearby creek where they disposed of another seven. Evidently satisfied with their expedition, they stayed at Wiseman's station for a few days before dispersing.[126] Billy was allowed to return to Myall Creek with two women.

[126] This account of the Myall Creek massacre is based on the depositions taken by Day during his visit to the Liverpool Plains in July-August 1838 (Muswellbrook Bench-book 1838-43, NSWA, 4/5601, pp. 85-149) and reports of the two trials of the Myall Creek men in *The Australian* of 17 and 29 November and 1 and 6 December 1838.

Surprisingly little has been written about the massacre. Bill Wannan, *Very Strange Tales* . . . , Melbourne 1962, pp. 191-223 has a popular account that is not always reliable in detail and Brian W. Harrison, *The Myall Creek Massacre and its Significance in the Controversy over the Aborigines* . . . (BA hons thesis, University of New England, Armidale, 1966) concentrates more on the newspaper controversy which the trials created. L. L. Payne, *Correlation of known and attested facts from the past and the present concerning the infamous Myall Creek massacre* (duplicated typescript, Bingara 1965) includes a useful summary of local traditions about the massacre and is the first attempt to place the incident in the context of a number of similar events in the Gwydir area. Reactions to an Apex Club proposal to build a gate commemorating the massacre and to the display of a pair of massive gate-hinges discovered by Payne on the site of the Myall Creek stockyards in July 1964 indicated that there were many people in the Bingara district who either did not want details of the massacre revived or refused to believe that it had ever happened. Shortly after a controversy in *The Bingara Advocate* in early 1965 (see issues for 20 and 27 January), the tombstone of one John Blake in the local cemetery was smashed to pieces. Blake, who was acquitted in the first Myall Creek trial, is believed to have later returned to the district and married into one of the families there.

The local tradition is that there were two major massacres in the district during early settlement, one at Myall Creek and another at about the same time at Slaughterhouse Creek. However, the two have sometimes been confused as in C. F. Boughton, 'Early History of Moree and Adjacent Districts' (extracts from the Moree *North-West Champion*, ML, p. 32). Boughton could not believe that there had been two major massacres, although the evidence indicates that there were probably as many as ten if Major Nunn's efforts are included. Unfortunately, I have not been able

On 15 June Hobbs called at Dight's on his way back to Myall Creek and learnt of the massacre from the hutkeeper Bates. Parry had told Bates that 'the blacks' had been 'settled' but Oates had said that 'it was a thing he did not like and would never have a hand in the like again'. Returning to Myall Creek, Hobbs questioned Anderson, Kilmaister and Davey and then together with the Aboriginal stockman followed the horsemen's clearly discernible tracks to the ridge beyond the stockyards where the bodies had been burnt.[127] There he was able to count twenty-eight heads and skulls but some of the bodies had not been consumed by the still-burning fire and the stench was almost overpowering. Birds of prey and dingoes had been feeding on the remains. The next day he inspected the place again, this time with Foster, and they discussed the best means of informing the authorities. Unable to leave their posts, they later agreed to the proposal of a neighbouring squatter, Frederick Foot, that he should inform the police magistrate at Invermein (Scone) 150 miles away while on his journey to Sydney. Kilmaister, who at first claimed that he did not know what had happened to the Aborigines and later that he took no part in the massacre, was extremely perturbed when Hobbs read out a letter which he was sending to Dangar. 'I hope, Sir, you won't report', he implored. 'For Jesus Christ sake, don't report it.'[128]

---

to establish if there are Aboriginal traditions about Myall Creek and the other massacres although it is known that, with a few exceptions, Aborigines have since avoided the district.

[127] On his way to the site, Hobbs discovered a basket which had been dropped by one of the victims. In it were a piece of opossum skin, pipe clay, belts and 'some small crystal stones which the blacks set great value on'. The basket almost certainly belonged to Daddy who would normally have been custodian of the quartz crystals.

[128] At least one overseer, McCormick of Eaton's, also asked Hobbs not to report the incident. Foot, who evidently announced in the neighbourhood that he intended making a report, received 'very threatening and abusive language' from 'Hall's servant' (Oates?) and 'would have brought him up for punishment had he an opportunity' (letter from C. J. Williams, clerk of the Bench at Muswellbrook, to Deas Thomson, 28 June 1838, *CSIL*, Governor's Minutes, 1838(2), M4329, 4/1014). In September 1838 Threlkeld reported that a 'gentleman' who had made a deposition before a magistrate on the murder of Aborigines was suffering harassment:

Intimidation is held out to drive him from his pasturage by a lawless banditti of free and bond, who can readily unite in such measures against those who possess not a spirit so diabolical, murderous and ungodly as their own!

Although he had not mentioned it to Anderson or Hobbs earlier, Kilmaister now claimed that the Aborigines who had been killed had been 'rushing' cattle on the station the day before the massacre. Hobbs then spent a few days with Kilmaister riding around the run but could find no sign that the cattle had been disturbed. In the meantime, three men had come back to the place where the bodies had been burnt and carried away most of the remains in sacks so that when Police Magistrate E. D. Day[129] inspected the site a month later during his investigation into the incident, only some children's jawbones, teeth and ribs could be found.

Contemporary evidence and local tradition suggest very strongly that the Myall Creek massacre was only one of a series which took place in the district commencing in 1836. According to Hobbs, the

---

('Memoranda', in Gunson, *Australian Reminiscences and Papers* of L. E. Threlkeld, Vol. I, p. 139.)

Foot is not known to have made a deposition but was certainly responsible for reporting the Myall Creek massacre to the authorities and was probably the 'gentleman' mentioned in Threlkeld's story. He was listed in the 1839 register as having a licence to depasture stock in the Liverpool Plains district and William Gardner's 1846 'Discription of a Map of the Five Northern Districts' described him as occupying 'Barrabba' to the south of Myall Creek.

129 Edward Denny Day (1801-76), son of an Anglican clergyman, was born in Kerry, Ireland. In 1820 he joined the 46th Regiment of Foot as an ensign and served until 1833 when he was appointed lieutenant in the 62nd Regiment with whom he served for a short time in India. Resigning from the army because of ill-health in 1834 he went to Sydney where he was first appointed Clerk of the Executive Council and then transferred to the Colonial Secretary's Department. In January 1836 he was made Police Magistrate for the Vale of Clwydd (Hartley-Lithgow) and from there was transferred to Maitland (January 1837) and to Muswellbrook (October 1837). In June 1838 he was despatched by Gipps to the Gwydir River to investigate the Myall Creek massacre and succeeded in capturing 11 of the 12 murderers. In December 1840, having left the magistracy, he demonstrated great personal courage by leading a police party in an attack on a well-armed gang of bushrangers led by Davis ('The Jew Boy') who had been raiding stations, including one owned by the Dangar family. Day had earlier been involved with Henry Dangar in the formation of the Maitland branch of the Australian Immigration Association which was committed to increasing migration from Britain. In 1844 he accompanied Gipps on a tour of the Paterson River and in 1846, his business ventures having been unsuccessful, he returned to Sydney as Superintendent of Police and commanded the guard of honour at Gipps' departure. He later served as stipendiary magistrate at Port Macquarie and Maitland where he retired in 1869. Ben W. Champion, 'Captain Edward Denny Day . . .', *JRAHS*, XXII, Pt V, 1936, pp. 345-57 and *ADB*, Vol. I, p. 300.

Aborigines at Myall Creek were harmless and would have been allowed to live,

> but success having attended *the first two massacres*, the murderers grew bold; and in order that their cattle might never more be 'rushed' it was resolved to exterminate the whole race of blacks in that quarter.[130]

Day told the 1839 Committee on Police and Gaols that

> It was represented to me, and I believe truly, that the blacks had repeatedly been pursued by parties of mounted and armed stockmen, assembled for the purpose, and that great numbers of them had been killed at various spots, particularly at Vinegar Hill, Slaughterhouse Creek, and Gravesend, places so called by the stockmen, in commemoration of the deeds enacted there.[131]

The first massacre was probably at Crawford's 'Ardgowan Plains' station on the Gwydir which was described by Aborigines to Crown Lands Commissioner Edward Mayne as having taken place twelve days before the murder of Cobb's two shepherds in November 1837:

> The blacks informed me that this was done in revenge for the murder in question. They explained the delay to have arisen from the difficulty of getting all the tribes together sooner; . . . I believe two or three attacks had been made on them by the overseers and stockmen within a few weeks on that part of the river. They stated, that finding it impossible to retaliate on the mounted stockmen, they determined to attack the shepherds and sheep.[132]

Following this, according to Threlkeld, the two shepherds' fellow servants 'armed themselves, overtook or came upon the tribe, found some with the clothes of the murdered shepherds on their backs, whom they hewed to pieces with their hatchets, and killed others'.[133] Mayne also visited a hill called 'Gravesend' ('after the

---

[130] *The Monitor*, 14 December 1838 (my emphasis).
[131] 'Report of the Committee on Police and Gaols', *V&P*, 1839, Vol. II, p. 224.
[132] Ibid., p. 24. However, Mr Len Payne believes that 'The Bushwhack' began with a massacre at a place now known as 'Pimpampa' station near Rowena and extended further east, culminating after five weeks in the massacres of 'tame blacks' at Myall Creek and McIntyre's. In the 1920s a large pile of bleached Aboriginal bones was something of a tourist attraction at 'Pimpampa'. One skeleton, strung together with wire, was seven feet in length.
[133] Gunson, *Australian Reminiscences and Papers of L. E. Threlkeld*, Vol. I, p. 144.

number of appearances of graves'), three miles from Cobb's head station, where as many as two hundred Aborigines were said to have been killed in another massacre before November 1837.[134]

Whether the Myall Creek men were involved in these two major incidents is difficult to ascertain but there are indications that they took part in at least one other massacre where between thirty and forty Aborigines were disposed of in similar fashion to those at Dangar's station. Describing this to Judge W. W. Burton[135] in February 1839, Threlkeld did not spare the gory details:

> the last that was murdered, was an elderly woman whose throat was cut as she stood, and then [they] let her run away, that the Blood spurted out, and when she fell they took her up while yet alive and cast her into the triangular log fire, and her infant child they threw alive without any previous injury into the flames. The Black *Davey* told it all with high glee and mimicked the struggles of the dying victims in the fire.[136]

The missionary had passed this story on to Gipps in October 1838 and the Governor, hoping that it was just another version of Myall Creek, asked him to compare notes with Day. However, both men were satisfied that there had been two distinct massacres committed by the same party. Threlkeld asked his son Joseph, who had a station on the Liverpool Plains, to fetch Davey and Billy so that they could give evidence but was told by his brother-in-law Thomas Arndell that the rumour was that Davey had been *'put out of the way'*.[137] The missionary believed that if the government established an inquiry into the behaviour of whites towards Aborigines in the interior

> A War of extirpation would be found to have long existed, in which the ripping open of the bellies of the Blacks alive;—the roasting of them in that state in triangularly made log fires, made for the very purpose;—the dashing of infants upon the stones; the confining of a party in a hut and letting them out singly through the door-way, to be butchered as they endeavoured to escape, together with many other

134 'Report of the Committee on Police and Gaols', *V&P*, 1839, Vol. II, p. 24.
135 For a biographical note on Burton, see p. 150.
136 Threlkeld to Burton, 9 February 1839, in Gunson, *Australian Reminiscences and Papers of L. E. Threlkeld*, Vol. II, p. 275. Mr Len Payne believes that this massacre took place after Myall Creek and in the vicinity of 'The Old Retreat', near today's Little Plain between Delungra and Inverell.
137 Gunson, *Australian Reminiscences and Papers of L. E. Threlkeld*, Vol. II, p. 275.

atrocious acts of cruelty, which are but the sports of monsters boasting of superior intellect to that possessed by the wretched Blacks![138]

In his mission report for 1838, Threlkeld claimed that while fifteen whites had been killed by Aborigines on the Liverpool Plains since 1832,

> a secret hostile process has been encouraged and carried on against the Blacks by a party of lawless Europeans, until it gained confidence, and unblushingly and openly appeared, to the loss of upwards of five hundred Aborigines within the last two years including the numerous massacres of men, women and children.[139]

This figure, provided by Day and confirmed by John Cobb and the Rev. Charles Wilton, included an estimated 'two or three hundred' killed during 'Major Nunn's campaign', but not the eighty believed by Threlkeld to have been killed in a separate incident by a party of Mounted Police led by a certain Sergeant Temple.[140] This massacre, mentioned to Joseph Threlkeld 'as a mere matter of course' by a stockman called Evans and his son who had accompanied the police party, may have been the 'Port Macquarie murders' reported in the *Sydney Gazette* shortly after Gipps' arrival in the colony and referred to again by that newspaper during the Myall Creek trials.[141]

Two other incidents from the Liverpool Plains related to Threlkeld by the stockman Evans indicated that the banding together of stockmen to 'punish' Aborigines was a common practice, although it did not always meet with the approval of their employers:

> In one instance a Stockman boasted to his master, that a bullock was speared, and that he went after the Blacks with a party, but outriding them, he overtook the blacks and killed 6 with his own hand! Instead of receiving the reward he expected from his Master for the exploit, his Master very properly discharged him. The other incident mentioned was this: Some cattle had been speared, the stockmen assembled, they went in search of the Blacks, found one; they knew not who he was, or whether guilty or not, they took him prisoner, tied his hands behind him, and fastened him to the stirrup of one of the horsemen and proceeded homewards. When they arrived near the huts the party separated, leaving the man to whom the black was

138 Ibid., Vol. I, p. 139.
139 Ibid., Vol. I, p. 145.
140 Ibid., Vol. I, pp. 136, 138.
141 In this instance, white constables were supposed to have returned with a number of Aborigines' ears as proof of the success of their expedition.

fastened to take him home to the hut; When the black found himself alone with the stockman he hung back, on which the stockman took out his pocket clasp knife, struck the Black through the throat, as he would a sheep, the Black fell down, the stockman rode away. It so happened that the Black had strength to crawl to Mr ———, a gentleman living at the Plains, not far distant. The Black told him his tale and then expired.

An enquiry was talked of, but the long journey to Sydney and consequent trouble and expense of attending court, where the inadequacy of the usual allowances to cover the actual costs is a serious drawback to the ends of justice, the loss of the services of the Stockman, together with the want of legal evidence of the fact, operated, it is said, to prevent the gentleman proceeding.[142]

There is some evidence that extensive depredations in the Liverpool Plains district commencing in July 1838 and reaching a climax in 1842-3 were motivated by a spirit of revenge arising from Myall Creek and other incidents. The Aborigines made concerted attempts to drive off the whites by destroying their stock and buildings, attacking them at every opportunity and killing horses so that the stockmen could not pursue them.

Day described the situation he found on the Liverpool Plains in July 1838 as 'a state of warfare' in which the whites felt that they were in an enemy's country and were afraid to venture outside their loopholed huts without firearms.[143] The Aborigines, he said, had been useful at first by helping to form the stations and by cutting bark and performing other services and he could only explain the subsequent hostility as arising from the stockmen's 'interference' with their women. When Mayne arrived a few months later the situation had not improved, there being very few stations where Aborigines dared show themselves:

such was the want of confidence subsisting between the Whites and the Blacks, that wherever they encountered each other, the Whites expected themselves or their cattle to be speared, and the Blacks expected to be fired at.

It seemed to be the general impression among the Overseers and Stockmen of the Upper District, that the Namoi and Gwydir Blacks would unite and make a general attack on the Herds and Stations. I think it probable that there were grounds for that impression. I con-

---

[142] Threlkeld to Burton, 20 July 1838, in Gunson, *Australian Reminiscences and Papers of L. E. Threlkeld*, Vol. II, pp. 267-8.
[143] 'Report of the Committee on Police and Gaols', *V&P*, 1839, Vol. II, p. 224.

*sider that the desire of revenge on the part of the Blacks originated in
various outrages committed on them by Stockmen and persons of that
class.* Previous to my arrival in the district, I believe many instances
occurred in which the whites fired upon the Blacks when merely meeting them on the runs. I am informed that the whites have been known
to rush them into the scrubs, and to fire on women and children; and
that the Stockmen and Hutkeepers always went about with firearms.[144]

Early in 1839 a number of attacks took place on the Gwydir
River within ten miles of where the Myall Creek Aborigines had
been murdered. Four hut-keepers were killed, despite the fact that
in one instance the attackers had just been supplied with food,
tomahawks and brass plates.[145] Although between 400 and 500 of
one squatter's sheep were killed, no part of any of them was taken
away. Similarly, a number of cattle were killed for their kidney fat
alone.[146] These appear to have been acts of sabotage, but in some
instances Aborigines obviously believed that the hanging of seven
of the Myall Creek men in December 1838 gave them immunity
against punishment. On 31 August 1839 *The Australian* published
a Galong correspondent's report that Aborigines arrested for sheep
stealing had told the constable who threatened to shoot them if they
ran away: 'You shoot me, the Governor hang you'. There were
numerous stories of a similar nature.

In February 1843 *The Sydney Morning Herald* was reporting
depredations in the southern parts of the Liverpool Plains which
had been peaceful for a number of years. The 'tame blacks' of the
Namoi, for example, had begun killing cattle on 'Rocky Creek'

---

144 Ibid., p. 23 (my emphasis).
145 The custom of distributing brass 'plates' or gorgets appears to have been
instituted by Macquarie in 1815 when he presented Bungaree with a 'badge'
inscribed with the coat of arms of New South Wales and the legend 'Chief
of the Broken Bay Tribe'. 'Badges of distinction' were presented two years
later to 'Chieftains' at the Parramatta 'feast' as part of Macquarie's plan to
create an Aboriginal political hierarchy responsible for the behaviour of their
race. 'Badges of merit' were also given to Aborigines who had performed
valuable services to the white community, e.g., tracking down bushrangers.
Brass plates were prized by the Aborigines only as a means of obtaining
rations from the whites and by the 1830s they were also being distributed
by settlers who chose their own 'kings'—usually Aborigines with a superior
command of English whose goodwill was valued. For further information,
see Reece, 'Feasts and Blankets'.
146 'Report from the Committee on the Crown Lands Bill', *V&P*, 1839, Vol. I,
pp. 9, 17.

station, and their numbers were reinforced by 'myalls' or 'wild blacks' from the northern end of the plains. In one instance an Aborigine who had just killed a hut-keeper and wounded his companion called out that he and his friends had killed all their horses and intended to kill or drive off all the 'whitefellows' from the Mooney, Macintyre and Severn Rivers.[147] In another, Aborigines announced their intention of killing every head of stock on the Gwydir, Boomi, Macintyre and Severn Rivers, as well as the northern part of New England.[148] During 1843, attacks on life and property became so serious that a number of squatters abandoned their stations on the Mooney River after suffering heavy stock losses. Following a number of clashes on the Barwon River, a punitive expedition of twenty-three men organized by squatters was ambushed one night by Aborigines who killed an overseer and a stockman and wounded three others.[149]

The unrelenting hostility of Aborigines in the northern part of the plains delayed effective settlement until 1846 and was eventually suppressed by a detachment of Native Police based at Warialda, north of Myall Creek. Alexander Harris was firmly convinced that execution of the seven Myall Creek men heightened racial strife by hardening white attitudes:

> From this time forward . . . the mischief increased. The blacks were driven out of the huts where hitherto they had always found countenance and kindness. They in retaliation either did, or, incited the wilder blacks to do, violence to the settler's property and to his men's lives. Then again, in return, the men and many of the masters shot them, with no more compunction than they would so many bush-dogs, in the secrecy of the bush, and left them there.[150]

He also claimed that in the areas where commissioners or employers banned the use of firearms, the consequent feeling of in-

[147] *The Sydney Morning Herald*, 1 February 1843.
[148] 'Reminiscences of Mrs. Susan Bundarra Young . . .', *JRAHS*, VIII, 1923, p. 399.
[149] *Maitland Mercury*, 9 September 1843, cited in James Jervis, 'Exploration and Settlement of the North-Western Plains', *JRAHS*, XLVIII, Pt V, 1962, p. 388.
[150] *Settlers and Convicts*, p. 221. This was corroborated by two other squatters: Gideon Scott Lang in his *Aborigines of Australia* . . . , Melbourne 1865, p. 45, and George Faithfull in Bride, *Letters*, p. 153; and by Protector James Dredge in his *Brief Notices of the Aborigines of New South Wales* . . . , Geelong 1845, p. 25.

security caused many whites to resort to poison as an alternative method of 'protection'.[151] Quantities of arsenic and mercuric compounds used for treating sheep diseases were readily obtainable and it would have been an easy matter to mix these in dampers or cakes to be given to the Aborigines.[152]

Hearsay reports of poisoning abound, but there is fairly good evidence of its use on Dr James Kilgour's 'Tarrone' station near Port Fairy in 1842 and on Evan McKenzie's 'Kilcoy' station northwest of Moreton Bay in the same year.[153] Although it was almost impossible for the authorities to obtain legal evidence of poisoning, it was, as Harris said, 'no less than the rumour of the whole country side'.[154] *The Monitor*, for example, recorded a revealing conversation in the barrack square shortly after the execution of seven of the Myall Creek men in December 1838:

Country Gentleman	—	So, I find they have hanged these men?
Town Gentleman	—	They have.
Country Gentleman	—	Ah—hem—we are going on a *safer* game now.
Town Gentleman	—	*Safer* game? how do you mean?
Country Gentleman	—	Why, we are poisoning the Blacks; which is much safer; and serve them right too.[155]

The Port Phillip Protectorate further embittered the squatters and their servants towards the Aborigines by causing depredations in the vicinity of the Protectors. A few squatters were antagonized by the resumption of parts of their stations for Protectorate reserves and most saw the Protectorate as evidence that the British and colonial governments were putting the interests of the Aborigines

---

[151] *Settlers and Convicts*, p. 211.

[152] *The Monitor*, 24 December 1838.

[153] GD, ML, MS.A1233, pp. 1397-1456. Further evidence of the 'Kilcoy' case was brought to light in Brisbane in 1861 by Captain John Coley and John Ker Wilson, witnesses before the Select Committee on the Native Police and the Condition of the Aborigines Generally, Queensland Legislative Assembly, *Votes and Proceedings*, 1861, pp. 425-6, 467.

[154] Harris, *Settlers and Convicts*, p. 211.

[155] *The Monitor*, 24 December 1838. Other versions of this story were recorded by the *Sydney Gazette* of 20 December 1838 and the *Commercial Journal and Advertiser* of 26 December 1838. In March 1840 Threlkeld informed Deas Thomson that a convict called Humphries had reported the poisoning of Aborigines with prussic acid at a station on the Beardy Plains (north of Armidale). There was no investigation although Gipps evidently promised one.

before those of the settlers. An important development was the collection of large numbers of Aborigines by Protector C. W. Sieve-wright in the Port Fairy district, without any adequate provision for their sustenance and control. Inevitably, the Aborigines raided the neighbouring stations, causing serious loss of life and property. The Port Fairy squatters claimed in a petition of 1842 that, in the first two months of the year, the Aborigines had stolen more than 4,000 sheep and 200 cattle, as well as robbing a number of huts, killing four men, and wounding seven.[156] They also claimed that the Aborigines had become more outrageous in their depredations in the belief that the Protectors had been specially appointed to 'protect' them against white reprisals.

The drought of 1837-45, the worst since 1828, had an important impact in the squatting districts and indirectly affected race relations. During 1837 and 1839 the western rivers dried up completely, the Murrumbidgee ceased to flow and even the Murray was 'almost dry'. 1840 and 1841 were 'fair seasons', but they were followed by renewed dryness which lasted in most areas until 1845.[157] One of the worst-affected was the Liverpool Plains where permanent water was always in short supply. In August 1842 Gipps noted that during the previous twelve months an estimated 30,000 sheep and 10,000 cattle had perished in that district alone because of their owners' inability to remove them quickly enough to water.[158] The shortage of water and pasture obliged many squatters to establish new outstations along the rivers where Aborigines were dependent on the little remaining water and associated game.

If the drought in Central Australia of 1924-9 is any guide,[159] that of 1837-45 probably had the following effects on Aborigines on the frontiers of the squatting districts who had been in contact with whites: some would choose to stay in the bush, although this might mean the deaths of some children and old people; others would travel long distances to outstations where they could obtain hand-outs of food and clothing; and finally, some would become more daring in their thefts of stock and stores.

---

[156] See Appendix I.
[157] S. H. Roberts, *The Squatting Age in Australia, 1835-1847*, 2nd edn, Melbourne 1964, p. 315.
[158] *HRA*, XXII, pp. 198-9.
[159] M. Meggitt, *Desert People: A Study of the Walbiri Aborigines of Central Australia*, Sydney 1962, pp. 24-7.

As squatters extended their outstations along the inland rivers they often came into conflict with Aborigines over water, especially during drought seasons. Along the Gwydir, Lachlan and Murrumbidgee, for example, many squatters would not allow Aborigines on their stations for fear of losing sheep and cattle. On the other hand, Mitchell described how cattle destroyed natural waterholes upon which the Aborigines depended not only for water, but for fish and the game which gathered there: 'These consequences', he wrote, 'although so little considered by the intruders, must be obvious to the natives . . . as soon as cattle enter on their territory'.[160]

Competition for water was particularly serious in the area of the Bogan, Gwydir, Namoi and Macintyre rivers. One of the most notorious encounters took place on the Bogan in early 1842 when increasing numbers of stock and a serious shortage of feed and water led a Bathurst squatter, William Lee, to direct his convict overseer to form a new outstation on the Bogan. Shortly after the station huts were built, the Aborigines killed seven of the eight men and the overseer, who had left the camp earlier, brought back the Border Police from Bathurst. It is said that in the ensuing vendetta almost all the males of the tribe involved were shot.[161]

High prices for flour and other commodities during the 1837-45 drought would also have reduced the settlers' ability to supply rations to Aborigines who could offer very little in return. When flour was costing squatters as much as £70 per ton[162] and prices of all kinds of imported goods had risen by fifty per cent,[163] the plundering of a drayload of stores, or even the theft of a few bags of flour from a hut, would have provided good reason for annoyance. Many squatters were already in financial difficulties due to their investment in stock at inflated prices in 1837, the collapse of the market in sheep and cattle stations, the fall in wool prices, the loss of sheep from scab, and the general lack of economic confidence which was gripping the colony by 1839. According to Strzelecki, sheep prices fell by ninety per cent between 1838 and 1843[164]

160 *Tropical Australia*, p. 413.
161 *The Sydney Morning Herald*, 24 August 1842; Edmund Milne, 'War on the Bogan Frontier', *Lone Hand*, June 1917, pp. 329-41; Mitchell, *Tropical Australia*, p. 30.
162 *The Australian*, 18 July 1839.
163 *The Australian*, 5 March 1839.
164 P. de Strzelecki, *Physical Description of New South Wales and Van Dieman's Land*, London 1845, pp. 368ff.

and many squatters sold their sheep to the boiling down works for
4s or 5s per head, which was more than they could obtain elsewhere.[165] In 1840, Robert Pringle of 'Rocky Creek' on the Liverpool
Plains even sold one of his stations to a neighbour for two horses.[166]

Conflicts over Aboriginal women were common, although there
is little evidence to support the claim of many contemporaries (and
of some modern historians)[167] that these arose principally from
'kidnappings'. The custom of lending wives to visitors was widespread in Aboriginal society[168] and many explorers and squatters
noted that Aborigines who had never seen whites before were
anxious to trade their women for axes and other European goods,
sometimes even offering them as tokens of goodwill. The whites,
especially the stockmen, shepherds and hutkeepers in the squatting
districts, were quick to take advantage of this and in the Wellington district it was reported as early as 1835 that every servant
possessed an Aboriginal mistress.[169] At the Moreton Bay German
Mission, the Rev. Wilhelm Schmidt was appalled at the way in
which 'the men carry on a regular trade . . . and offer their women
and daughters to any one',[170] while a squatter in the Loddon River
district claimed that 'the use of the women was offered by *themselves* and *their husbands* indifferently for a trifling amount'.[171]
Similar references from other areas indicates that practice was
common throughout the squatting districts and it was not only the
stockmen who were involved. According to Threlkeld's mission report for 1838

> There are also White Gentlemen whose taste, when in the Bush, leads
> them to keep Black Concubines:- no wonder that the unhappy convicts,

[165] R. N. Dawson, 'Pioneering Days in the Clarence River District', *JRAHS*,
XX, Pt II, 1934, p. 76.

[166] R. J. Webb, '*The Rising Sun*': A History of Moree and District, Moree 1962,
p. 21.

[167] S. C. McCulloch, for example, claims that 'real strife did not occur until
convict servants kidnapped native women'. ('Sir George Gipps and Eastern
Australia's Policy Towards the Aborigines 1838-46', *Journal of Modern
History*, XXXIII, 1961, p. 261.)

[168] A. P. Elkin, *The Australian Aborigines*, 3rd edn, Sydney 1954, pp. 129-30.

[169] 'Annual Report of the Mission . . . at Wellington Valley . . . 1835', *V&P*,
1836, n.p.

[170] 'Report of the Committee on the Condition of the Aborigines', *V&P*, 1845,
p. 960.

[171] Bride, *Letters*, p. 183.

whose state of bondage generally precludes marriage, should readily follow the example of their betters, for whose conduct no such plea exists.[172]

While repeating many instances of kidnappings and assaults on Aboriginal women, including girls of about 8 or 9 years of age 'taken by force by the vile men of Newcastle', Threlkeld drew a very different picture of conditions further inland:

> In the interior, the desolate Shepherd was glad to obtain by any means a female, irrespective of colour, to be his companion in his isolated position. This occasioned a reluctance in the frail dark-one to return to her sable lord, her treatment as a concubine being generally speaking far more humane than that which the Aboriginal wife received from her legal husband.[173]

Convinced that 'kidnapping' was one of the main causes of conflict between the races, Governor Sir Richard Bourke in 1837 prohibited whites from forcibly detaining Aboriginal women,[174] but this only had the effect of making them a little more careful. Commissioner Henry Bingham reported from Tumut in 1841 that 'The mode of proceeding now with the Servants is to visit the Native Camps in the Night as they are afraid to bring the Black Women to the Huts.'[175]

The new regulation also provided the whites with an additional motive for having their half-caste children destroyed at birth. Reports from many parts of the colony during the late 1830s and the 1840s indicate that large numbers of half-caste babies were killed by their mothers shortly after birth.[176] White fathers were rarely willing to support their offspring[177] and women who were pregnant, diseased or no longer in favour were turned away. Marriage seems seldom to have been considered.

The main reason for strife over women was the whites' refusal

---

[172] Gunson, *Australian Reminiscences and Papers of L. E. Threlkeld*, Vol. I, p. 146.

[173] Ibid., Vol. I, p. 49.

[174] *GG*, 16 September 1837, p. 413.

[175] Aborigines Papers, ML, MS.A611, p. 221. This sentence was omitted from Bingham's reply when it was printed as part of an Appendix to the 1841 'Report from the Committee on Immigration', *V&P*, 1841, n.p.

[176] Numerous references to this can be found in Bride, *Letters*, and the 'Report on the Condition of the Aborigines', *V&P*, 1845, pp. 937-1001.

[177] Captain William Oldrey to Deas Thomson, 7 May 1842, *CSIL*, 4/1133.3, 42/4201.

to supply relatives with food, tobacco and clothing upon request and to release the women when required. It is almost certain that very few whites understood the nature of the obligations which, in the eyes of the Aborigines, they had contracted. And when relatives continued to ask for hand-outs of food, tobacco and other items after the initial 'sale', whites often expressed their resentment and annoyance through insults and violence.[178] At the same time, it is unlikely that the Aborigines intended that their women should remain permanently on the stations and trouble may have arisen when they attempted to recover them. One tragic case described by a squatter in the southwestern corner of the Portland Bay district indicates the complications that could arise:

> Mr ——, of ——, on the Glenelg run, near me, kept a harem for himself and his men. The consequence was that he, like many more, had to sell out. All the men and masters got fearfully diseased from the poor creatures; they, of course, quarrelled with natives about their gins, and the natives, to be revenged for some of the insults, took away 48 ewes and lambs—they were followed by some of the neighbours and Mr ——'s own men. They rushed the camp, shot two of the natives, one of them a female, said to be Mr ——'s foremost black woman.[179]

Venereal disease was widespread by the early 1840s. According to Foster Fyans, Commissioner for Portland Bay, it had been introduced from Van Diemen's Land and while 'hardly a shepherd was without disease',[180] two-thirds of the Aborigines of the Port Phillip district had been destroyed by the infection. Bingham at Tumut and settlers in the Albury district also testified to its prevalence.[181] Sometimes referred to as 'native pox' or 'black pox', the disease was believed by the whites to have originated from the Aborigines[182] and it undoubtedly caused a good deal of bitterness between the races. At 'Glenormiston' in the Western District, Niel Black was told 'it is no uncommon thing for these rascals to sleep all night with a

---

[178] Elkin, *The Australian Aborigines*, pp. 129-30.
[179] Bride, *Letters*, p. 31.
[180] Ibid.
[181] Aborigines Papers, ML, MS.A611, p. 220; *GD*, ML, MS.A1236, pp. 697-8.
[182] In fact there can be little doubt that syphilis and gonorrhoea were brought to Australia by whites including the sealers and whalers who called along the eastern and southern coasts. However, the diseases may have also entered Australia from the northern coasts of the continent following Bugis and other contacts much earlier.

Lubra—and if she poxes him or in any way offends him perhaps shoot her before 12 next day'.[183]

Their association with whites also gave Aboriginal women a new status which was almost certainly resented by their menfolk and the frequent attacks on women attached to the stations may have been due to the need to enforce tribal discipline as well as the inevitable shortage of tribally 'correct' marriage partners. There is some evidence that Aboriginal men found this new situation destructive of their authority and monopoly of ritual. In 1835 a convict shepherd on the Williams River near Dungog evidently persuaded the Aboriginal woman with whom he lived to obtain one of the sacred quartz crystals used in ritual. When this was discovered, the men of the tribe gathered together and appointed a man called 'Charley' to kill them both. After killing the shepherd (the woman having escaped) Charley was subsequently caught by the police and hanged.[184] There were probably many more cases of whites violating ritual objects and places or refusing to allow Aborigines access to them and the small amount of information available is almost certainly due to the ignorance of the offenders who invariably ascribed Aboriginal hostility to 'treachery'.

The character of the whites with whom the Aborigines came into contact on the fringes of settlement had a profound effect on race relations. For the most part these men were convict servants and ex-convicts whose undisciplined and violent behaviour among themselves can be seen from the colony's annual return of criminal offences and the most cursory examination of contemporary newspapers. In remote districts such as the Liverpool Plains where very few squatters even visited their stations,[185] the hut-keepers, shepherds and stockmen were under the somewhat relaxed supervision of overseers who were often ex-convicts themselves. They commonly carried arms and were able to use their masters' horses.

During the first years of settlement in the Port Phillip district, most of the convicts and ex-convicts came with their masters from

---

183 Margaret Kiddle, *Men of Yesterday: Social History of the Western District of Victoria 1834-1890*, Melbourne 1961, p. 121.

184 Gunson, *Australian Reminiscences and Papers of L. E. Threlkeld*, Vol. I, pp. 51, 122. See also the Rev. James Günther's 'Notes on the Aborigines of New South Wales', BP, No. 85.

185 Of the 23 licence-holders listed in 1837 as depasturing stock in the Liverpool Plains district, not one appears to have lived any closer than Scone, more than 150 miles from Myall Creek.

Van Diemen's Land where they had learnt to fear and hate not only the local Aborigines with whom there had been a virtual state of war for some years, but the mainland Aborigines used to track down convict 'bolters', the most notorious of these being Musquito[186] who had been transported from Sydney for murder and whose skill led convicts to describe him as 'a hangman's nose'.[187] The readiness of Van Diemonian convict 'old hands' or 'Tasmanians' to shoot Aborigines on sight was noted by E. M. Curr who took over 'Tongala' station on the Goulburn River in 1841. One morning shortly after his arrival in the area, Curr noticed three Aborigines on the other side of the river:

> Their appearance on the scene caused some little trepidation in my old Tasmanians, whose idea, as I heard one of them express it, was 'to kid (entice) them over and shoot the lot'.[188]

On another occasion he had to restrain two of his men who wanted to shoot some Aborigines, giving as their reason that this would 'save trouble' later.

Convict attitudes north of the Port Phillip district were similarly influenced by the use of Aborigines as trackers. Three members of the Newcastle tribe, including the famous McGill, were used to track 'bolters' from the penal settlement at Port Macquarie after 1821.[189] In 1840 Threlkeld recommended to Deas Thomson that an Aboriginal boy called 'William Burd' who had successfully tracked down a gang of bushrangers should be rewarded by the Governor with a suitably inscribed brass plate. At the same time he revealed that the bushrangers had threatened to kill all the Aborigines they met out of retaliation.[190] George Henderson noted the same vindictive attitude among convicts on the McLeay River who had been at Port Macquarie.[191]

---

[186] See the broadside 'A true Account of the Notorious Musquito . . .' in G. C. Ingleton, *True Patriots All!* . . . , Sydney 1952, pp. 99-101. Charles Macalister, *Pioneering Days in the Sunny South*, Goulburn 1907, p. 91, also records that Aborigines from Argyle County tracked down the famous bushranger *Jacky Jacky* (William Westwood) and other convict escapees in Van Diemen's Land.

[187] M. C. I. Levy, *Governor George Arthur*, Melbourne 1953, p. 101.

[188] *Recollections of Squatting in Victoria*, Melbourne 1883, p. 84.

[189] Cunningham, *Two Years in New South Wales*, Vol. II, p. 27.

[190] Threlkeld to Deas Thomson, 29 December 1840, in Gunson, *Australian Reminiscences and Papers of L. E. Threlkeld*, Vol. II, p. 287.

[191] Henderson, *Excursions*, Vol. II, p. 10.

Two further examples illustrate the dread in which convicts held Aborigines on the frontiers of settlement. In May 1836 Major Mitchell and an exploring party consisting mostly of convicts found their progress along the Murray River impeded by a large group of Aboriginal warriors who showed open hostility after their attempts at pilfering around the camp caused Mitchell to send them away. 'Jemmy Piper', a Bathurst Aborigine, and his wife who were accompanying Mitchell then revealed that some of the group had come all the way from the Darling River to kill Mitchell and all his party in revenge for the death of a man who had been killed by a member of the Major's previous expedition. By this time the men were so nervous that they would not even undress at night and none was willing to leave the camp to tend to the bullocks. Hoping to precipitate a confrontation, Mitchell divided the party into two and although he ordered that no one was to fire unless they were attacked, a substantial number of Aborigines were shot and others wounded without even a spear or a boomerang being thrown.[192]

As the explorer Edward Eyre moved down the Murrumbidgee with his party of convicts and stock in December 1838, he learnt that the stockmen had been making raids on the Aborigines but the particulars were impossible to ascertain. When he reached the lowest stations the reports became 'more constant and less satisfactory'. By the time Devlin's station—the last on the river and 420 miles from Sydney—was reached, his men were very worried about the Aborigines: 'indeed they talked of nothing else and there was great furbishing of arms'.[193]

After a West Indian negro attached to the party had been speared, the men wanted to shoot every Aborigine they saw in retaliation and, according to Eyre, would certainly have done so had he not been there to restrain them:

> No doubt this principle has very often been acted upon and thus innocent punished for the guilty. Occasionally too, I believe the natives have been shot at even without provocation merely because the white men were afraid of them and it was easier to shoot at them at a distance and thus drive them off than it was to allow them to come near and

192 An account of the incident is contained in *GG*, Supplement, 21 January 1837, pp. 59-74. Mitchell named a nearby peak 'Mt Dispersion' in commemoration. See pp. 119-21.
193 Eyre, 'Autobiographical Narrative', p. 151.

have to watch them with vigilance and treat them with kindness.[194]

Later parties of overlanders were not as scrupulous as Eyre and both races took indiscriminate revenge. One overlander described two fierce encounters on the Murrumbidgee and Murray in 1839 in which at least thirty Aborigines and three whites were killed.[195] Although the squatter in charge of the party was anxious that the bodies of the Aborigines should be buried, his convict servants 'positively refused to dig a grave for them, and merely dragged the corpses to a gully at hand, and cast them into the scrub'.[196]

There can be little doubt that fear and insecurity played an important part in determining the attitudes of whites in remote areas such as the Liverpool Plains where they were greatly outnumbered by Aborigines. Stockmen and hutkeepers must have been apprehensive when parties of Aborigines appeared without warning from the bush and it is not surprising that after earlier clashes they should have preferred to shoot on sight rather than risk attack. Besides, the Faithfull massacre and many other stories made Aboriginal 'treachery' an article of faith in frontier life.[197]

We know very little about what these men felt but Judith Wright has written of

> the deep emotional repulsion that was half attraction for a way of life so unconscious and unquestioning. It was the repulsion of will and intellect from their own opposites—the kind of fear that had prompted the white men to kill and kill, not because of the little damage the blacks could do them materially, but because of a threatened deeper damage, the undermining of a precarious way of life that existed by denying what the aboriginals took for granted.[198]

Isolated from the comparative comfort of the towns and confronted with the harsh realities of lonely bush life, they manned the outposts of a potentially dominant but still thinly represented civilization. While the frontier gradually extended, they nevertheless felt embattled by a people whom they knew only well enough to fear and hate. It was a harsh and brutalizing environment for men al-

[194] Ibid., p. 253. From a number of contemporary reports it appears that Negroes, Chinese and Indians were regarded by the Aborigines as special objects of contempt.
[195] Byrne, *Twelve Years' Wanderings*, Vol. II, pp. 230-2, 250-2.
[196] Ibid., p. 253.
[197] This question is dealt with more fully in Chapter 2.
[198] *Generations of Men*, Melbourne 1959, p. 89.

ready hardened by their own society and its penal system and it is not surprising that they should have expressed themselves through physical violence. In Professor A. P. Elkin's words, 'the [whites'] sense of power and superiority was tinged and modified by a feeling of fear and uncertainty . . . [which] was expressed in harshness and force'.[199]

A good example of this fear and uncertainty was an incident related by Commissioner Mayne to the Committee on Police and Gaols in 1839. A party of about six Aborigines arrived at one of the Hall brothers' stations on the Gwydir River and asked the hutkeeper for food. Frightened out of his wits, he barricaded himself in his hut and then flung out some bread and meat.[200] The Aborigines were thoroughly enraged by this and, according to Mayne, would have sought revenge if he had not used his influence with them.

On the other hand, 'tame' Aborigines attached to the stations provided convenient targets for the aggressive behaviour of convicts and ex-convicts who otherwise possessed few opportunities to assert themselves. They evidently ridiculed those Aborigines who retained a proud demeanour despite their new state of economic dependence. E. M. Curr observed that

> Like the gentleman reduced by circumstances to the necessities of menial labour, the aborigine was a good deal bullied by the white labourer, who lost no opportunity of asserting his superiority over him.[201]

Another factor which should not be overlooked is that life on remote stations was a monotonous and uneventful routine and an expedition against 'the blacks' must have been a welcome diversion and a splendid source of yarns for the camp fire as well as an insurance policy for the safety of stock. In his poem 'The Spectre of the Cattle Flat', which he said was 'substantially true', Charles Harpur described just such a group of stockmen vying to tell the most bloodthirsty story:

> While not a noisy tongue lacks
> To tell of drunken brawls:
> But most of battle with the Blacks
> Some bloody tale appals.

---

[199] *The Diocese of Newcastle . . .* , Newcastle 1955, p. 52.
[200] 'Report of the Committee on Police and Gaols', *V&P*, 1839, Vol. II, p. 25.
[201] *Recollections of Squatting*, p. 299.

One tells of how, after a fierce fray,
A wounded Chief he found
Dark-lying, log-like, on his way,
Sore gashed with many a wound,

And how, as there alive he lay,
He staked him to the ground.
Or how in the elbow of a creek
That ran 'neath crag-walls grey,

A tribe entire, with many a shriek,
Was pent, and held at bay,
Till there, like sheep, in one close heap,
Their slaughtered bodies lay.[202]

One of the stockmen, Ned Connor, wins greatest acclamation with his story of how he promised to give an Aboriginal boy a knife if he would guide him home, and how he then shot him dead when they reached the station. Shortly after telling this chilling tale, Connor goes to the creek for water and sees the boy's ghost which chases him, causing him to die of fright. Connor's story is similar to one mentioned by Threlkeld in his mission report for 1838 and the third stanza quoted is probably based on a massacre at Slaughterhouse Creek in the same year. Harpur lived for some time in the Singleton district where he would have heard many such anecdotes.

Some, of course, were 'tall stories', just as squatters and their overseers exaggerated stock and property losses to support their demands that Border Police should be stationed in their areas. Day told the 1839 Committee on Police and Gaols that an overseer who 'complained loudly' of his employer's extensive cattle losses could only point out five or six carcasses in a day's ride over his run,[203] and Mayne remarked in 1846 that despite reports from two squatters of extensive cattle spearing on the McLeay River, only two working bullocks had been killed. He also noted that numbers of sawyers on the river were absconding from employers to whom they owed money on the pretext of 'troublesome blacks'.[204]

[202] *Miscellaneous Poems*, Harpur MSS, ML, MS.A97.
[203] 'Report of the Committee on Police and Gaols', *V&P*, 1839, Vol. II, p. 225.
[204] Mayne to Deas Thomson, 27 June 1846, *CSIL*, 4/2719, 46/5195. W. H. Wright, Crown Lands Commissioner for Wellington, reported that the injury done to cattle owned by William Lawson Jr of 'Warran' was due to mismanagement by his superintendent and not to Aboriginal attacks. *HRA*, XXIII, p. 588.

Stockmen sometimes deliberately antagonized Aborigines by shooting their women and children. They were then able to claim additional wages or rations from employers for holding off attacks from 'treacherous blacks' who were probably relatives seeking revenge. Commissioner Richard Bligh gave this description of such tactics in the Gwydir River area in the 1840s:

> The method pursued has been that of stealing by night in large parties upon the natives when sleeping in their camps at the stations of the few individuals who offered them protection, and discharging upon them a volley of firearms.
>
> The victims selected have been almost without exception females and infants and generally valuable servants to the residents of stations which they frequented, and this selection in itself proves that the object is not the punishment of offenders, but the exasperation of the natives and the gratification of the wanton brutality of the assailants by the degree of moral pain inflicted on the survivors. . . . the stockmen have a twofold reason for keeping up the irritation of the natives, which is, of course, most effectively done by shooting their women and children. In the first place the natives when peaceable diminish the rate of wages and the demand for labor; and in the second place the pretext of 'the Blacks' serves as an easy method of accounting to the proprietor for any cattle lost by the negligence of the stockman, or killed or stolen by himself and his friends for their own purposes.[205]

It can be safely said that the fundamental cause of conflict in the squatting districts was the expropriation of the Aborigines' traditional lands by the whites and their introduction of European commodities for which the Aborigines soon developed a powerful desire. However, the variety of complicating factors already indicated makes it impossible to offer any simple analysis of the tragic contact between the two races. The bewildering history of 'aggressions' and 'reprisals' from the very foundation of the colony of New South Wales led one magistrate to conclude in 1839 that:

> As civilization spread, constant differences, followed by acts of aggression, occurred, till it became quite impossible to assign to each its act of provocation.[206]

[205] 'Report on the State of the Aborigines in the District of Gwydir . . . 8th January, 1849', *CSIL*, 4/2843, 49/1201.
[206] 'Report of the Committee on Police and Gaols', *V&P*, 1839, Vol. II, p. 75.

CHAPTER TWO

Christianization and Civilization

In all their ignorance they lay
Before the Saviour's piercing eye;
And he who makes the darkness day,
Thus pitied all their misery:
'Proclaim to yonder savage race
The tidings of redeeming grace.

'Let the wild savage know the God
Whose Providence his life sustains,
And Him who shed his precious blood
To save him from eternal pains;
So shall his brutal warfare cease,
So shall he learn the arts of peace.'

J. D. LANG

Black men—we wish to make you happy.
But you cannot be happy unless you love
God who made Heaven and earth and men
and all things.

Love white men. Love other tribes of
black men. Do not quarrel together.
Tell other tribes to love white men, and
to build good huts and wear clothes.
Learn to speak English.

COL. GEORGE GAWLER

THE 'IMPROVERS'

The handful of people in Great Britain and New South Wales concerned about the welfare of the Aborigines had been shocked by the moral degradation, physical decline and depopulation which invariably followed contact with the whites. Some insisted that because the representatives of European civilization in New South Wales were for the most part men who had been judged unworthy to remain in their mother country, the Aborigines should be completely segregated if they were to be successfully Christianized and civilized. In this isolation, it was argued, they would absorb the teachings of the Gospel and the technical skills of civilization which would prepare them to enter colonial society immunized against its vices and capable of supporting themselves economically. Others believed that segregation from the whites was necessary for the Aborigines' very survival because of their tragic susceptibility to European diseases.

In 1819 the Rev. Robert Cartwright suggested to Governor Lachlan Macquarie that the Native Institution,[1] a residential school for

---

[1] William Shelley (1774-1815), a former South Seas missionary and trader, addressed Macquarie in early 1814 on the possibility of civilizing the Aborigines and was invited by the governor to submit plans. In December 1814 he was appointed superintendent and principal teacher of the Native Institution which commenced work on 18 January 1815, His Majesty's birthday, with an enrolment of twelve Aboriginal girls and boys. Shelley died in July 1815 after establishing the school and it continued under Mrs Shelley's direction until 1823. Macquarie expressed satisfaction with its progress in his 1822 report (*HRA*, X, p. 677) but his views should be contrasted with those of Mrs Shelley in her evidence to the 1838 Committee on the Aborigines Question (*V&P*, 1838, pp. 54-5), and of Barron Field in his 'Narrative of a Voyage to New South Wales' in *Geographical Memoirs on New South Wales*, London 1825, p. 436. After its removal to Black Town under the Rev. George Clarke's supervision in January 1823 the Institution had a chequered and undistinguished history. Clarke soon moved to New Zealand and was succeeded by the Wesleyan missionary William Walker and his wife who took only the girl students while the boys went to the Rev. Robert Cartwright at Liverpool. Brisbane, who had never shared Macquarie's personal interest in the Institution, dissolved its committee in 1825 and the remaining girl students went with Walker when he took over his new post as master of the Female Orphan School. It was revived in 1826 under the auspices of the newly established Clergy and Schools Corporation when Thomas Hobbes Scott decided that Aborigines from the Male and Female Orphan Institutions should be placed there. The Rev. William Hall of the Church Missionary Society was appointed superintendent, bringing with him some Maori children who had been under his charge at the Rev. Samuel Marsden's Parramatta school. In January 1827 there were only four Maoris and nine Aborigines and the experiment was finally abandoned in 1829, the remaining Aborigines being sent to the Male Orphan School where Richard Sadleir had been appointed master. So far there has been no complete account of the Native Institution although it has been dealt with briefly in Barry Bridges, 'Aboriginal Education in Eastern Australia (N.S.W.) 1788-1855', *The Australian Journal of Education*, Vol. 12, No. 3, October 1968, pp. 231-3; A.

Aboriginal children which had been established at Parramatta in 1815, should be kept separate from the whites until the work of civilization was sufficiently advanced 'as to be proof against the evil practices and examples of our depraved countrymen'.[2] The Institution was removed three years later on the recommendation of its committee to a reserve sixteen miles north of Parramatta, soon to become known as 'Black Town'. However, the Rev. George Clarke who was appointed schoolmaster and supervised the removal told the Church Missionary Society that his work was made difficult by the 'prejudice excited by the Heathenish conduct of those around them calling themselves Christians'.[3]

Cartwright's choice of the Cow Pastures as a site for the special Aboriginal enclave which he suggested to Macquarie[4] was also influenced by his view that parts of the district 'would be for years shut out by the River, etc. from all communication with white people'.[5] Macquarie expressed enthusiasm for the plan but wanted to have the enclave in the 'New Country' recently discovered by Captain Charles Throsby. This, he told Lord Bathurst, would bring it closer to where the Aborigines were living 'and at the same time render it less subject to be disturbed by Vagrants than if it were placed in the Settled Districts'.[6]

The Rev. William Walker, who was sent out by the Wesleyan Missionary Society to work with the Aborigines in 1821, also em-

---

Duncan, 'A Survey of the Education of Aborigines in New South Wales . . .', MEd thesis, University of Sydney, 1969, Chs 1 and 2 and Gunson, *Australian Reminiscences and Papers of L. E. Threlkeld*, Vol. I, pp. 11-13. For a sentimental view of its failure, see Charles Tompson, 'Elegy Written in the Verandah of the Chapel of the Deserted Hamlet of "Black Town" . . .' in his *Wild Notes from the Lyre of a Native Minstrel*, Sydney 1826, pp. 42-7.

[2] Cartwright to Macquarie, 6 December 1819, *HRA*, X, p. 26.

[3] 'Report of the Committee of the Church Missionary Society, May 4, 1824', *BT*, Miss, Box 54, p. 1817.

[4] The principles of this plan were outlined in Cartwright's two letters to Macquarie dated 6 December 1819 and 18 January 1820, *HRA*, X, pp. 263-72. Cartwright also submitted to the governor a poem entitled 'Macquarie City' which he saw as 'the best means of exciting public attention to a thing I have for a long time past had so much at heart, but have wanted courage to make known'. The poem won Macquarie's approbation and Cartwright announced his intention of sending it to his son in Cambridge for publication. However, neither the poem nor the plan was heard of again.

[5] Cartwright to Macquarie, 6 December 1819, *HRA*, X, p. 267.

[6] Macquarie to Bathurst, 24 February 1820, ibid., p. 263. Macquarie was referring to the Moss Vale and Sutton Forest area.

phasized the importance of segregation. After a short spell as super-intendent of the Native Institution he and his assistant, John Har-per, made a point of 'itinerating' with Aborigines who had little previous contact with whites. They chose Wellington Valley as the site for a permanent mission because of its isolation, and when an unprecedented flood led them to abandon the idea as impracticable, Harper set off to explore the south coast. In 1827 he recommended Bateman's Bay as an alternative:

> Let the mission be established at a place where the blacks are not in communication with the whites, and, my soul for any man's, but this mission will prosper.[7]

In the same year Richard Sadleir,[8] who had been despatched by Archdeacon Thomas Hobbes Scott to investigate the condition of Aborigines in Argyle County, followed Cartwright in recommend-ing the establishment of government reserves 'as remote as possible from the White Population'.[9] No doubt this influenced Scott's suc-cessor, Archdeacon William Grant Broughton, in his selection of the former government agricultural settlement at Wellington Valley for a Church Missionary Society venture in 1831.[10]

The virtual disappearance of the Aborigines of Van Diemen's Land and rapid depopulation on the mainland lent further weight to the segregation argument by suggesting that only complete re-moval from the whites could save the Aborigines from imminent extinction. The Rev. Joseph Orton emphasized this in 1836 when he told the Wesleyan Missionary Society that in order to be sure of success, a mission would have to be established at least 500 miles from Sydney and beyond all the stations.[11] So anxious was Arch-bishop John Bede Polding for the success of the newly-arrived Passionist missionaries in 1843 that he sent them to Stradbroke Island, Moreton Bay, in the vain belief that since the island was barren, whites would never want to use it.[12] One philanthropist even recommended the removal of all the Aborigines to the Buc-

---

[7] Quoted by J. S. Needham, *White and Black in Australia*, London 1935, p. 70.
[8] For a biographical note on Sadleir, see p. 117n.
[9] Scott to Darling, 27 March 1828, *HRA*, XIV, p. 59.
[10] Broughton to Darling, 14 June 1831, *PP*, 1837, Vol. VII, No. 425, pp. 21-2.
[11] *BT*, Miss., Box 54, p. 1970.
[12] 'Report of the Select Committee on the Condition of the Aborigines', *V&P*, 1845, p. 949. For the history of Dunwich mission, see O. Thorpe, *First Catholic Mission in Australia*, Sydney 1951.

caneer Archipelago off the northern coast of Western Australia where they would be remote from disease and the 'blasting influence of European morals' which had provided an 'insuperable obstacle' to the improvement of their condition and their acceptance of Christianity.[13] Unlike the missionaries, he did not foresee an ultimate mingling of the Aborigines with white society.

Nevertheless there were others who, while regretting the worst features of contact, opposed even temporary segregation as undesirable, holding that contact with a superior civilization must ultimately benefit the Aborigines. This belief in 'attachment' had been prevalent since the founding of the settlement—indeed from the beginning of European overseas expansion and contact with indigenous peoples.

The two attitudes were clearly contrasted when the colonization of the southern coast of the continent was first discussed. Once the settlement of Port Phillip appeared inevitable, concern was expressed that there should not be a repetition of the racial strife which had racked Van Diemen's Land. In 1834 Governor Sir George Arthur offered to visit any new settlement on the mainland and station a small military party under an officer who would act as Protector of the Aborigines. He also recommended the establishment of schools for Aboriginal children.[14] Arthur was influenced in this by the initial success of Robinson's Aboriginal Establishment at Flinders Island where the remainder of the Aborigines of Van Diemen's Land had been taken after Robinson had mustered them in a number of epic journeys between 1830 and 1834. He envisaged a similar scheme for the mainland where the tribes would be 'collected' by travelling protectors and civilized with the assistance of 'Aboriginal graduates' from Flinders Island. Naturally, Robinson saw himself as commander-in-chief of this grand enterprise.

Captain Alexander Maconochie, secretary to Arthur's successor Sir John Franklin, visited Flinders Island where Robinson's use of Aborigines as police led him to devise a rather different plan.[15]

---

[13] Anon., *Plan to Ameliorate the Condition of the Aboriginal Inhabitants and Prevent their Extermination*, Sydney 1839, p. 119.

[14] Arthur to Thomas Fowell Buxton, 18 September 1834, *PP*, 1836, Vol. VII, No. 538-679.

[15] 'Observations on the treatment of Aborigines, New South Wales', *Extracts from the Papers and Proceedings of the Aborigines' Protection Society*, No. 1, London, May 1839, pp. 109-15.

He recommended the formation of a corps of Native Police, led by white officers, which would protect whites and Aborigines from each other on the frontiers of settlement as well as civilizing its members through constant contact with upstanding members of white society.

For Maconochie, the principles of treatment of a native population were

> their exaltation, intermixture with ourselves, beneficial employment, religious conversion, instruction in our language, and thereby the progressive development of their mind and understanding.[16]

He attacked the idea of protective segregation because it implied inferior status and created distrust by keeping the Aborigines 'out of harm's way, as children'.[17] The whites, he said, were under a moral obligation to raise the status of the Aborigines and this could best be achieved by employing them in the public service where 'the whole imitative faculties of the race would be devoted to good, instead of . . . to vice and folly'.[18]

Maconochie claimed that Providence had provided these 'faculties' to enable the Aborigines to be 'drawn up' to a civilized condition. He recommended that they should be taught English as soon as possible because the Creator had endowed savage man with a facility for acquiring languages.[19] Employment as police possessed the further advantage of being easily reconciled with their own wandering habits, although Maconochie hoped that the Aboriginal troopers would ultimately settle in established villages. He felt that the foundations of civilized life would be laid when the Aboriginal troopers were instructed in habits of neatness, decency and cleanliness. Furthermore, they would learn the basic virtue of self-discipline which was 'implied by the voluntary performance of what is yet felt to be a task'.[20] They were to be weaned gently from their own customs which were not to be trampled on, but while

[16] Ibid., p. 114.
[17] Ibid., p. 112.
[18] Ibid., p. 111.
[19] Maconochie's thinking may have been influenced by the pioneer German ethnologist Gustav Klemm's division of humanity into 'active' and 'passive' races, a dichotomy of the species which could only be overcome by the latter 'copying' the former whilst in a state of 'discipline'. Robert H. Lowie, *The History of Ethnological Theory*, London 1937, pp. 11-16.
[20] 'Observations', p. 112.

their 'superstitions' were to be respected, systematic attempts should be made to introduce Christianity. 'There is no bond of social unison', wrote Maconochie, 'stronger than a community of worship, nor any civilizer like a perception of Christian faith and morals'.[21]

Sir Richard Bourke, another opponent of segregation, was enthusiastic about Maconochie's plan and gave a former army officer, C. L. J. de Villiers, the task of recruiting and training a small force for the Port Phillip district. After many difficulties, including de Villiers' resignation, and a period of supervision by the missionary, George Langhorne,[22] the experiment was discontinued until 1842 when Gipps agreed that 'in the civilization of savages, military discipline, or something nearly approaching it, may advantageously be employed'.[23]

A more comprehensive plan to civilize the Aborigines at Port Phillip was devised by Bourke himself with the assistance of Judge W. W. Burton[24] of the Supreme Court of New South Wales, both men having had some experience of the Kaffirs at Cape of Good Hope. Returning some papers relating to the governor's proposal in November 1835,[25] Burton recommended that the tribes be gathered 'into one' and that land be reserved for 'Black Villages' with a special portion in each village for children and the infirm. The building of a hut for the 'Chief', he said, would induce the other Aborigines to settle down. Missionaries were to live in the villages and there were to be schools where the teaching of English would

[21] Ibid., pp. 113-14.
[22] Langhorne, who arrived in N.S.W. in 1832, became a catechist for the Church Missionary Society and shared the secretaryship of its revived Auxiliary with the Rev. Richard Hill. In 1836 he was appointed catechist to the Aboriginal prisoners at Goat Island, Sydney, and taught them to read English. In November he took six conditionally released prisoners to Threlkeld's establishment at Lake Macquarie where they promptly took to the bush. Appointed by Bourke to take charge of the new government mission establishment at Port Phillip, he arrived in Melbourne in January 1837. After its failure he joined his brothers who had become overlanders and squatters and was later accepted into the Anglican priesthood. In 1837 he had married the eldest daughter of the Rev. Robert Cartwright. Gunson, *Australian Reminiscences and Papers of L. E. Threlkeld*, Vol. I, p. 35, Vol. II, p. 324.
[23] Quoted by E. J. B. Foxcroft, *Australian Native Policy, Especially in Victoria*, Melbourne 1941, p. 87.
[24] For a biographical note on Burton, see p. 150n.
[25] 'Extract of a Letter from The Honble Mr. Justice Burton to His Excellency Major General Sir Richard Bourke', Sydney, 22 November 1835, Gurner MSS, ML, MS.A1493, pp. 31-4.

be a high priority. Burton noted from his observations at the Cape where only the Moravians had been successful that it was important to separate the roles of missionary and teacher.

Bourke did not accept all the judge's ideas but Captain William Lonsdale subsequently received instructions[26] from the Colonial Secretary, Alexander McLeay, that the Aborigines were to be conciliated by kind treatment and presents and established in villages where they would be encouraged to work for their food and clothing. Finally, William Buckley,[27] a former convict who had lived with the Aborigines at Port Phillip for thirty-two years, was to be employed as an intermediary and the Aborigines were to be told that they were amenable to British law. In his December 1836 memorandum to Langhorne, who was placed in charge of the experiment, Bourke added further details. Land was to be allocated to the Aborigines either on a family basis or to each village so that it could be managed along the lines of Robert Owen's socialist

---

[26] McLeay to Lonsdale, 14 September 1836, ibid.

[27] William Buckley (1780-1856), best known of the 'wild white men', was a farmer's son from Cheshire who joined the 7th Regiment and was wounded while serving in the Netherlands. In August 1802 he was sentenced to transportation for life for receiving a stolen roll of cloth and in 1803 was taken to Port Phillip in Lieutenant-Governor David Collins' party. There he absconded with two other convicts, both of whom were lost when they tried to return to camp. Buckley, whose massive physique must have impressed the Aborigines, was 'adopted' by the Watourong tribe and lived with them for thirty-two years before giving himself up to J. H. Wedge's party in July 1835. During that time he learnt the language and customs of the Watourong and was given a wife. Buckley was initially regarded by members of the Port Phillip Association as a useful intermediary with the Aborigines and after receiving a pardon from Governor Arthur was employed as an interpreter, first by John Batman and then by the government which assigned him to Langhorne. However, his close connection with the Watourong made dealings with other Aborigines difficult—the Yarra tribe, for example, regarded him as an enemy—and he disappointed his employers. After assisting the Rev. Joseph Orton for some time he went to Hobart in 1837. Buckley's lack of education caused John Pascoe Fawkner to regard him as 'a mindless lump of matter' but the botanist John Lhotsky was impressed and Orton described him as 'a man of thought and shrewdness, a proof of which he exhibited in the policy he has adopted towards the natives, particularly in carefully avoiding to mix in any of their party feuds, by which means he has remained on terms of friendship with all'. Langhorne, 'Reminiscences of William Buckley', La Trobe Library, Melbourne; Orton, *Aborigines of Australia*; John Morgan, *The Life and Adventures of William Buckley*, Hobart, 1852; John Lhotsky, 'My "Conference" with Buckley', *Tasmanian And Review*, 26 January 1838, p. 29; *ADB*, Vol. I, pp. 174-5.

establishment at New Lanark in Lancashire. 'The great object', he concluded, 'will be gradually to wean the Blacks by proving to them experimentally the superior gratifications to be obtained in civilized life'.[28]

Bourke's favourite theory was that the two races could be 'amalgamated' by bringing the Aborigines into contact with the lower classes of whites[29] and he rejected Langhorne's opinion that the projected mission would only be successful if it was isolated from white settlement. Consequently it was established on the River Yarra about three miles from the township rather than at French Island, Westernport, which Langhorne regarded as 'the most eligible nucleus'. After some initial success, the mission rapidly became little more than a temporary home for Aborigines attracted to Melbourne from all over the Port Phillip district. Gipps refused Langhorne's request for it to be removed and in January 1839 the missionary urged that it be abandoned. In retrospect he wrote:

> I have ever been convinced that nothing short of isolation from intercourse with the whites would suffice to save a remnant of the aborigines from destruction and the event has proved I was right.[30]

A more practical scheme of 'civilization' had been suggested some years earlier by John Helder Wedge,[31] one of the members of the Port Phillip Association. Wedge hoped that the new colony would soon become independent and his plan for the Aborigines was based on the assumption that the colonists would control revenue from the sale of Crown lands. He believed that the Aborigines had 'an undoubted claim upon the land'[32] and recommended that one-fifth of all revenue from Crown land sales be set aside for their

---

28 'Memorandum to serve as Instructions for Mr. Langhorne on undertaking the employment of Missionary for the Civilisation of the aboriginal Natives at Port Phillip', Gurner MSS, ML, MS.A1493, p. 39.

29 Notes by Langhorne, ibid., p. 91.

30 Langhorne's statement of the Port Phillip mission, ibid., p. 66. An account of the mission can be found in H. N. Nelson, 'Early Attempts to Civilize the Aborigines of Port Phillip District', MEd thesis, University of Melbourne, 1966.

31 'Scheme for civilising and bringing into industrious habits the Aborigines of New Holland', typescript, La Trobe Library. See also, Wedge to Russell, 18 January 1840, Enclosure, Russell to Gipps, 24 January 1840, HRA, XX, pp. 487-9. As part of the Port Phillip Association's campaign to curry support for its land claim at Port Phillip, the scheme can be regarded as the thin end of the wedge.

32 Ibid.

material and spiritual support. Assuming that, as in Van Diemen's Land, they would be driven from their hunting grounds and consequently deprived of the means of sustenance, he suggested the establishment of three or four government reserves where they could obtain a daily supply of flour and potatoes, together with an annual dole of two blankets per person and occasional gifts of tomahawks and trinkets. They would be encouraged to live in huts and become agriculturalists while settlers who succeeded in domesticating Aborigines on their stations were to be rewarded with a reduction in the upset price of land.

Wedge recognized that it would be difficult to accustom the Aborigines to agriculture but he believed that since they relied on women for most of their food, and since women could obtain food from the government stations, they 'might by degrees be estranged from their wandering mode of life'.[33] He was unaware of the inter-tribal antagonisms which would make such collectivization impossible and his assumption that the Aborigines would retreat before white settlement was largely incorrect. Nevertheless, the plan was forwarded to the Colonial Office through Sir George Arthur and may well have influenced Lord Glenelg's decision to establish a system of Aboriginal Protectors in New South Wales.

By far the most penetrating comments on the problem of civilizing the Aborigines were made by that seasoned explorer, Captain George Grey. During his voyage to England in 1840, he set down his views and forwarded them to the Colonial Office. These were based on what he saw to have been the two greatest obstacles so far—the failure both in bringing English law to the Aborigines and in employing them usefully.

He claimed that although they had been made amenable to English law in relation to their attacks on white property and persons, a grave mistake had been made in allowing them to maintain their own customs. Countering the argument that as a conquered people they should be allowed to retain their own laws, he insisted that the 'savage and traditional customs' of the Aborigines should not be mistaken for 'a regular code of laws'.[34] He described these

---

[33] Ibid.
[34] 'Report upon the best means of promoting the civilization of the Aboriginal Inhabitants of Australia', Enclosure, Russell to Gipps, 8 October 1840, *HRA*, XXI, p. 35.

customs as an anti-civilizing force which allowed the tribal elders to deter those who would otherwise adopt civilized habits. Furthermore, he argued, the inconsistency of law enforcement created the impression among the Aborigines that certain actions were undesirable only when they occurred within white society. For these reasons he recommended that both races should be equally amenable to English law and that unsworn evidence given by Aborigines should be accepted when it was supported by strong circumstantial evidence. As a corollary to this, he recommended the careful policing of the thinly-settled squatting districts where whites were liable to take the solution into their own hands if they were not provided with adequate protection, and where Aborigines were encouraged in their depredations when their raids on stock and property went unpunished.

Secondly, he pointed out that Aboriginal labour had never been properly utilized. Payment in kind[35] had prevented Aborigines from realizing that different skills and amounts of labour were of different value and unscrupulous employers had taken advantage of this unsatisfactory arrangement. He recommended that an indenture system should be introduced on the stations and that in the settled districts, Aborigines should be encouraged to gather in numbers since under these conditions they worked more readily and were more easily controlled and protected (although this would be imprudent in remote areas where the white population was small). Finally, he thought that they should be employed in occupations suitable to their temperament, such as road-blazing, hunting and fishing, until they could be persuaded to take up pastoral or agricultural work.

There was a further division of colonial opinion on the desirability of coercion in the civilizing process. The Rev. William Watson's policy of keeping Aboriginal children against their parents' wishes precipitated a dispute with his fellow missionary, James Günther, at Wellington Valley. In 1840, after being dismissed by the Church Missionary Society, Watson left the mission station with most of the Aborigines and established the new Apsley mission on a piece of ground made available by one of the very few co-operative local squatters. In the same year, and again in 1843,

---

[35] The standard payment for a large sheet of bark was a 'plug' of tobacco. Other payments were made mostly in rum, flour, sugar and old clothing.

George Arden, editor of the *Port Phillip Gazette*, outlined his system of 'coercive Education and Employment' by which Aboriginal children were to be educated in complete isolation from their parents. The remainder were to be confined to reserves where the sick, aged and infants would be provided with rations and the able-bodied left to subsist by hunting and tilling the soil.[36]

Whether they believed in 'attachment' or segregation, coercion or coaxing, these colonial philanthropists assumed that the Aborigines were capable of 'improvement'. Some, like Dr Charles Nicholson, even referred to a 'psychological law, that civilization is progressive, and that it must take several generations to procure a high degree of intellect'.[37] Polding, too, noted encouragingly that after three generations of Christian influence, the intellect of the South American Indians had been greatly elevated.[38]

There was general agreement that Christianity had been closely related to the successful development of Western European civilization and that it was the primary factor in the process of 'improvement' of savage races. For example, the Rev. Francis Tuckfield of the Wesleyan mission at Buntingdale near Geelong believed

> That civilization would proceed in a ratio proportionate to the moral influence of Christian instruction, is demonstrable by the universal concurrence of all historical testimony.[39]

But the Rev. John Dunmore Lang, who castigated the early missionaries for placing initial emphasis on civilizing rather than on Christian teaching,[40] saw Christianity as possessing a more complex significance. Lang believed that the original state of man was one of 'comparative civilization' in which he enjoyed the knowledge of God and a pure and holy religion. As a consequence of his apostasy, man had become a savage and the only rational and effective means of dispelling his moral and intellectual darkness and restoring him to his pristine state was to 'captivate his heart and his understanding with the truths of revelation'.[41] In his *View of the*

---

[36] 'Civilization of the Aborigines', *Arden's Sydney Magazine*, October 1843, pp. 65-82.
[37] 'Report of the Select Committee on the Condition of the Aborigines', *V&P*, 1845, p. 950.
[38] Ibid., p. 950.
[39] *GD*, ML, MS.A1231, p. 695.
[40] *The Colonist*, 12 November 1835.
[41] *The Colonist*, 5 November 1835.

Origins and Migrations of the Polynesian Nation in 1834 Lang wrote:

> The voice of history, whether sacred or profane, proclaims to us that man was originally no barbarian. And, as it was, doubtless, through his having forgotten the author and object of his being, that man has in any instance fallen from this high estate of primitive civilization into the abject condition of a savage, it is unquestionably the most rational mode of attempting to lead him back to that primitive state to direct his intellectual vision to these objects again.[42]

He thought of the Aborigines as being among the last to benefit from the moral and intellectual transformation which only Christianity could bring about. Threlkeld, too, noted that 'the most scientific man in the world, if deprived of the knowledge of God . . . would soon develop himself, even worse than a monkey, and be counted of God as a Fool'.[43]

Reasoning within Bishop Ussher's chronology which gave mankind a history of less than 6,000 years since Creation, Lang, Threlkeld and their contemporaries were unlikely to regard environmental factors as an explanation for the condition of the Aborigines. Instead they grasped the only explanation available to them —the prophecy of Noah that the sons of Ham would suffer for their father's sin. As the Rev. William Walker told Richard Watson of the Wesleyan Missionary Society in 1821, the Aborigines were 'the progeny of him who was cursed to be "a servant of servants to his brethren" ' and 'emigrants from the same stock that *shall soon stretch out its hands unto God*'.[44]

The Evangelicals' belief in progressive moral and intellectual degeneration led them to interpret the apparent backwardness and depravity of the Aborigines as evidence that they were in fact a degenerate civilization. Having studied some of the carvings in the Sydney area together with Police Superintendent W. A. Miles, Threlkeld wrote:

---

[42] London 1834, pp. 246-8. This contains Lang's 'Verses Written Within Sight of the North-East Cape of New Zealand, August 1830' in which he expounded his views on the primacy of evangelization over the teaching of civilized arts and habits.

[43] 'Reminiscences' in Gunson, *Australian Reminiscences and Papers of L. E. Threlkeld*, Vol. I, p. 59.

[44] Walker to Watson, 5 October 1821, *BT*, Miss, Box 51, p. 198. Quoted by Gunson in his Introduction, p. 9.

It is evident from these very engravings upon the rocks that the aborigines have degenerated, and will continue to do so, until the few remaining individuals shall have become extinct, like so many other portions of the human family, who are now no more . . .

There may possibly be ruins of very ancient buildings lying hid in Australia, which remains to be discovered by some future traveller, who, if unprejudiced against the Aborigines, may find out many remnants of an ancient people now absolutely becoming, all but totally extinct.[45]

The Rev. James Günther at Wellington Valley thought that he had found evidence of a superior past civilization in the fact that the Aborigines were now apparently unable to imitate the stencilling which covered the walls of caves at *Dabu* nearby and that there was also a tradition of a great flood during which the survivors hid in a cave near Wellington Valley. 'The aborigines themselves', he wrote, 'have the impression that their ancestors knew much more than themselves'.[46] Threlkeld concluded that the Aborigines were 'but the remnants of an all-but-exhausted nation, the origin of which it is difficult at present to trace'.[47]

While upholding the doctrine that the Aborigines were descended from Adam and Eve, the Evangelicals vilified their customs and even their appearance in a way rivalled only by the squatting interest. Influenced by a doctrinal predisposition to view the Aborigines as the special victims of God's wrath, they also shared the other whites' revulsion for the Aborigines' way of life.

Practically all the first missionaries were Evangelicals and their response was made clear as early as 1799 by William Henry whose

---

[45] 'Reminiscences' in Gunson, *Australian Reminiscences and Papers of L. E. Threlkeld*, Vol. I, pp. 59-60. Miles (*Remarks upon the Language, Customs, and Physical Character of the Aborigines of Australia*, Sydney, n.d. Public Library of N.S.W., Pamphlets, Vol. E, MJ252.) came to similar conclusions: Either Etymology is a fallacy, a tissue of extraordinary coincidences, or else these our brethren carved in ebony are a race of most extraordinary antiquity, retrograded long ago and wearing out, going to the tomb of the Capuchets unfeathered Bimanal Dodos, who in a few years will not even find a niche in History.

[46] Letter Book, ML, MS.A1450, p. 14.

[47] Threlkeld to Richard Cull, 25 June 1856, in Gunson, *Australian Reminiscences and Papers of L. E. Threlkeld*, Vol. II, p. 298. This theory of moral and intellectual degeneration, most succinctly expressed by William Hull's *Remarks on the Probable Origin and Antiquity of the Aboriginal Natives of New South Wales . . .* , Melbourne 1846, was repeated well into this century.

duties in the Parramatta district had involved some contact with the Aborigines. He told the London Missionary Society:

> I am heartily sick of this place and have been so for some time on a variety of accounts, but chiefly from the little prospect I see of my usefulness among the inhabitants, and the still less prospect, yea, I may say, the almost impossibility of being useful among the poor Natives, who are truely the most writched and Deploreable beings my eyes have ever yet beheld. I think the Greenlanders, Labradorians, or the inhabitants of Terra de Fuego, cannot be much more sunk to a level of Brute creation than they. O Jesus, when shall thy Kingdom come within power amongst them? When shall the rays of thine Eternal gospel penitrate the gross darkness of their minds (well represented by their faces) and illumine their benighted souls.[48]

Similarly, the Rev. George Clarke who had been sent out by the Church Missionary Society for the South Seas in 1822 and was diverted to teaching at the Native Institution at Parramatta wrote in 1824: 'The Natives are . . . the poorest objects on the habitable globe. I have seen the miserable Africans come from the holds of the Slave Ships; but they do not equal, in wretchedness and misery, the New Hollanders'.[49] The influential Samuel Marsden told the Church Missionary Society that the Aborigines were 'the most degraded of the human race . . . all addicted to drunkenness and idleness and vice . . .' and that 'the time is not yet arrived for them to receive the great blessings of civilization and the knowledge of Christianity'.[50]

Many of the most vehement denunciations of Aboriginal 'depravity' proceeded from a desire to publicize the Aborigines as an urgent case for missionary activity. Writing from Hobart in 1836 the Rev. Joseph Orton told his English Wesleyan audience that the Aborigines were 'degraded in some respects far below the brute creation', and 'cannibals . . . of the grossest and most shocking description':

---

[48] Henry to S. Pinder, 29 August 1799, London Missionary Society, South Seas Letters, L.M.S. Archives, London. I am indebted to Dr W. N. Gunson for this reference.

[49] 'Report of the Committee of the Church Missionary Society, May 4, 1824', *BT*, Miss, Box 54, p. 1817.

[50] Marsden to Rev. J. Pratt, 24 February 1819, in J. R. Elder (ed.), *The Letters and Journals of Samuel Marsden 1765-1838* . . . , Dunedin 1932, pp. 231-2. Marsden's similarly pessimistic report to Archdeacon Scott in 1826 can be found as an Appendix in W. N. Gunson, *Australian Reminiscences and Papers of L. E. Threlkeld*, Vol. II, pp. 347-9.

It would seem that the intellectual as well as the moral debasement of the Aborigines of Australia is so great, that long-continued intercourse with them, if not some degree of religious culture, is necessary, before any information can be obtained from them, relative to the superstitious notions which they cherish.[51]

The Aborigines, wrote Orton, opened the door to 'an interesting field of missionary operation'. The same kind of motivation no doubt lay behind another missionary pamphlet based on a letter from Perth in the same year:

We think no heathens more worthy the compassion of Britons; for we believe it is the universal opinion of all who have seen them, that it is impossible to find men and women sunk lower in the scale of human society. With regard to their manners and customs, they are little better than the beasts that perish. They neither wear clothes, build houses, nor cultivate the ground, but depend entirely upon their dexterity in fishing and hunting for their food; nor do they ever provide for the morrow. Polygamy is tolerated amongst them. They have not the most distant idea of any supreme Being; and before the arrival of the white people, it is a matter of doubt whether they had any idea of existence after death in any state whatever.[52]

And at the first meeting of the Society in Aid of the German Mission in Sydney in May 1838 the Rev. W. P. Crook told the assembled audience that

The heathen are so sunk in ignorance as to have no idea of moral guilt, They have a word for *sin*, but signifies only an offence against the priests and their idolatrous customs. To rob and plunder is with them no crime for they have a god of thieves, of whom they tell long tales . . . War, murder, fornication, and all uncleanliness, are with them no crime; for they are perfectly consistent with their gross mythology.[53]

Many of the missionaries in the field were no less condemnatory. The Wellington Valley mission report for 1835 noted that the Aborigines 'have no law against murder, and consequently no punishment for it—A man may murder his wife, or child, or any other relative with impunity'.[54] The harshest judgements seem to

51 *Aborigines of Australia: Copy of a letter from the Rev. Joseph Orton, dated Hobart Town, Van Diemen's Land, August 1836.*
52 *Aborigines of Australia: Extract from a Letter, dated Perth, Swan River, Western Australia, July 17, 1836.*
53 *The Colonist*, 23 May 1838.
54 'Wellington Valley Report for 1835', *V&P*, 1836.

have come from the German missionaries at Moreton Bay whose national temperament possibly made them less tolerant than their British counterparts. For Christopher Eipper, the 'savage nature' of the Aborigines was 'clearly evinced in their intercourse with each other when they are excited by hatred, jealousy, or carnal passions'. As for religion: 'Their God is their belly: their will, or rather their passions, are their law, as long as they are able through violence and cruelty to maintain their point'. But for prostitution, a practice particularly prevalent at the Moreton Bay settlement and a constant source of righteous indignation on the part of the Germans, there was 'that shocking malady which Divine Providence has wisely ordained as the due reward of profligacy'.[55] Even Threlkeld whose knowledge of the Awakabal language enabled him to learn more about Aboriginal culture than any of his missionary contemporaries, was prepared to believe the worst about the Aborigines. He claimed to have prevented a woman from being buried alive and when seeing a man cremating his mother's body, complete with clay pipe, suspected that she was still alive when cast into the flames.[56]

At a more serious level, the missionaries bitterly resented the strength of Aboriginal tradition and the authority of tribal elders which made their task of proselytization well-nigh impossible. At Wellington Valley, for example, Günther learnt enough about the Aborigines to conclude that there were no 'chiefs' in the political sense, but that the tribal elders exerted a powerful influence:

> The old men are obstinately adhering to their own habits and customs and use various means to deter the young men from abandoning the old ways whilst the women old and young are in slavish subjection to the will of the old men.[57]

At this time of unquestioning faith in the supremacy of British Christian civilization and its automatic benefits for the wretched and benighted savage, only a few voices were raised in doubt. The Polish explorer and naturalist, Paul de Strzelecki, observed that

---

[55] Christopher Eipper, *Statement of the Origin, Condition and Prospects, of the German Mission to the Aborigines at Moreton Bay* . . . , Sydney 1841, pp. 7, 9, 10. The Protector James Dredge took a similar view in his *Brief Notices of the Aborigines of New South Wales*, Geelong 1845, p. 12.

[56] Gunson, *Australian Reminiscences and Papers of L. E. Threlkeld*, Vol. II, p. 258.

[57] Letterbook, p. 36.

since Christianity sapped the strength of Aboriginal institutions and thereby destroyed the Aborigines' morale, it was necessary that some form of civil organization should precede their adoption of the new faith.[58] Quoting this with evident approval, the sociologist William Westgarth added that the 'applications of the abstract truths of religion are probably little adapted to forward practically the cause of Aboriginal civilization'.[59] He argued that assumptions about the role of Christianity in the civilizing process were derived not from a study of past efforts, but from theoretical deductions made from religious principles. Strzelecki and Westgarth thought that the Aborigines would soon be extinct and that in the meantime all they wanted was to be left to their own habits and customs. Westgarth went so far as to recommend in 1846 that all the remaining Aborigines in the Port Phillip district should be gathered together on large reserves where they could roam in their natural state.[60]

Nor did everyone regard the Aborigines as degenerate remnants of some lost and forgotten civilization or as simpletons unable to learn from the European example. Robert Dawson, the enlightened manager of the Australian Agricultural Company, recognized the importance of their separation from the rest of mankind. Although unwilling to subscribe to any particular theory of their origin and migration, he believed that sufficient time had elapsed since their arrival in New Holland

> to have rendered them a distinct people, and to have caused in them those peculiarities both of mind and form, which time and circumstance have every where produced as the distinguishing characteristics between the several races of mankind.[61]

The poet Richard Howitt saw them as products of their environment:

> A great deal of nonsense has been talked about the aborigines, as it regards their social and moral condition. Had they been in a more civilised state it would have been singular; for no country on the face of the earth . . . has been so destitute of the means of fixed residence,

---

[58] P. de Strzelecki, *Physical Description of New South Wales and Van Dieman's Land*, London 1845, p. 349.
[59] *A Report on the Condition, Capabilities and Prospects of the Australian Aborigines*, Melbourne 1846, p. 34.
[60] Ibid., p. 38.
[61] *The Present State of Australia* . . . , London 1830, p. 342.

corn and fruits, for the localisation of a people. It is easy to call a native a fool for not providing himself with a house, but it is not so easy to furnish him with a fixed maintenance. It is not all at once that even Europeans can change their own fixed habits. The mode of life of the natives of New Holland is the natural result, age after age, of the one compelling necessity of roaming over the land in search of food. The blandness of the climate, too, tends to perpetuate such a kind of existence. Their desires are simple as their food, and easily satisfied.[62]

In Strzelecki's remarks stressing the validity of Aborigines' way of life there was even a glimpse of the Natural Man whom Cook had seen seventy years earlier:

> To any one . . . who shakes off the trammels of a conventional, local, and therefore narrow mode of thinking . . . who studies and surveys mankind . . . by personal observation, —it will appear that Providence has left as many roads to the threshold of contentment and happiness as there are races of mankind . . . Placed by the Creator, in perfect harmony with the whole economy of nature, in his allocated dwelling and destiny, the Australian is seen procuring for himself all that he wants, regulating all his social affairs, and securing all the worldly happiness and enjoyment of which his condition is capable.[63]

THE 'REALISTS'

Many squatters probably agreed that Christianity was the foundation of their own society, but when they spoke of 'civilizing' the Aborigines they often meant 'pacifying' them and making them 'civil' or submissive. Their principal claim was that the only 'rule' the Aborigines understood was that of superior force. Robert Scott told the 1838 Committee on the Aborigines Question:

> Among themselves they have no governing principle but force; superior strength alone commands obedience; each person is free to do any thing within his own daring, personal fear is his only control . . . Men so constituted, cannot be kept in check, except by force, and the certainty of instant retaliation. It is useless to deceive ourselves—it is wicked to do so.[64]

[62] *Impressions of Australia Felix* . . . , London 1845, p. 197. Richard Howitt was the son of William Howitt whose *Colonization and Christianity*, London 1838, publicized the situation of the Aborigines.

[63] *Physical Description*, p. 342.

[64] 'Report from the Committee on the Aborigines Question', *V&P*, 1838, pp. 16-17.

It was argued that the Aborigines' unaccountable love of bloodshed and their 'treacherous' disposition towards the whites, as well as their fellows, meant that these 'anti-civilizing propensities' had to be subdued before they could enter white society. James Macarthur developed this view at some length during the Legislative Council debate on the William Lee case in 1842:

> when civilized man was brought into contact with savages, it became absolutely necessary that those savages should be . . . thoroughly convinced of the irresistible nature of the power they had to contend with, that it was absolutely necessary that the savage should be compelled to submit himself to that power before it was attempted to introduce him to any of the refinements of our social system.[65]

It was almost universally believed among the squatting fraternity that tolerance and kindness on the part of the whites were interpreted by the Aborigines as signs of weakness or cowardice and only served to embolden them in their outrages. According to Scott, the Aborigines

> cannot comprehend forbearance, they attribute it to fear, impunity urges them to renewed aggressions, success gives them new courage, until at last the patience of the Europeans is exhausted, they fly to arms, and then follow those scenes which must be expected when men are driven to take the law into their own hands.[66]

It was held that the only sensible policy was to punish depredators in such a way that they would be deterred from committing the same offence again. To use the contemporary cliché, the 'blacks' had to be 'taught a lesson' and this was the advice given to would-be settlers by Lieutenant W. H. Breton, R.N., after a visit to the colony:

> In case of any serious affray with the blacks, it really would be the most judicious plan, to make upon them at once, a strong impression, for if only one or two be killed, the sole effect is to instigate them to revenge their companions, whereby a series of murders on both sides is the consequence.[67]

A number of squatters expressed the same view with varying degrees of explicitness. For Alexander Harris, it was 'a simple question

[65] *The Sydney Morning Herald*, 24 August 1842.
[66] 'Report from the Committee on the Aborigines Question', *V&P*, 1838, p. 16. See also, *The Colonist*, 16 February 1839.
[67] *Excursions in New South Wales, Western Australia and Van Diemen's Land* . . . , London 1833, pp. 199-200.

of intimidation (nothing more) between the musket and the spear'.[68] He argued that servants on stations should all have firearms since

> the consciousness of power, whilst on the one hand it intimidates the aborigines, on the other placing the white man out of fear, keeps his mind clear of that bitter enmity to the blacks which otherwise takes possession of it, when . . . 'he lives in hourly fear of his life from them'.[69]

When conflicts along the Gwydir River became worse after Myall Creek a local squatter wrote, 'You must either shoot a few of them by way of example, or you must abandon the country altogether'.[70]

It was also argued by Scott and others that a little 'civilization' could be a dangerous thing. Many of the raids on stock and stores were led by Aborigines who had spent some time on stations before returning to the bush where they put their new-found knowledge of white society to practical use. Another squatter pointed out that two or three of the Aborigines outlawed by Macquarie in 1816 'had been bread up in European Families and became the most despirate Murderers'.[71]

Finally, there were those who believed, or found it convenient to claim, that the spiritual and intellectual degradation of the Aborigines was beyond the elevating power of Christianity. Unlike the South Sea islanders (wrote the journalist George Arden), 'the mind of the poor New Hollander is too feeble, too frivolous to comprehend and be moulded by the grand truths that have worked such wonders elsewhere'.[72]

The prevailing colonial attitude to the 'improvement' of the Aborigines was one of open pessimism; by the early 1820s most of the whites in New South Wales believed that it was impossible. They pointed out that despite the activity of numerous clergymen and missionaries since the founding of the colony, there had been no permanent conversions. Moreover, attempts to encourage Abor-

---

[68] *Settlers and Convicts*, London 1847, pp. 214-15. See also, Gardner, 'Productions and Resources', Vol. II, p. 79, ML, MS.A176$_2$.

[69] *Settlers and Convicts*, p. 206.

[70] *The Colonist*, 16 February 1839, letter from 'Stat Umbra'.

[71] George Bowman's Memorandum for Robert Scott, 5 January 1839, *BP*, No. 102.

[72] 'Civilization of the Aborigines', *Arden's Sydney Magazine*, October 1843, p. 82.

igines to wear European clothing, adopt settled habits and support themselves by means of steady labour had been conspicuously unsuccessful.

Pessimists and critics could produce a great deal of evidence to support their views. James Macarthur expressed the sentiments of the squatting interest when he pointed out in 1836 that after almost fifty years of contact, very little progress had been made towards Christianization and civilization. Referring to the annual reports of the Lake Macquarie and Wellington Valley missions for 1835, he emphasized that no converts had yet been made and that not even the children had shown any 'real spiritual-mindness'. He argued that if the colonists were to continue financing the missions, their methods would have to be radically revised in order to achieve even the slightest results.[73] Similarly, in 1843 Arden listed all the experiments in civilization and Christianization from Bennelong[74] to 'Bob' and 'Jack', two of the 'graduates' of the Flinders Island Aboriginal Establishment who had been brought across by Robinson to civilize the Aborigines of Port Phillip, only to be executed in 1841 for the murder of two whalers at Westernport. He attributed the failure of all these schemes to a 'fallacious view of their physical sympathies and mental capabilities'.[75]

For most contemporaries, signs of advance towards civilization were thought to consist in an appreciation of the main tenets of Christianity, a disposition to adopt European standards of personal cleanliness, dress and housing, and a desire to accumulate money and material possessions. After fifty years of contact with European civilization the Aborigines, even children brought up by white families, had developed none of these qualities and the natural inference drawn by the colonists was that they possessed certain 'anti-civilizing propensities' which prevented change. It was agreed, for example, that their wandering habits constituted an important obstacle to civilization, and that their lack of 'shame' of nakedness,

[73] New South Wales: Its Present State and Future Prospects, London 1837, Appendix 55, p. 259.
[74] For a note on Phillip's protégé, see ADB, Vol. I, pp. 84-5.
[75] 'Civilization of the Aborigines', p. 67. Arden himself set an interesting example of 'civilized' behaviour: the Port Phillip Gazette of 16 March 1842 reported that he had been fined for drunkenness on a race course, drunkenness and obscene language at a concert, and fighting and cursing at a public dinner.

tantamount to a lack of knowledge of good and evil, impeded an appreciation of Christianity.

There appears to have been little demand for intellectual demonstration of the commonly accepted view that the Aborigines were incapable of 'improvement', although a number of authorities could be invoked if necessary. Principal among these was Barron Field who had been on the Committee of the Native Institution and had helped to found the short-lived Society for the Propagation of Christian Knowledge among the Aborigines but became convinced that the Aborigines, unlike the South Sea islanders, would 'never be other than they are'. Field generally accepted Blumenbach's[76] analysis of hair, skin-colour and the shape and capacity of the skull to distinguish five varieties of the human race: Caucasian, Mongolian, Ethiopian, American, and Malay. Of these the Caucasian was the highest and most 'primitive' form from which all the others had 'degenerated'—the Ethiopian occupying the bottom of the scale and possessing no capacity for civilization.[77] According to Blumenbach, the Aborigines of Van Diemen's Land and the northwest coast of New Holland were of the Ethiopian type while all the others were Malay. Field, however, believed that no such distinction could be made and that they were all Ethiopian. 'The skull, the genius, the habits, of the Australians', he told a meeting of the Australian Philosophical Society in Sydney in January 1822, 'appear to me . . . to have, in all of them, the degenerate Ethiopian character, like those of the Andamaners, and the negro races of the Indian Islands'.[78]

The crucial fact, in Field's view, was that the Aborigines had no aptitude for civilization and were still in the same condition that whites had found them:

[76] Johann Friedrich Blumenbach (1752-1840), a German physiologist and comparative anatomist, established modern physical anthropology with his *De Generis Humani Varietate Nativa*, Göttingen 1775 and his *Collectionis Suae Craniorum Diversarum Gentium Illustratae Decades*, Göttingen 1790-1828. His five-fold classification of mankind was made public in 1781. Although Blumenbach was the first to place such reliance on skull form to determine race, theories of Negro inferiority annoyed him and he 'argued in favour of the essential physical unity and emotive and intellectual unity of all mankind'. Donald G. Macrae, 'Race and Sociology in History and Theory' in his *Man, Race and Darwin*, London 1960, p. 79.

[77] T. K. Penniman, *A Hundred Years of Anthropology*, London 1952, p. 55.

[78] 'On the Aborigines of New Holland and Van Dieman's Land' in *Geographical Memoirs*, p. 197.

We have now lived among [the Aborigines] for more than thirty years; and the most persevering attempts have always been made, and are still making, to induce them to settle, and avail themselves of the arts of life; but they cannot be fixed, nor is it possible by any kindness or cherishing to attach them. They have been brought up by us from infancy in our nurseries, and yet the woods have seduced them at maturity, and at once elicited the savage instincts of finding their food in the trees, and their path through the forest, —propensities which civil education had only smothered.[79]

While exchanging their stone axes and shell fish-hooks for ones of steel, they had not developed European skills and would never become builders, mechanics, mariners or cultivators as the Maoris and South Sea islanders had done. 'Perhaps it is better', Field wrote, 'that their names should pass away from the earth. They will not serve and are too indolent and poor in spirit ever to become masters. They would always be drones in the hive of an industrious colony'.[80]

Field also seems to have been the first to use phrenology, the new 'science' of human behaviour, to account for the failure of all attempts to Christianize and civilize the Aborigines, and for their gradual extinction. Based on the physiological researches of two

[79] 'On the Aborigines', ibid., pp. 224-5. Similar observations on the American Indians were made by Dr Samuel George Morton whose *Crania Americana* of 1839 was modelled on Blumenbach's work. Morton did not think that the Indian was physically degenerate, but that he was 'incapable of servitude, and thus his spirit sunk at once in captivity, and with it his physical energy', while 'the more pliant Negro, yielding to his fate . . . bore his heavy burthen with comparative ease'. Quoted by William Stanton in *The Leopard's Spots: Scientific Attitudes Towards Race In America 1815-59*, Chicago 1960, p. 34.

[80] 'Narrative of a Voyage to New South Wales' in *Geographical Memoirs*, p. 435. Field and his contemporaries believed in what might be called 'social devolution' but a rival theory of evolution, already developing in Europe, took note of the fact that some races could not survive contact with Europeans and were doomed by Nature to extinction. In 1837 Charles Darwin noted during his visit to N.S.W. that 'the varieties of man seem to act on each other in the same way as different species of animals—the stronger always extirpating the weaker'. (*Journal of Researches*, London 1890, p. 521.) Evidence of the rapid extinction of the Aborigines of Van Diemen's Land and the Indians of North America and British Guiana given by witnesses before the 1837 Aborigines Committee of the House of Commons led a noted anatomist, Dr James Cowles Prichard, to address a meeting of the British Association in Birmingham in 1839 on 'The Extinction of Some Varieties of the Human Race'. However, Prichard's *The Natural History of Man . . .* , London 1843, concluded that there was only one human species.

Viennese physicians, Franz Gall and Gaspard Spurzheim, phrenology had been developed by an Edinburgh lawyer, George Combe, into a 'character Science' which could explain the differences in national as well as individual character. Assuming that mental phenomena are brought about by natural and ascertainable causes, phrenology claimed that man possessed thirty-seven independent 'faculties' directly related to different parts of the brain. The size of these areas was supposed to indicate the degree of development of the faculties and since the outer skull was assumed to correspond to the pattern of the brain, the observer was able to analyse the character of any person, alive or dead, from the 'bumps' of his skull.[81]

Phrenology divided the human race into four psychological types: 'lymphatic', 'sanguine', 'bilious', and 'nervous', whose behavioural characteristics also corresponded to physical criteria. Implicit in phrenological writing was the assumption that there was a close relationship between brain size and intelligence, although this was offset to some extent by the belief that it was within an individual's powers consciously to develop socially desirable characteristics and to suppress undesirable ones.

Field appears to have ignored this, concluding from his own study of Aboriginal skulls that the Aborigines were constitutionally incapable of being Christianized and civilized—a view which was supported by an unnamed French 'Medical Philosopher' who examined a number of Aborigines during his visit to Sydney in 1825.[82] When informed by Attorney-General Saxe Bannister[83] that this confirmed his own opinion of the 'innate deficiency of these poor people', Threlkeld at the newly-established Lake Macquarie mission declared that he was

exceedingly happy that the French examination ended in the head for

---

[81] Jacques Barzun, *Race: A Study in Modern Superstition*, London 1938, p. 56. A more detailed account of phrenology and its relevance to attitudes to the American Indian and the Negro can be found in J. D. Davies, *Phrenology: Fad and Science, a 19th Century American Crusade*, New Haven 1955.

[82] It has not been possible to identify this man but Dr W. N. Gunson has suggested to me that he was probably connected with the visits of either La Thetis (Bougainville) or L'Esperance (du Campeir) between June and September 1825.

[83] Bannister to Threlkeld 15 September 1825, in Gunson, *Australian Reminiscences and Papers of L. E. Threlkeld*, Vol. II, p. 186. For a biographical note on Bannister, see p. 110.

my business lies solely with an organ which has escaped their notice, namely the *heart*, but had they even searched and found an *innate deficiency* in that organ I would have then smiled and retorted my trust is in him who has said: 'A new heart will I create within them'.[84]

More pointedly, he added that his recent difficulties in learning the language of the Lake Macquarie Aborigines might well cause them to think that there was 'an innate deficiency in the bulk of white men's sculls which prevents their attainment of the native language'.[85]

Lang, too, referred to 'gentlemen of intelligence' in the colony who had 'professed to be in doubt, whether they ought to consider the Aborigines of New Holland as a superior order of beings to the ourang-outang of the neighbouring islands of Borneo and Sumatra'.[86] While admitting that the spectacle of Aborigines searching for and eating *cabra* (wood grubs) might lead people to conclude that 'the difference between the two classes of animals does not appear to be very remarkable', he emphasized that their ability to give appropriate names to groups of stars and to commemorate the heroic achievements of their tribe in poetry created a very strong impression of their humanity:

> Instead . . . of reasoning downwards, (which . . . is the easiest thing in the world), and showing how closely the New Holland savage assimilates to the brutes, let the New Holland philosophers reason upwards, and show us how closely the brutes assimilate to the New Hollander in his higher moods. Let them only inform us by what names any of the inferior animals have ever designated any of the constellations. Let them only show us 'A poem in fifteen stanzas by an ourang-outang'. No! Even in the times of ancient paganism, men entertained ideas on this subject much more accordant with common sense and with the proper and exclusive dignity of man.[87]

Phrenology was certainly the most popular theory explaining Aboriginal 'inferiority'. Although Field, Alexander Berry, Major Mitchell and a number of others were familiar with its principles in the early 1820s, general interest was insignificant until 1836 when Dr William Bland presented a collection of sixty 'phrenological busts' to the Sydney Mechanics' School of Arts. Subsequently

---

[84] Threlkeld to Bannister, 27 September 1825, ibid., p. 187.
[85] Ibid.
[86] *View of the Origins and Migrations of the Polynesian Nation*, p. 247.
[87] Ibid., pp. 247-8.

G

public lectures were given on the subject by Dr F. L. Wallace,[88] Dr A. a'Beckett and by James Hamilton, a professional 'practical phrenologist' from Glasgow. One of the School of Arts weekly debates in 1844 was on the subject of 'whether the doctrine of Phrenology is true or not?',[89] and the 'science' was defended in the *New South Wales Magazine*, the *Colonial Literary Journal* and other periodicals of the educated classes. Part of the appeal of 'practical' phrenology lay in its simplicity. Armed with Combe's phrenological charts and a rudimentary knowledge of cranial anatomy, the enthusiast could confidently 'manipulate' a subject's skull and analyse his business prospects as well as his character. *The Sydney Morning Herald* of 4 November 1846, for example, carried the information that

> Mr Moreau, The Ultra-Phrenologist, may be consulted on the natural temper and disposition, but more particularly on all questions which involve loss or gain, such as any cause at issue, the quality of bonds, bill and sureties, on the expediency of opening life policies, speculative operations, horse-racing, etc.

The colonial exponents of phrenology attributed to the cranial structure of the Aborigines traits of behaviour which had already been noticed for some time and could now be explained 'scientifically' in terms of the under- or over-development of certain 'organs' of the brain. The most thorough colonial application of phrenology to the Aborigines was undertaken by 'Aeneas', a contributor to *The Colonial Literary Journal*, in 1844.[90] His first point was that like all savage races, the greater part of the Aboriginal brain lay in the back of the head which housed the passions and 'inferior sentiments'. Consequently their moral and intellectual faculties were, with a few exceptions, 'very deficient', and their general indolence could easily be explained:

> The disposition of the Aborigines . . . exhibits a considerable proportion of lymphatic temperament, and . . . such a quality predisposes to inactivity and sluggishness, for which they are noted—being roused

---

[88] Reported in *The Sydney Herald*, 29 August 1838.

[89] By 1842 the School of Arts library contained Combe's *Phrenology*, Spurzheim's *Lectures on Phrenology* and Roget's *Outlines on Physiology and Phrenology*.

[90] 29 August and 5 September 1844. The following quotations are taken from these two articles.

from their slothful torpor only by the trumpet-voice of passion, or the cravings of continued hunger.

A deficiency in 'constructive ingenuity' was supposed to account for their technological primitiveness and consequent material wretchedness. But while their gunyahs and canoes were considered to be crude and frail, they displayed great skill in the making of weapons since their faculties of 'Destructive and Combativeness' were strongly developed:

> The talent of constructing will always, if the mind is allowed to follow its own bias, be employed in what is most congenial to the feelings of the constructor; and in this instance the Aborigines only imitate the custom of all barbarous nations.

However, their survival in warfare amongst themselves had been guaranteed by the thickness of their skulls ('the strength of the Aboriginal head-piece in resisting the most powerful blows of their waddy is well known'), and the strong development of their organ of 'Caution'. Providence, wrote 'Aeneas', had also endowed the Aborigines with a large organ of 'locality'—a talent for remembering places and finding their way through the bush which was indispensable to their particular mode of life. The same organ, however, was responsible for their apparently insuperable aversion to permanent settlement. A strong organ of 'Individuality' rather than superior eyesight accounted for their skill in observation, and the development of these two organs accounted for the prominence of the lower forehead.

As might be expected, the 'reflective faculties', housed in the upper forehead, were thought to be undeveloped. 'Ideality' (creative imagination) was considered weak, although it was admitted that the Aborigines had poets. Perhaps the clearest rationalization of a European response to the Aborigines' culture was 'Aeneas'' analysis of their music:

> Time is much more largely developed in their foreheads than Tune— hence their comparative skill in the modulations of time displayed in their grotesque dances and corrobories and the almost total want of anything like melody in the discordant noises which form their national music.

Unlike other critics, 'Aeneas' was prepared to concede that the Aborigines' migratory habits arose *at first* from necessity, but qualified this by admitting that 'their passion for roaming exists, independently of any extraneous influence'. More importantly, he saw some hope for the Aborigines who, although 'inferior in the great endowments of the mind', were nevertheless capable of improvement. If, as was thought by some, New Holland was a continent of recent origin, Europeans should be more lenient towards the barbarisms of a race which had had little time to improve itself. 'Numerous instances of intelligence and even refinement' showed that the 'organs' and 'faculties' of the Aborigines could be developed. Although 'Aeneas' constantly confused these two terms, he seems to have accepted Combe's principle that once a man's weaknesses were diagnosed, the path lay clear through education to 'improvement'.

For those whose acquaintance with phrenology was more tenuous, the common conclusion was that the Aborigines possessed 'an innate deficiency of intellect rendering them incapable of instruction'. As one writer put it:

> The virgin page of the savage mind cannot retain our characters, in other words . . . the black scull does not possess the faculties necessary for the purposes of civilized life.[91]

Two influential landholders with more than twenty years of experience of the Aborigines, used phrenology as a crude anatomical explanation which linked their behaviour with intellectual 'inferiority'. The Aborigines' nomadic habits were attributed by Alexander Berry to the over-development of 'locomotive propensities',[92] and by Robert Scott to the complete absence of the 'organ of inhabitiveness'.[93] Others spoke of the Aborigines' 'instinctive' aversion to labour.

It was claimed that the Aborigines could only be civilized by 'breeding out' these and other inherent weaknesses through miscegenation with the whites. The Rev. David Mackenzie observed that 'by intermixture with Europeans some of the phrenologically bad points disappear in the Australian blacks'[94] and it was even believed that an Aboriginal woman who had sexual intercourse

---

[91] 'A Few Words on the Aborigines of Australia', *The New South Wales Magazine*, I, No. 2 February 1843, 57.
[92] 'Recollections of the Aborigines', *BP*, No. 83.
[93] 'Report from the Committee on the Aborigines Question', *V&P*, 1838, p. 18.
[94] *The Emigrant's Guide: or Ten Years' Practical Experience in Australia*, London 1845, p. 242.

with a white man was thereby 'improved' to the extent of no longer being able to have a child by an Aboriginal man.[95] Everyone agreed that half-caste Aborigines were superior by virtue of their 'white' blood. Mrs Shelley told the 1838 Committee on the Aborigines Question that from her experience at the Native Institution the half-caste children were quicker to learn and more tractable than the full-bloods.[96] Berry remarked that 'the cross bred are distinctly an improved race'[97] and many others noted that the half-caste's faculties were 'of a different order from those of a pure black' and therefore sufficient to equip him for civilized life.[98] A correspondent signing himself 'A Phrenologist' wrote to *The Colonist* in October 1838 that the only means of raising the 'debased' Aborigines was 'crossing them with European blood' and proposed that 600 white females from the Parramatta 'factory' should be distributed among the tribes and an equivalent number of Aboriginal females among the white stockmen and shepherds. Noting the recent lecture in which Dr Wallace had emphasized the striking resemblance between the skull of an Aborigine and that of a monkey, 'A Phrenologist' concluded that 'the native American savages, and native New Hollanders, cannot, with their present brains, adopt Christianity or civilization'.[99]

In a leading article ten days later entitled 'Are the Aborigines Men?', *The Colonist* regretted the revival of 'what we thought had become an obsolete doctrine, that because the skulls of the New Hollanders fall short of the intellectual beau-ideal set by the curious in bones, they are physically disqualified for the acquisition of civilized life'.[100] It continued:

> That the Aborigines are our fellow-*men*, might be regarded as a self-evident proposition were it not for the notorious fact, that its truth has been somewhat more than questioned by certain fanatics calling themselves philosophers.[101]

[95] P. de Strzelecki, *Physical Description of New South Wales and Van Dieman's Land*, London 1845, pp. 346-7. This claim was later demolished by Dr T. R. Heywood Thomson, 'Observations on the Reported Infecundity of the "Gins" or Aboriginal Females of New Holland . . .', *Journal of the Ethnological Society of London*, Vol III, 1854, pp. 243-6.
[96] 'Report from the Committee on the Aborigines Question', *V&P*, 1838, p. 54.
[97] 'Recollections of the Aborigines'.
[98] 'A Few Words on the Aborigines of Australia', p. 59.
[99] *The Colonist*, 13 October 1838.
[100] Ibid.
[101] Ibid.

The controversy aroused by the Myall Creek trials and executions persuaded Threlkeld that phrenology could no longer be dismissed so lightly. In his mission report for 1838 he wrote:

> The fashionable philosophy of the day, speculating on the intellectual powers of the Aborigines, as manifested in the Bumps of the Brain, is a splendid specious fallacy leading away the mind from the hope of the influence of God's holy spirit regenerating the Heart opening the eyes of their understanding, and turning them from darkness to light, from the power of Satan unto God; and instead of depending as christians, on the promised divine secret influence of the Holy Spirit, this specious science, contemplates only the quantity of accumulation of matter in the formation of the brain, the depositions of bone in the various corresponding concavities and convexities of the skull, sets aside a positive declaration, to assume an hypothesis, amusing in theory, but dangerous in practice.
>
> The miserable attempt to deduce from such a science, falsely so called, that these Black human beings, 'have an innate deficiency of intellect rendering them incapable of instruction', would arrive at the natural conclusion that it would be useless to attempt it, and consequently the Blacks being part and parcel of the brute creation, being deficient of intellect, there can be no responsibility attached to their destruction, more than there is to the extirpation of any other animal whose presence is obnoxious to the possessor of the soil! It is to be lamented that such sentiments have most likely had their influence on men of corrupt minds, who gladly avail themselves of any specious argument to enable them to gratify their love of cruelty, which has ended in blood and the consequent forfeiture of life to Justice in the recent execution of the wanton murderers of the Aborigines. Nor, have some . . . who are termed well educated minds, escaped the contagion of the mental poison, which insidiously perverts the judgement, and has led to the adoption of means and arguments alike discreditable to Christian honor.[102]

Threlkeld evidently believed that this 'scientific' proof of physical and intellectual inferiority was being used to justify treating the Aborigines as something less than human, and that it could also be invoked by all those who opposed expenditure on Aboriginal missions and other enterprises and argued that such endeavours would always be fruitless.[103]

---

[102] Gunson, *Australian Reminiscences and Papers of L. E. Threlkeld*, Vol. I, p. 148.

[103] In 1858 a Committee of the Victorian Legislative Council actually called in a Bourke Street phrenologist to give his opinion on the capabilities of the Aborigines. 'Report of the Select Committee of the Legislative Council on

Ironically, a theory which had been designed partly to attack the idea that there were different species of men was transformed into a vulgar 'science' lending respectability to the popular belief that the Aborigines were inferior beings who could justifiably be treated by another set of moral standards. It would be misleading to suggest that all the colonial exponents of phrenology were pandering to popular prejudices, but there is no doubt that by correlating certain cultural characteristics with physical 'deficiencies', they lent spurious authority to the popular view that the Aborigines were 'lowest in the scale of humanity' and could never be 'improved'.

There is evidence to suggest that particularly after the Myall Creek arrests in July 1838 the squatting interest attempted to lessen the seriousness of killing Aborigines by denying their humanity. In October, for example, *The Sydney Herald* published a letter from 'Anti-Hypocrite', a native-born Murrumbidgee squatter who wrote of

> these hordes of Aboriginal cannibals, to whom the veriest reptile that crawls the earth holds out matter for emulation, and who are far, very far, below the meanest brute in rationality, and every feeling pertaining thereto.[104]

Although no one ever published any explicit claim that the Aborigines were animals or that they were the product of a separate creation, the climate of opinion during the latter part of 1838 was such that *The Colonist* and a number of Protestant clergymen felt the necessity of stressing their essential humanity. Replying to 'Anti-Hypocrite' and others, the Rev. John Saunders told the Sydney Baptists that the whole of the human race was of one species, descended from Adam and Eve.[105] In November, just before the first trial of the Myall Creek men, J. D. Lang reminded his congregation in Scots Church that the Aborigines were 'bone of our bone and flesh of our flesh—formed originally after the image of God . . . and guilty only . . . of an Ethiopian skin, and an untutored soul'.[106]

---

the Aborigines', *Victorian Legislative Council Papers*, 1859. Phrenology continues to survive as part of the stock-in-trade of certain private vocational guidance consultants in Australia.

104 *The Sydney Herald*, 5 October 1838.

105 *The Colonist*, 20 October 1838.

106 This sermon was printed as a pamphlet entitled *National Sins the Causes and Precursors of National Judgements* . . . , Sydney 1838 (p. 15).

The Rev. W. Hamilton also offered Presbyterians in the squatting districts various learned proofs that 'all mankind, not excepting the New Hollanders, are descended from common parents'.[107]

The Colonist went to the heart of the matter in an editorial of 16 January 1839:

> Sordid interest is at the root of all this anti-aborigines feeling. Because the primitive lords of the soil interfere, in some of the frontier stations, with the easy and lucrative grazing of cattle and sheep, they are felt by the sensitive pockets of the graziers to be a *nuisance*; and the best plea these 'gentlemen' can set up for their rights to abate the nuisance by the summary process of stabbing, shooting, burning, and 'poisoning', is, that the offenders are below the level of the white man's species.

However, for some of the educated, Christian gentlemen among the squatting class, the argument that the Aborigines were less than human was probably more than just expediency. For those whose consciences troubled them, it may have been very convenient to believe that killing an Aborigine was a very different thing from killing a man.[108]

THE POPULAR VIEW

It is unlikely that more than a handful of those in closest contact with the Aborigines were familiar with colonial vulgarizations of Combe and Blumenbach, but the general belief was that they were 'lowest in the scale of humanity'. White disapproval of the Aborigines was most commonly expressed in disgust at their physical appearance, but the exaggerated and emotional character of many descriptions also suggest a desire to emphasize the 'inferiority' or 'degradation' of the Aborigines.

It has already been mentioned that the Aborigines' habit of rubbing themselves with fish-oil against mosquitoes and marsupial fat against the cold endowed them with a strong odour. One squatter recommended that because of their failure to wash (except in the middle of summer when they dived into the nearest water-hole), 'the safe plan, and that which the bushman usually adopted,

---

[107] 'The Obligation of the Scottish Presbyterian Church of New South Wales to use Means for the Salvation of the Aborigines of the Territory' in his *Practical Discourses Intended for Circulation in the Interior of New South Wales*, Sydney 1843, p. 137.

[108] C. D. Rowley makes this point in 'Aborigines and other Australians', *Oceania*, XXXII, No. 4, June 1962, pp. 248-9.

is to keep to the weather side of them, even on horseback'.[109] So powerful was the smell, it was claimed, that cattle bred and imported by English settlers would run away from Aborigines 'with every symptom of disgust'.[110]

Little distinction was made between the Aborigines of the interior and those who had taken up semi-permanent occupation on the stations or outside the towns. The newly-arrived immigrant's first impression was of

> a number of half-naked dusky savages . . . lounging down the street with spears and waddies in their hands, filthy, and slimy, and greasy, leaving behind them an odour enough to turn the stomach of the stoutest dog.[111]

Some whites reacted strongly to the Aborigines' physical appearance:

> their features, which were most repulsive—the low, or I might almost say *no* forehead of most of them—the shaggy eyebrows protruding over and almost hiding the small keen eyes—the flabby nose, unnaturally distended by a long white bone inserted through the nostrils—the thick lips and the snow-like teeth, common to cannibals—all inspired me with a dislike for them, that time and almost daily intercourse have not removed.[112]

Furthermore, the custom of wearing pieces of wood or bone through the nostrils was seen as sheer perversity, 'as though they were not sufficiently ugly'.[113] Aboriginal women were found to be especially objectionable:

> at the age of six or seven and twenty they present the most hideous appearance imaginable; they are mere outlines of humanity. Their loathsome appearance is, in time of mourning, increased by the custom of tearing off the skin of their cheeks, and literally besmearing their black foreheads with white pipeclay.[114]

[109] J. O. Balfour, *A Sketch of New South Wales*, London 1845, p. 9. For a similar reaction from a more recent visitor, see Charles Chewings, *Back to the Stone Age*, Sydney 1936, pp. 109-10.
[110] J. F. O'Connell, *A Residence of Eleven Years in New Holland and the Caroline Islands* . . . , Boston 1836, pp. 86-7.
[111] E. Lloyd ['A Squatter'], *A Visit to the Antipodes* . . . , London 1846, pp. 83-4.
[112] Balfour, *A Sketch of New South Wales*, pp. 7-8.
[113] Breton, *Excursions*, p. 26.
[114] G. T. Lloyd, *Thirty-Three Years in Tasmania and Victoria* . . . , London 1862, p. 468.

Naturally, disease made them even more unattractive. On the lower Murrumbidgee in 1829 Captain Charles Sturt found the 'loathsome conditions and hideous countenances' of Aboriginal women 'a complete antidote to the sexual passion'.[115]

Many whites appear to have found the Aborigines' nakedness quite shocking and repulsive. J. O. Balfour wrote of his first encounter with the Bogan tribe that he would 'never forget the disgust with which I first saw these savages, in all the majesty of nature, without the slightest covering'.[116] No doubt their frank sexuality and lack of 'shame' horrified many whites and affected their attitudes to Aboriginal customs. Balfour likened a corroboree which he had seen to 'a ballet executed by the denizens of the zoological gardens'[117] and Breton found part of one 'far too disgusting to bear a description'.[118] He was repelled by 'libidinous gestures' and 'yelling in concert in the most hideous manner imaginable'.[119] Polygamy, too, was found highly offensive and Balfour recorded his disgust at the sight of fathers and sons fighting for the possession of women. He claimed that polygamy had no limits, old warriors having at least seven or eight wives.[120] It was also rumoured that initiation ceremonies were little more than opportunities for tribal elders to indulge in unnatural practices with the young men.[121] 'Speaking of them collectively', wrote Breton, 'it must be confessed I entertain very little more respect for the aborigines of New Holland, than for the ourang-outang; in fact, I can discover no great difference.'[122]

Perhaps the most explicit summary of popular knowledge of the

---

[115] *Two Expeditions into the Interior of Southern Australia . . .* , 2 vols, London 1833, Vol. II, p. 126.

[116] *A Sketch of New South Wales*, p. 7.

[117] Ibid., p. 16.

[118] *Excursions*, p. 202.

[119] Ibid.

[120] *A Sketch of New South Wales*, p. 13.

[121] Breton, *Excursions*, p. 202. Attitudes to Aboriginal ceremonies were coloured by the fact that large gatherings presented a threat to stock. One squatter reported in 1842 that the tribes from the Gwydir, Macintyre and Namoi had come together for a *bora* (initiation) ceremony and had killed between ten and twelve cattle each day for food. One of the *Herald*'s correspondents explained that 'on these occasions they do not look for food in the usual manner, but attack the first cattle they can find'. *The Sydney Morning Herald*, 27 October 1842. See also, Mitchell, *Tropical Australia*, p. 21.

[122] *Excursions*, p. 196.

Aborigines was set out in Maclehose's *Picture of Sydney and Stranger's Guide in New South Wales* for 1838:[123] they were homogeneous in race but not in language; their government was 'patriarchal' but no 'laws or regulations' could be discovered, other than an agreement on tribal territories; they practised polygamy, wife-stealing and cannibalism (fathers killing and eating their own children) and were instinctively averse to work, although they delighted in war; religious forms were unknown to them, but they possessed 'superstitions' and their corroborees resembled the 'devilworship' of mountain tribes in Ceylon; finally, drawings by John Carmichael illustrated the claim that they were incomparably inferior to the New Zealanders and were rapidly being destroyed by disease and internecine war.

There was a wide audience for sensational anecdotes[124] and it was commonly believed that Aborigines killed and ate whites, as well as each other.[125] The story which seems to have gained widest currency, especially amongst the convict class, was given credibility by none other than Charles Sturt on the Murrumbidgee in 1829:

> The parties were two Irish runaways, who thought they could make their way to Timor. They escaped from Wellington Valley with a fortnight's provisions each, and a couple of dogs, and proceeded down the Macquarie. About the cataract, they fell in with the Mount Harris tribe, and remained with them for some days, when they determined on pursuing their journey. The blacks, however, wanted to get possession of their dogs, and a resistance on the part of the Europeans brought on a quarrel. It appeared, that before the blacks proceeded to extremities, they furnished the Irishmen, who were unarmed, with weapons, and then told them to defend themselves, but whether against equal or inferior numbers, I am uninformed. One of them soon fell, which the other observing, he took his knife out, and cut the throats of both dogs

---

[123] Sydney 1838, pp. 159-64.

[124] Michael Roe, *Quest for Authority in Eastern Australia 1835-1851*, Melbourne 1965, p. 27.

[125] It is likely that the Aborigines of eastern Australia did occasionally take part in the ritual eating of certain internal organs of dead babies and young women, and the skin of warriors killed in battle. This would almost certainly have been restricted to a few people of prescribed relationship to the deceased and there is no reliable evidence to suggest that Aborigines went out of their way to eat human flesh. However, infanticide was common, especially in bad seasons when the mother was still suckling another child, or if the child had a European father. It is conceivable that Aborigines in times of extreme drought and famine might have killed babies for food, but this is not likely to have happened in the area covered by this study.

before the blacks had time to put him to death. He was, however, sacrificed; and both the men were eaten by the tribe generally. I questioned several on the subject, but they preserved the most sullen silence, neither acknowledging nor denying the fact.[126]

Repeating the story, Breton commented: 'We have no decided proof of this being true',[127] but for the majority of the white population, proof was unnecessary. A rumour that the botanist Richard Cunningham's kidney fat had been removed after he had been killed by Aborigines near the Bogan River in 1835 gained wide currency, although once again there was no evidence. A few years earlier, similar significance had been attached to Captain Bishop's discovery of the clean-picked bones of a stockman allegedly killed in Argyle County.[128]

Sturt also recorded a story of cannibalistic infanticide related to him at O'Brien's station on the Yass plains by a stockman who

> pointed out two blacks to me at a little distance from us. 'That fellow, sir', said he, 'who is sitting down, killed his infant child last night by knocking its head against a stone, after which he threw it in the fire and devoured it'. I was quite horror-struck, and could scarcely believe such a story. I therefore went up to the man and questioned him as to the facts, as well as I could. He did not attempt to deny it, but slunk away in evident consciousness. I then questioned the other that remained, whose excuse for his friend was that the child was sick and would never have grown up, adding that he himself did not patter (eat) any of it.[129]

It seems that Sturt was anxious to believe the story, regardless of its veracity, being

> as firmly persuaded of the truth of what I have stated as if I had seen the savage commit the act . . . *The very mention of such a thing among these people goes to prove they are capable of such an enormity*.[130]

In the same year that the second edition of Sturt's *Two Expeditions* appeared, Dr George Bennett, a noted English anatomist, repeated a similar tale. Having heard such claims previously, he had decided to make his own investigations while on a visit to the Murrumbidgee district:

---

[126] *Two Expeditions*, Vol. I, p. 114.
[127] *Excursions*, p. 243.
[128] Cunningham, *Two Years in New South Wales*, Vol. II, p. 17.
[129] *Two Expeditions*, Vol. II, p. 222.
[130] Ibid., p. 223 (my emphasis).

I succeeded in ascertaining that infants were frequently destroyed; sometimes the reason assigned was some personal defect in the infant . . . or the mother not wishing to have the trouble of carrying it about. The female children were more frequently destroyed than the males. I heard of a weak and sickly child having been destroyed, and even eaten; the reason given by the unnatural parents was, that they were very hungry, and the child no use and much trouble.[131]

Other more sensational and popular accounts described the Aborigines' brutality and their deficiency in the natural affections of husband for wife, parents for children and children for parents. In *A Narrative of the Sufferings of Jas. Loveless, Jas. Brine and Thomas & John Standfield, Four Of the Dorchester Labourers . . .* it was claimed that the Aborigines

When suffering from hunger . . . have been known to eat their own male offspring, and frequently are the whites speared, roasted and devoured by them. Their aged and infirm, when no longer able to travel and obtain their own food, are disposed of in the following way: the younger portion of the tribe pile a quantity of dry wood together, leaving on one side a hole similar to the mouth of an oven, into which the aged and infirm are thrust, the wood set on fire, and thus they are left to perish.[132]

Perhaps the most celebrated account of 'atrocities' inflicted by Aborigines on whites derived from the wreck of the *Stirling Castle* north of Moreton Bay in 1836 when Captain James Fraser and his first officer were murdered but his wife, Eliza, and three male survivors lived with the Aborigines of the Wide Bay district for some time before escaping. The subsequent publication in London of newspaper accounts, broadsides and books[133] gave wide publicity to Mrs Fraser's misadventures and reinforced colonial interest in the incident. There was even an American version of the story made to resemble other accounts of white women held captive by Indians by adding an episode in which Mrs Fraser's subjection to

[131] *Wanderings*, Vol. I, p. 124.
[132] London 1838, p. 15.
[133] *Shipwreck of Mrs. Fraser and the Loss of the Stirling Castle*, London 1837; John Curtis, *Shipwreck of the Stirling Castle . . . to which is added the Narrative of the Wreck of the Charles Eaton . . . ,* London 1838; *The Wreck of the Stirling Castle—Horrib Treatment of the Crew by Savages,* J. Catnach, [London] 1838. The latter, a broadside ballad, is reproduced together with various illustrations and contemporary material in Michael Alexander, *Mrs. Fraser on the Fatal Shore*, New York 1971.

the brutal passions of the Aboriginal 'chief' was narrowly averted by the opportune arrival of a rescue party.[134]

In 1838 the 'narratives' of Mrs Fraser and three other survivors were collated by a London writer, *Times* journalist John Curtis, in a sensational piece of hagiography[135] depicting them as slaves subjected by the Aborigines to all manner of diabolical tortures. Forced to collect food for the tribe, they were only allowed to eat rotten offal and when they displeased their masters, fire-brands were applied to the soles of their feet and other sensitive parts 'and every device was resorted to by which pain could be created, in order that their joy might be enhanced at the writhing of their victims'.[136] Mrs Fraser's summary of her experiences emphasized that the Aborigines were evil beyond all previous expectations:

> The stories which we have read in our childhood, and the representations of savage life we have seen in the theater in our riper years, are mere trifles and faint representations, when compared with the facts of life which I and my unfortunate companions were eye-witnesses. When I first beheld the countenance of these savages, and heard their frightful yell, I expected nothing but destruction—although my life has been spared, I never expected to witness the scenes I have beheld, and the abominable insults I have undergone. To me it appears, that as to decency of conduct, and sensibility of mind, there is no difference between them and the beasts of the forest, or if there be, it consists in the latter being less ingenious in their cruelty.[137]

No one questioned the authenticity of her story, or those of her companions, although it is quite likely that she was deranged. The 3rd Officer of the ship which took her back to England noted in his diary that the Aborigines had burnt the *Stirling Castle*'s mate to death and made 'soup and hash' of the others, but his eagerness

---

[134] *Narrative of the Capture, Sufferings, and Miraculous Escape of Mrs. Eliza Fraser* . . . , New York 1837. An abridged version of this chapbook can be found in Ingleton, *True Patriots All*, pp. 176-9. Rumours of a white woman living with Aborigines in eastern Gippsland excited popular fancy in the mid 1840s and a number of expeditions were sent out to rescue her. The 'woman' was eventually discovered to be the female figurehead from the wreck of the *Britannia*.

[135] *Shipwreck of the Stirling Castle* . . . Curtis, whose report of Mrs Fraser's story appeared in *The Times* of 24 August 1837, had earlier covered the sensational 'Murder in the Red Barn' case about which he also wrote a book. Alexander, *Mrs. Fraser on the Fatal Shore*, pp. 137-8.

[136] *Ibid.*, p. 78.

[137] *Ibid.*, p. 157.

to hear the story from the heroine's own lips was prevented by her indisposition: 'she is quite lost at times I hear'.[138] Curtis himself admitted that she had 'evinced symptoms of aberration of mind . . .'.

Curtis also included in his book the 'Narrative of the *Charles Eaton*', a ship which had been wrecked in 1834 on a reef near the Sir Charles Hardy Islands off Cape York where its survivors were supposedly devoured by natives. Both stories lent support to the popular rumour that the Aborigines of the northern coasts were more prone to kill and eat whites than were those in other parts of the continent. This belief was implicit in J. D. Lang's suggestion in the late 1830s that a mission be established in the Moreton Bay area so that the northern coasts might be made safe for the survivors of future shipwrecks.[139] Lang's father had been a passenger on a small coastal vessel which disappeared in 1830 on a voyage from Newcastle to Sydney and it is likely that this event influenced his plan.[140] Curtis, too, expressed the hope that his book would stimulate missionary operations.[141]

Another case widely reported in the colonial press was that of the brigantine *Maria* which was wrecked on Bundin's Reef near the mouth of the Murray River in September 1840.[142] Of the twenty-six passengers and crew, ten bodies were found of survivors who had evidently been killed by Aborigines and it was assumed that most of the remainder had suffered a similar fate, although there was no suggestion of cannibalism. The colonists applauded the action of Major T. O'Halloran and his mounted police who hastened to the area from Adelaide and promptly hanged two members of the 'Big Murray' or Milmenrura tribe without going through the niceties of a magistrate's inquiry. While it was asserted by O'Halloran that the Milmenrura were notorious among the Aborigines themselves for their brutal and fierce character, no significance was attached to the cruel exploits of a whaler, Roach, and his companion who had been

---

[138] Henry Wren, Journal. ML, MS.A763.
[139] *Appeal* . . . on behalf of the German Mission, Sydney 1839. For a history of the 'German Mission', see W. N. Gunson, 'The Nundah Missionaries', *Royal Historical Society of Queensland Journal*, Vol. VI, 1960-61, pp. 511-39.
[140] *HRA*, XIX, pp. 9-10. Lang himself had travelled to N.S.W. on the *Stirling Castle* and Captain Fraser had officiated at his marriage at Cape Town. Lang later chartered the ship to bring out Scots immigrants.
[141] *Shipwreck of the Stirling Castle*, p. vi.
[142] *The Australian*, 1 September; 10, 13 October 1840.

murdered by Aborigines in the same area a short time before.[143] Some years earlier, members of the same tribe had distinguished themselves by rescuing the crew of another ship but the activities of the whalers may have radically changed their attitudes to whites.

Even before the *Stirling Castle*, it was almost automatic practice to attribute the disappearance of ships' crews and overland expeditions to Aboriginal attacks motivated by cannibalism. The loss of Captain Stewart's ship-wrecked party in the Twofold Bay area in 1819[144] was immediately put down to the Aborigines, as was the disappearance of Cunningham and of J. T. Gellibrand and G. B. Hesse near Geelong in 1836.[145] In 1845 the colonial press was filled with rumours that the explorer Ludwig Leichhardt had suffered a similar fate. The Faithfull massacre and the Lee case were also produced as proof that even apparently friendly and helpful Aborigines could not be trusted.

Some contemporaries were acutely aware of the injustice of these charges. During Robert Dawson's term as manager of the Australian Agricultural Company's establishment at Port Stephens, there was a rumour that several whites had been killed and eaten in the area and Dawson was 'exceedingly glad to have it in my power to contradict a tale which was fabricated solely to excite prejudice against the natives there'.[146] Referring to the number of stories of cannibalism that came from the Aborigines themselves, he explained that 'the natives cannot, in any way, so much degrade their enemies in the eyes of white people, as by calling them cannibals'.[147] Breton, too, in spite of his generally low opinion of the Aborigines, dismissed stories of cannibalism as

> greatly exaggerated, probably utterly false; because whenever any of them have been killed by the convicts, and others, the latter have invented all sorts of ridiculous tales . . . in order that they may be furnished with an excuse for taking away their lives.[148]

Robinson's exposure of false reports and rumours in 1845 prompted the liberal *Weekly Register* to ask whether these had actually been

---

[143] *The Australian*, 1 September and 10, 13 October 1840.
[144] David Blair, *The History of Australasia*, Glasgow 1878, pp. 136-7.
[145] The Aborigines' own account of what happened to Gellibrand and Hesse can be found in *The Weekly Register*, 27 July 1844.
[146] *The Present State of Australia*, London 1830, pp. 334-5.
[147] Ibid., p. 336.
[148] *Excursions*, p. 243.

concocted with the intention of 'exciting hostile feelings against the Aborigines, or . . . to obtain a stronger police force'.[149]

However, these and other stories were widely circulated among a pastoral population who saw the Aborigines as dangerous animals —and were as readily accepted by an urban population who, for the most part, saw them as inferior and worthless brutes. As 'Anti-Hypocrite' put it:

> Before they are made Christians you must make them men . . . every man of common experience knows that the aboriginals of my native country are the most degenerate, despicable and brutal race of beings in existence, and stand as it were in scorn to 'shame creation'—a scoff and a jest upon humanity—they are insensible to every bond which binds man to his friend—husband to wife—parent to its child—or creature to its God. They stand unprecedented in the annals of the most ancient and barbarous histories for the anti-civilizing propensities they put forth.[150]

Such was the climate of opinion in New South Wales when the British government was making a well-meaning, if belated, attempt to Christianize and civilize the Australian Aborigines.

[149] *The Weekly Register*, 21 June 1845.
[150] *The Sydney Herald*, 5 October 1838.

H

CHAPTER THREE

The Background of Official Policy

> A governor could neither ignore colonial opinion nor dispense with colonial administrators, and often he had to function as a buffer between colonial opinion and Colonial Office opinion, the one coloured largely by realism, the other by idealism. In these circumstances, a certain degree of procrastination and lukewarmness was to be expected.
>
> G. R. MELLOR

THE EARLY GOVERNORS AND THE COLONIAL OFFICE

The arrival of Governor Sir George Gipps in New South Wales in February 1838 coincided with the British government's first serious attempt to supervize the welfare of the indigenous inhabitants of its colonies. A curious blend of philanthropy and arbitrary force had characterized all previous attempts on the part of colonial authorities to regulate relations between the two races in New South Wales, reflecting the British government's lack of sustained interest and the variety of understanding and temperament displayed by individual governors upon whose initiative any attack on the problem inevitably depended.

For the first fifty years of the colony's history, official British policy towards the Aborigines was embodied in the instructions given to Captain Arthur Phillip and his successors:

> To endeavour by every means in his power to open an intercourse with the natives, and to conciliate their good-will, requiring all to live in amity and kindness with them; and if any of our subjects should wantonly destroy them or give them any unnecessary interruption in the exercise of their several occupations, it is our will and pleasure that you do cause such offenders to be brought to punishment, according to the degree of the offence.[1]

[1] *HRA*, I, pp. 13-14. This appears to have been based on Charles II's instructions to the Council of Foreign Plantations of 30 July 1870, quoted by Saxe

Phillip was also required to report on their numbers and the best means of turning intercourse with them to the colony's advantage. The British government, influenced no doubt by the vast size of an evidently sparsely populated continent, does not appear to have thought that there would be very much contact with the indigenous inhabitants. Sir Joseph Banks had assured the 1779 Committee on Transportation that due to their cowardice and small numbers 'there would be little Probability of any Opposition from the Natives'.[2] There had been no signs of fixed habitation and cultivation of land to suggest that the Aborigines occupied any place permanently, nor had they expressed any interest in engaging in trade for European goods. The main reason for promoting 'amity and kindness' was probably to facilitate further colonial expansion and to prevent their being suborned by a foreign power.[3] Nevertheless, it seems to have been assumed that some Aborigines would 'attach' themselves to the settlement after a time.

New South Wales was a possession of the British Crown by right of discovery and the Aborigines were not regarded as having the status of a 'conquered nation' with their own rights and traditions. Indeed, for all legal purposes the territory was regarded as having been uninhabited at the time of discovery. But as inhabitants of a Crown colony the Aborigines were, in theory at least, British subjects and accordingly entitled to the rights of British citizenship, including the protection of British law. In fact, this status was not spelled out until 1837 and 'protection' was a fiction. For example, in two of the three instances before 1838 when whites were convicted of murdering Aborigines, their sentences were either commuted by the governor or quashed by the British government.

In 1799, Governor Sir George Hunter attempted to bring to justice five Hawkesbury settlers who had 'most barbarously murdered' two Aboriginal boys near Windsor. Although a court martial was unanimous in finding them guilty, a vote of four to three referred the question of sentence over the Governor's head to the Secretary of State for Colonies. In a despatch to the Duke of Port-

---

Bannister, *Humane Policy; or Justice to the Aborigines of New Settlements*, London 1830, pp. 22-3.

[2] C. M. H. Clark (ed.), *Select Documents in Australian History 1788-1850*, Sydney 1950, pp. 13-14.

[3] A. C. V. Melbourne, *Early Constitutional Development in Australia . . .* , R. B. Joyce (ed.), Brisbane 1963, p. 7.

land which included a full account of the trial, Hunter feebly protested that the reference was an 'incorrect procedure' since the power to confirm or commute criminal sentences had been delegated to him. Bending with the colonial wind, he had released the convicted men on bail, explaining that he was 'unwilling to show to the colony that any difference is likely to take place between the judicial and executive authorities, particularly when in the smallest degree inconsistent with lenity'.[4] However, he told Portland that much of the hostility shown by the Aborigines was due to provocation from the whites. The murder of the two boys had led to threats of crops being burnt and the murder of an Aboriginal mother and her child by a constable had resulted in hostility towards the military. He also remarked on the injustice of a situation where a 'host of evidence' could be brought forward to prove how many whites had been killed by Aborigines:

> but cou'd we have brought with equal ease such proofs from the natives as they are capable of affording of the wanton and barbarous manner in which many of them have been destroy'd . . . we shou'd have found an astonishing difference in numbers.[5]

Shortly afterwards Hunter was recalled and Lord Hobart instructed Acting-Governor P. G. King to issue pardons for the five men. He had taken into account the circumstances of the trials and the difference of opinion among members of the court, but most important of all was 'the length of time which has elapsed'. However, he added, 'It should . . . be clearly understood that on future occasions any instance of injustice or wanton cruelty towards the natives will be punished with the utmost severity of the law'.[6] In a proclamation of 30 June 1802 in which he announced Hobart's decision, King expressed very clearly the terrible contradiction underlying government policy towards the Aborigines:

> But at the same time that His Majesty forbids any act of Injustice or wanton Cruelty to the Natives, yet the Settler is not to suffer his property to be invaded, or his existence endangered by them; in pre-

---

[4] King to Portland, 2 January 1800, *HRA*, II, p. 402.
[5] Ibid., p. 402. According to the surgeon Molloy, 26 whites had been killed and 13 wounded on the Hawkesbury in the four years preceding the Windsor case.
[6] Hobart to King, 30 January 1802, *HRA*, III, p. 367.

serving which he is to use effectual, but at the same time the most humane, means of resisting such attacks.[7]

The significance of the case's outcome can not have been lost on the settlers and an important precedent had been established.

By this time the idea of 'attachment' had been found quite impracticable. In 1796 large numbers of Aborigines congregated near farms in the Hawkesbury district where they stole or destroyed crops, cattle and property and even killed some whites. In a Government Order, Hunter indicated that it was the 'amity and kindness' of the settlers which was the cause of all the trouble. 'There can be no doubt', the Order stated, 'but that had they never met with the shelter which some have afforded them they would not at this time have been so very troublesome and dangerous'.[8] In future, settlers were not to allow Aborigines on their farms and were to 'mutually afford their assistance to each other by assembling without a moment delay whenever any numerous body of the natives are known to be lurking about the farms'.[9] However, they were not to fire wantonly on the Aborigines and kill them. Such an act would be considered 'deliberate murder' and be subject to punishment.

Further precedents for the use of force were established by King. When large groups of Aborigines gathered around Parramatta, George's River and Prospect Hill in April 1801, the governor ordered that they were 'to be driven back from the settlers' habitations by firing at them'.[10] In November of the same year he instructed a detachment of soldiers sent to protect wheat crops at George's River to 'fire on any native or natives they see. . . Every means is to be used to drive them off, either by shooting or otherwise'.[11] In the early part of 1805 the murder of some settlers 'whose hospitality appears to have drawn upon them the most barbarous treatment' caused Captain William Bligh to distribute detachments of soldiers among the remote settlements 'for their protection against those uncivilized Insurgents'.[12] He also issued a Government Order which forbade Aborigines to visit the farms or houses of

[7] *HRA*, III, p. 593.
[8] *HRA*, I, p. 688.
[9] Ibid., p. 688.
[10] *HRA*, III, p. 250.
[11] Ibid., p. 446.
[12] Government Order dated 19 April 1805, *BP*, No. 4.

settlers until the murderers were given up. Settlers were to be prosecuted if they 'harboured' natives and were 'required to assist each other in repelling those visits'.[13] However, a number of Aborigines who were well known around Prospect and Parramatta were exempted from this restriction after they had placed themselves under the protection of the Parramatta magistrates. Later, more Aborigines successfully applied to be allowed to return to Parramatta and Sydney, although trouble continued along the Hawkesbury and George's rivers.[14]

Hobart had been sufficiently interested in the problem of the legal status of the Aborigines to request a report from King. He in turn passed on the request to the colony's Judge-Advocate, Richard Atkins, whose opinion was naturally accepted by colonial magistrates and judges:

> The Natives are within the Pale of H.M. protection; but how can a Native, when brought to Trial, plead Guilty or Not Guilty to an Indictment, the meaning and tendency of which they must be totally ignorant of? Plead they must before Evidence can be adduced against them, and Penal Laws cannot be stretched to assure a particular exigency . . . the natives of this Country (generally speaking) are at present incapable of being brought before a Criminal Court, either as Criminals or as Evidences; that it would be a mocking of Judicial Proceedings, and a Solecism in Law; and that the only mode at present when they deserve it, is to pursue them and inflict such punishment as they merit.[15]

For some time the British government was evidently satisfied to accept this pronouncement in spite of its clear implications. However, the 1812 Committee on Transportation remarked on the inequitable application of the law to whites and Aborigines and in his Report on the State of Agriculture and Trade in New South Wales Commissioner J. T. Bigge recorded that Macquarie had authorized the execution of a convict for the murder of an Aboriginal constable at Newcastle.[16]

Moved by genuine sympathy for the wretched remnants of the 'Sydney blacks', Macquarie was the first governor to concern himself conscientiously and constructively with Aboriginal welfare.

13 Ibid.
14 Government Orders dated 3 May 1805 and 8 January 1806, BP, Nos 4 and 3.
15 Enclosure No. 2, King to Earl Camden, 20 July 1805, HRA, V, pp. 503-4.
16 This is evidently the same case mentioned by Saxe Bannister in *Humane Policy*, Appendix 5, p. ccxl, but I have been unable to obtain further information about it.

Despite the depressing evidence visible in Sydney, he believed that contact with a superior civilization must of necessity benefit a primitive, benighted race. In December 1814 he announced his intention of establishing a school for Aboriginal children at Parramatta and an annual 'feast' or 'congress' which would serve the dual purpose of reuniting the pupils with their relatives and demonstrating His Majesty's goodwill with presents of roast beef, plum pudding, slop clothing, blankets, pipes and tobacco. Accordingly, the Native Institution was opened in January 1815 under the supervision of the former South Seas missionary William Shelley and his wife. Macquarie also established 'King' Bungaree and the remnants of the Broken Bay tribe on a reserve of land at George's Head on the northern side of the harbour.

However, like earlier governors, Macquarie answered with alacrity requests for protection from outlying settlers. When severe drought caused Aborigines to plunder farms along the Hawkesbury and its tributaries in 1815 and early 1816, killing a number of whites, Macquarie despatched three detachments of the 76th Regiment to arrest the depredators. The force under Captain James Wallis attacked a camp near Appin at night, killing fourteen Aborigines including the notorious 'chief', Carnabyagal or Carnanbigal, who had been credited with leading the depredations. Subsequently Macquarie compiled a set of Regulations which were published as a proclamation on 4 May 1816.[17] Aborigines were not to appear armed within a mile of any settlement or farm and no more than six were allowed to 'lurk or loiter' near any farm. Assemblies of large numbers near any settlement 'on the Plea of inflicting punishments on Transgressors of their own Customs and Manners' were abolished as a 'barbarous Custom repugnant to the British laws, and strongly militating against the Civilization of the Natives'. Finally, those Aborigines who desired the protection of the British government and who conducted themselves in a suitable manner were to be supplied with 'Passports or Certificates' signed by the

[17] *HRA*, IX, pp. 141-5. (The following quotations are from this source.) Macquarie issued two further proclamations on the Aborigines: one on 20 July 1816 outlawing 10 'Most Violent and Atrocious Natives' and another on 1 November offering an amnesty to those who had not already been killed and confirming the holding of a 'General Friendly Meeting' at Parramatta on 28 December. *HRA*, IX, pp. 362-6.

Governor and issued by the Colonial Secretary on the first day of each month. But the vital point made in the Proclamation was that settlers were empowered to use force of arms if *in their judgement* the Aborigines had contravened the Regulations, and to apply to a magistrate for military assistance if the situation was beyond their means.

At the same time, Macquarie reiterated the positive aspect of his policy. To those Aborigines who were 'inclined to become *regular settlers*' he was prepared to grant land in locations of their choice, as well as tools, seed and stores of food and clothing for six months. Five areas were set aside as agricultural reserves for the settlement of tribes in the Sydney area. At George's Head and Elizabeth Bay huts were built, gardens laid out and convicts assigned to assist in their cultivation, but to no avail. Not to be discouraged, Macquarie re-established Bungaree and his 'vagrant train' at George's Head in 1821 and announced to Lord Bathurst his intention of setting aside for the Aborigines 10,000 acres of land in the 'New Country' recently discovered by Captain Charles Throsby.[18] By this time, Macquarie seems to have become convinced that very little could be achieved unless the Aborigines were kept apart from the whites. 'Attachment' had not been a success.

In August 1824, on Attorney-General Saxe Bannister's[19] advice, Governor Sir Thomas Brisbane declared martial law for the entire area west of Mount York after Aborigines had stolen large numbers of sheep and killed seven shepherds. The Aborigines of the Bathurst area evidently resisted the expansion of white settlement and

---

[18] Macquarie to Bathurst, 24 February 1820, *HRA*, X, p. 263.

[19] Saxe Bannister (1790-1877), barrister and Attorney-General of N.S.W. 1824-6, was not opposed to the use of military force against the Aborigines but expressed concern that it should always be preceded by the proper legal formalities protecting soldiers and police from otherwise necessary prosecution for manslaughter. In 1826 Bannister successfully prosecuted three convicts for the murder of an Aboriginal boy at Port Stephens and was highly critical of Darling's failure to have their sentences carried out. Disagreement with Darling over the status of the Aborigines appears to have become one of the reasons for the governor's refusal to increase his salary, resulting in his return to England. He became one of the earliest champions of the rights of indigenous peoples of British colonies, producing a number of books and pamphlets on the subject and giving evidence before the Aborigines Committee in 1836. He was also apparently an early member of the British and Foreign Aborigines' Protection Society. See *ADB*, Vol. I, pp. 55-6 and *DNB*, Vol. III, pp. 142-3.

PLATE I 'Natives of N. S. Wales. As seen in the Streets of Sydney'—Augustus Earle, *Views in New South Wales And Van Diemens Land*, London 1830

PLATE II 'Annual Meeting of the Native Tribes at Parramatta, N.S.W.'—Augustus Earle

PLATE III 'A Native Family of N. S. Wales Sitting down on an English Settler's Farm'—Augustus Earle

PLATE IV 'A Native Camp of Australian Savages near Port Stevens, N.S.W.'— Augustus Earle

PLATE V 'Bushman's Hut'—S. T. Gill

PLATE VI Aborigines attacking a shepherd's hut—from an undated newspaper illustration

PLATE VII 'Danger's Station, Mayal Creek'—J. G. Sawkins, *Sketches of Australian Scenes*

PLATE VIII 'Natives spearing the overlanders' cattle. 1846'—George Hamilton

PLATE IX 'Mrs. Fraser and the crew of the *Stirling Castle* assaulted by aborigines'—from *Shipwreck of Mrs Fraser and the loss of the Stirling Castle*, London 1837

PLATE X 'Mrs. Frazer's Escape From The Savages'—from John Curtis, *Shipwreck of the Stirling Castle . . .*, London 1838

PLATE XI   John   Hubert   Plunkett,   Attorney-General   of   New   South   Wales,
1836-56

PLATE XII   William Westbrooke Burton,
Judge   of   the   Supreme   Court   of   New
South Wales, 1832-44—from *Australian
Men of Mark*, Sydney 1889

PLATE XIII   Henry Dangar, proprietor
of   Myall   Creek   Station,   Liverpool
Plains—from *Australian Men of Mark*,
Sydney 1889

PLATE XIV   Sir George Gipps, Governor
of New South Wales, 1838-46

PLATE XV 'Distribution of flour at Moorunde'—from E. J. Eyre, *Discovery into Central Australia*

PLATE XVI 'Hawker at an Aboriginal Station, Australia'—from *Illustrated Australian News*, 1876

PLATE XVII   '45 Natives driven to Police Court by the Police for trespassing 1845'—William Anderson Cawthorne

PLATE XVIII   Native police, Queensland

'Saturday', described by Brisbane as 'their great and warlike chief', is said to have boasted openly of killing fifteen whites with his own hand. Following the imposition of martial law, however, roving bands of soldiers and police, assisted by settlers and stockmen, 'dispersed' the Aborigines who had collected near Bathurst, possibly killing as many as one hundred.[20] Subsequently Saturday decided to make his peace and in December 1824 the Rev. Daniel Tyerman and George Bennet of the London Missionary Society observed him at the Parramatta feast:

> On some understood assurance of good treatment, he has ceased from his acts of violence, and arrived today to make his submission; for which purpose, and that it might be done with due solemnity, he rode into town upon a horse, bearing an olive branch in his hand. On presenting himself to the governor he was graciously received and forgiven, on condition that he would never offend again in the like manner[21].

All of Saturday's party were then treated to roast beef, plum pudding and half a pint of rum as well as gifts of pipes, tobacco, slop clothing and blankets.

[20] Threlkeld gave this account of the Bathurst affair:

> One of the largest holders of Sheep in the Colony [William Cox], maintained at a public meeting at Bathurst, that the best thing that could be done, would be to shoot all the Blacks and manure the ground with their carcases, which was all the good they were fit for! It was recommended likewise that the women and children should especially be shot as the most certain method of getting rid of the race. Shortly after this declaration, martial law was proclaimed and sad was the havoc made upon the tribes at Bathurst. A large number were driven into a swamp, and mounted police rode round and round and shot them off indiscriminately until they were all destroyed! When one of the police enquired of the Officer if a return should be made of the killed, wounded there were none, all were destroyed, Men, Women and Children! the reply was;—that there was no need for a return. But *forty-five* heads were collected and boiled down for the sake of the skulls! My informant, a Magistrate, saw the skulls packed for exportation in a case at Bathurst ready for shipment to accompany the commanding Officer on his voyage shortly afterwards to England.

('Reminiscences' in Gunson, *Australian Reminiscences and Papers of L. E. Threlkeld*, Vol. I, p. 49.) Sadleir, *The Aborigines of Australia*, Sydney 1883, p. 48, mentions an 1826 meeting where 'it was declared by men of position that the blackfellow was not a human being and that there was no more guilt in shooting him than in shooting a native dog'. This was evidently the same meeting but it has not been possible to obtain further information.

[21] James Montgomery (ed.), *Journal of Voyages and Travels by the Rev. Daniel Tyerman and George Bennet, Esq. . . . ,* 2 vols, London 1831, Vol. II, quoted by Gunson, Vol. II, p. 340.

When there were rumours of further gatherings of Aborigines in the Bathurst district in June 1826, Bannister advised Darling to proclaim martial law as Brisbane had done. As it happened, the rumours were false but in the Hunter River district Aborigines subsequently killed two stockmen and an overseer and in early September a number of landholders petitioned Darling to send soldiers or to recall the Mounted Police who had gone to Newcastle.[22] Learning of this, Bannister again advised martial law, pointing out that otherwise soldiers and settlers would not be protected 'in certain cases of possible mistake' or when the Aborigines refused to hand over individuals known to have committed murder.[23] When Darling informed him that Lieutenant Lowe and a party of soldiers had already been sent to Hunter River and that this was in accordance with 'Instructions', Bannister asked to see these Instructions and emphasized that Darling's action had placed him in a very difficult position:

> I have thought, that indiscriminate slaughter of offenders, except in the heat of immediate pursuit or other similar circumstances, requires preliminary solemn acts; and that to order soldiers to punish any outrage in this way, is against the law.[24]

For the governor, who had previously described his Attorney-General to Sir John Hay as 'eccentric and enthusiastic',[25] this insistence on legal niceties was the last straw. Informing Hay that he would no longer communicate with Bannister, he ridiculed the latter's sensitivity in the 'cause of the natives' and the declaration of martial law against 'a few naked Savages, who, however treacherous, would not face a Corporal's Guard'.[26] Besides, Darling's action had been well within his rights. In a despatch a year earlier, Lord Bathurst had told him that

> In reference to the discussions, which have recently taken place in the Colony respecting the manner in which the Native Inhabitants are to be treated when making hostile incursions for the purpose of plunder, you will understand it to be your duty, when such disturbances cannot

---

[22] *HRA*, XII, p. 576.
[23] Bannister to Darling, 5 September 1826, ibid., p. 578.
[24] Bannister to Darling, 9 September 1826, quoted by Bannister in his *Statements and Documents relating to proceedings in New South Wales in 1824, 1825 and 1826 . . .* , Cape Town 1827, p. 99.
[25] Darling to Hay, 26 July 1826, *HRA*, XII, p. 446.
[26] Darling to Hay, 11 September 1826, ibid., p. 575.

be prevented or allayed by less vigorous measures, to oppose force by force, and to repel such Aggressions in the same manner as if they proceeded from subjects of any accredited State.[27]

Replying to the petition, Darling told the landholders that they should take vigorous measures for their own defence and that they could be assured of all necessary help from the government. At the same time, however, he remarked that most of the eleven signatories were resident in Sydney and that their presence at Hunter River would be the best means of ensuring the safety of their property and supervizing their convict servants to whose 'irregularities' he attributed much of the trouble.[28]

During Lowe's expedition to the Hunter River an Aborigine supposed to have killed Bowman's stockman was shot dead by members of the party at Wallis' Plains (Maitland) and it was popularly believed that he had been tied to a stake and used as a live target. In a report to Bannister, Threlkeld wrote:

> The Black who is supposed to have committed the murder was taken at or near Mr Bowman's farm and brought down at night to the new jail at Wallis's plains, a distance of upwards of 40 miles. The next morning he was brought out, tied to two saplings and the Officer commanded the Soldiers to shoot him—One fired at him, the ball hit him on the back of the neck, the black turned round his head and looked at him, the next fired, and the bullet cut along the jaw, and broke the bone; the black turned his head round again [,] another soldier stepped up and blew his head to pieces.—They then buried him by the privy belonging to Government house. The Officer mounted his horse and went in pursuit of two other Blacks.[29]

Darling despatched the Chairman of Quarter Sessions to investigate but he was shipwrecked and had to return to Sydney. Following this, Darling told Hay, the Acting Attorney-General himself visited Wallis' Plains, only to find that the 'indisposition of everyone to give information on the subject' rendered his journey 'totally abortive'.[30] Enough evidence was eventually found for Lowe to be committed for trial on a charge of manslaughter but the case was

27 Bathurst to Darling, 14 July 1825, ibid., p. 21.
28 Darling to the Landholders at Hunter's River, 5 September 1826, ibid., p. 577.
29 'Memoranda' in Gunson, *Australian Reminiscences and Papers of L. E. Threlkeld*, Vol. I, p. 92.
30 Darling to Hay, 23 March 1827, *HRA*, XIII, p. 179.

dismissed on the grounds that the convict witnesses were 'not . . . entitled to credit'. Darling explained that the case presented a number of difficulties, 'the inhabitants of every class being at least indifferent to the fate of the Natives, and unwilling that anyone, that has been actuated by the same feelings, should be made answerable for his conduct'.[31]

Threlkeld reported that shortly after the Maitland incident a further three Aborigines were killed by the Mounted Police, one of them at Bowman's where another white had been wounded:

> a black, one of the tribe was taken, brought to Mr Bowman's hut, a rope was borrowed from a person[,] tied round the Black's neck, and he was marched nearly a mile to a suitable tree, he was then ordered to climb it, he did so, he was ordered to crawl to the extremity of a bough of the tree, when he had done this, he was ordered to tie the rope tight to the branch, the other end being tied fast around his neck; this he did and sat crouched on the tree: one then fired at him wounded him, another fired and wounded him again: A volley was then fired which knocked him off and left him suspended by the neck on the tree.[32]

The missionary told Bannister that the three killings were said to have been carried out either on the authority of a letter from a judge or as the result of a private understanding involving the governor himself, and that these malicious rumours had been responsible for a great deal of bloodshed.[33] In the meantime Aborigines, infuriated by the imprisonment of one of their number in Newcastle jail and the shooting at Bowman's, were threatening to burn all the houses of the whites and Threlkeld warned of the possibility of 'war'.

It had proved impossible to bring Lowe to justice but when three convict servants, Samuel Chipp, John Ridgway and Edward Colthurst were found guilty in September 1826 of murdering an Aboriginal boy called 'Little Tommy' at Port Stephens,[34] Darling had procrastinated. Although the Executive Council decided that

---

[31] Ibid., p. 179. An account of Lowe's trial can be found in the *Sydney Gazette*, 21 May 1827.

[32] 'Memoranda' in Gunson, *Australian Reminiscences and Papers of L. E. Threlkeld*, Vol. I, p. 95.

[33] Ibid.

[34] According to Bannister, the conviction was secured 'through the integrity and right feeling of a private individual, Mr Pennington'. *Humane Policy*, Appendix 5, p. ccxl.

Chipp should be hanged at Port Stephens and the other two men transported for life, his execution was delayed until Thomas Stanley, another principal in the crime, was arrested and tried. Stanley was duly found guilty and condemned to death and the Council decided in March 1827 that he and Chipp should be hanged together at Port Stephens. For some reason, however, the executions were delayed and the Council decided in April that the men should be imprisoned to await His Majesty's pleasure. In May, Darling recommended to Bathurst that the sentences be commuted to transportation to Norfolk Island for life. He told the Secretary of State that he had intended to make an example of the men in order to prevent ill-treatment of the Aborigines, 'but the events, which from time to time interfered to prevent the orders being given for their Execution being carried into effect, induced the public at length to take an interest in their fate'.[35] Indeed, opinion had been vehemently opposed to their execution and as Chief Justice Sir Francis Forbes explained to R. Wilmot Horton in the Colonial Office, 'the feelings of the public here would be wounded by seeing the law put into force after so long'.[36] Subsequently William Huskisson informed Darling that His Majesty would recommend commutation but expressed dissatisfaction with the governor's handling of the case. He complained that Darling had not sent a report of all the evidence presented at the trials, nor had he given details of the various delays in executing the two men.[37]

Bannister, who had prosecuted three of the men at the first trial before returning to England, published in 1830 *Humane Policy: Or Justice to the Aborigines* in which he wrote that 'a more unmitigated case was never presented to a court of justice'. Bannister recalled the outcome of the 1799 case and requested that all details relating to Lieutenant Lowe's expedition and prosecution should be laid before Parliament. He also quoted the complaint of a colonial magistrate[38] about the killing of a 'principal native' called 'Tong' by a constable at Port Stephens and that the remission of sentence on

---

[35] Darling to Bathurst, 13 May 1827, *HRA*, XII, p. 301.
[36] Forbes to Wilmot Horton, 15 May 1827, Chief Justice Forbes. Private Letters to R. Wilmot Horton, 1825-7, ML, MS.A1819, p. 172.
[37] Huskisson to Darling, 29 November 1827, *HRA*, XIII, p. 626.
[38] Probably Robert Dawson who was in charge of the Australian Agricultural Company's establishment at Port Stephens at that time and was known for his enlightened attitude towards the Aborigines.

the men convicted of killing 'Little Tommy' made the prosecution of such offenders pointless. Bannister concluded:

> The English rules of evidence, the absence of interpreters, and the ill-conduct of the people (both settlers and convicts, with special exceptions,) render it exceedingly difficult to cause the law to be put in force against murderers and other heinous wrong-doers towards the natives; and when, by any concurrence of favourable circumstances, conviction has been obtained, the government has sympathized too much with the oppressing class, and too little with the oppressed, to permit justice to have its course.[39]

Meanwhile the Evangelical missionary societies of Great Britain had begun to take a new interest in the Aborigines. In August 1824 George Bennet and the Rev. Daniel Tyerman of the London Missionary Society arrived in Sydney with Threlkeld after inspecting the Society's establishments in the Pacific Islands. They discussed with Brisbane the possibility of establishing a mission to the Aborigines. A site was chosen near a place known (somewhat unpropitiously) as 'Reid's Mistake' on the shores of Lake Macquarie and a deed was drawn up appointing a number of trustees. Bathurst agreed to Brisbane's request and 10,000 acres were set aside at Lake Macquarie for the use of the mission on condition that the land would revert to the Crown if the mission was a failure. In response to the London Missionary Society's initiatives, a Corresponding Committee of the Church Missionary Society was formed in Sydney in 1825 with the special object of working among the Aborigines and a request for a similar grant of land was apparently met by Brisbane before his departure. But in the following year Darling refused an application from the Wesleyan Missionary Society until the two earlier projects were shown to be successful. Meanwhile Threlkeld who had been appointed by the London Missionary Society to take charge of the Lake Macquarie mission was hard at work at Bahtabah.

Evidently this burst of missionary activity aroused some official interest since the Instructions issued to Darling in July 1825 contained the new requirement that special provision should be made for the Christianization and civilization of the Aborigines.[40] Darling

---

[39] Bannister, *Humane Policy*, Appendix 5, p. ccxl. The magistrate's remarks were taken from an article in the *Westminster Review*, January 1830.
[40] *HRA*, XII, p. 125.

passed on the responsibility to Archdeacon Thomas Hobbes Scott and in July 1826 Scott sent Richard Sadleir,[41] the Rev. Robert Cartwright's son-in-law, to Argyle County southwest of Bathurst where there had recently been a number of conflicts between Aborigines and stockmen. Scott required information on the numbers of Aborigines, their ages, leaders and the goods which they desired most, as well as details of their relations with the whites. He told Sadleir that

> It would be very desirable for you to possess yourself with the *reasons* they have . . . for their ceremonies and usages, motives for wars, as well as for declining to become civilized, or parting with their children; and whether they are permanently susceptible of being aware of the advantages held out to them. Under this head, inquiries as to the capacities, especially with our own people, and whether there has been and still is any intercourse with them, to what extent, its nature and the effects produced by it would be most desirable.[42]

In his monthly reports[43] to Scott, Sadleir evidently indicated that while the Aborigines would appreciate gifts of food and clothing, they were interested neither in Christianity nor in civilized habits and simply wished to be left alone. Nevertheless, Sadleir recommended the establishment of four government stations beyond the frontiers of settlement where the Aborigines could be educated and Christianized in government schools.

Scott, who was hard-pressed to find money for the education of white children, realized the expenditure that would be involved and made it clear to Darling that the Aborigines should not receive

---

[41] Lieutenant Richard Sadleir R.N. had some experience with the Indians in Canada before coming to N.S.W. in 1825. This probably interested him in the Aborigines and no doubt it was his father-in-law who recommended him to Scott. After his expedition he was granted land on the Hunter River and served as a catechist to the Aboriginal and white population. In 1829 he was appointed master of the Orphan School at Parramatta where a number of Aboriginal children were cared for after the abandonment of the Native Institution. Sadleir was an important witness before the 1838 Committee on the Aborigines Question and his evidence and tabled correspondence can be found in the Committee's Report, *V&P*, 1838, pp. 27-50. His reminiscences of this early period, together with various scraps of information about the Aborigines, were recorded in his *Aborigines of Australia*.

[42] Scott, Letterbooks, ML, MS.A851, p. 291.

[43] These were lost some time before 1838 when they were called for by the Legislative Council's Committee on the Aborigines Question. However, Scott's summaries of them can be found in *HRA*, XIV, pp. 57-62.

any priority.[44] Sadleir's plan was shelved and government activity continued to be restricted to the annual feast at Parramatta and the distribution of blankets and other gifts. Attempts by Scott and Broughton to arouse interest among the 'principal persons' of the colony were unsuccessful and Lord Goderich, agreeing that there were objects of greater importance, directed that the Archdeacon should restrict himself to collecting information about the numbers and condition of the Aborigines.[45]

There were signs of change in 1834 when T. Spring Rice wrote to inform Bourke of a recent House of Commons address requesting

> that His Majesty will take such measure, and give such directions to the Governors, and Officers . . . of His . . . Colonies . . . as shall secure to the Natives the due observance of justice, and the protection of their rights, promote the spread of Civilization among them, and lead them to the peaceful and voluntary reception of the Christian Religion.[46]

While Rice emphasized that these principles were not being laid down for the first time, he gave a broad hint that there was increasing British interest in the Aborigines.

Two incidents in 1836 must have demonstrated very clearly to Bourke that the 'important, and interesting duty' of looking after the interests of the Aborigines could be an extremely complex and difficult one. In April the three judges of the Supreme Court considered the case of 'Jack Congo Murral' and 'George Bummery', two Aborigines charged with murdering two other Aborigines, Jabinguy or 'Pat Cleary' and 'Cary', while drinking outside a public house on the Windsor Road. 'Bowen Bungarree', brother-in-law of the dead man, had asked Threlkeld to tell the Supreme Court that he and his tribe wished the men to be tried by the 'English'.[47] On Murral's behalf, it was argued by the barrister Sidney Stephen that the Aborigines were not His Majesty's subjects, that they continued to be regulated by their own laws, and consequently were not sub-

---

[44] Scott to Darling, 9 December 1826, Enclosure, Darling to Bathurst, 22 December 1826, *HRA*, XII, pp. 796-7.

[45] Goderich to Darling, 6 July 1827, *HRA*, XIII, p. 434.

[46] Spring Rice to Bourke, 1 August 1834, *HRA*, XVII, p. 491.

[47] Threlkeld to Attorney-General, 6 February 1836, *BP*, No. 41. At the trial later, Bummery explained through Threlkeld that he had killed 'Cary' because the latter had killed one of his own people. He also asked that a jury of Aborigines should be empanelled for the case. *Sydney Gazette*, 14 May 1836.

ject to English law. In accordance with Aboriginal custom, however, Murral could be 'exposed to such and so many spears as the
Friends and relatives of the said Jabinguy . . . may think proper to
hurl and throw against . . . him . . .'[48] This plea was rejected by
Attorney-General John Kinchela who prosecuted the case and
Judges Burton, Dowling and Forbes found that the jurisdiction of
the Court extended to all offences committed by the Aborigines
inter se. The Aborigines, Burton explained when handing down
judgment, 'had not attained . . . to such a position in point of
numbers and Civilization, and to such a form of Government and
Laws, as to be entitled to be recognised, as so many *sovereign states,
governed* by *laws* of *their own*'.[49] At the same time, Burton dis-
counted the difficulties arising from the increased business for
magistrates and others involved in the administration of justice as
a result of the decision. If difficulties did occur, he said, they could
only be to the benefit of the Aborigines. Besides, he added,

> the greatest possible inconvenience and scandal to this Community
> would be consequent, if it were to be holden by this Court that it has
> no jurisdiction in such a case as the present—to be holden in fact that
> crimes of murder, and others of almost equal enormity may be com-
> mitted by those people, in our streets without restraint so they be
> committed only upon one another! and that our laws are no sanctuary
> to them.[50]

Public opinion continued to be divided on the issue, the *Sydney
Gazette*, for example, describing the forthcoming trials as 'legal murder'.[51] As it happened, Murral was acquitted since it could not be
proved that he struck the fatal blow and Bummery was discharged
because the evidence against him was identical. Nevertheless, the
highest court in the colony had established an important precedent
in finding that the Aborigines were amenable to the laws of the
white man in their own affairs and that their own laws and customs
did not merit serious consideration.

The second incident took place in May when Major Mitchell's

---

[48] *BP*, No. 42.
[49] *BP*, No. 47. Burton's complete notes and judgment in this case can be found
in Nos. 47 and 48. See also, J. G. Legge, *A Selection of Supreme Court Cases
in New South Wales, from 1825 to 1862*, 2 vols., Sydney 1896, Vol. I, pp.
72-3.
[50] *BP*, No. 108.
[51] 5 May 1836.

convict retainers fired several volleys on Aborigines near Lake Victoria on the Murray River, killing at least seven. Writing to Deas Thomson later, Mitchell described what had happened:

> Attacked simultaneously by both parties, the . . . [Aborigines] betook themselves to the river; my men pursuing them and shooting as many as they could. Numbers were shot in swimming across the Murray, and some even after they had reached the opposite shore, as they ascended the bank. Amongst those shot was the chief (recognised by a particular kind of cloak he wore, which floated after he went down). Thus, in a very short time, the usual silence of the desert prevailed on the banks of the Murray, and we pursued our journey unmolested.[52]

Bourke was so struck by the 'abruptness' of this passage that he had it omitted from the report of the expedition when it was published in the *Government Gazette* on 5 November and at the same time instituted an Executive Council inquiry. 'Considerable anxiety has been expressed by the Public on the subject', he told Glenelg, 'and it will be proper to make the result of the investigation known immediately on its conclusion'.[53]

The Council found a number of discrepancies between Mitchell's account in his letter to Deas Thomson and the evidence obtained from members of his party, noting in particular the explorer's 'design of drawing the Blacks after him, and then turning to attack them. . .'.[54] However, in his own Memoranda submitted to the Council, Mitchell argued that 'instances of necessary chastisement have occurred with the Aborigines wherever the colonization of New Holland has hitherto been extended'. Citing the experiences of Macquarie in the 'Carnanbigal war' and those of the Bringelly magistrate and respectable settlers on the Hunter, together with

---

[52] Mitchell to Deas Thomson, 24 October 1836, *GG*, Supplement, 21 January 1837, p. 59. Mitchell also recorded the incident in *Three Expeditions*, Vol. II, pp. 102-3.

[53] Bourke to Glenelg, 15 November 1836, *HRA*, XVII, pp. 590-1. The *Sydney Gazette* in particular demanded a public inquiry into what it described as 'this wholesale slaughter of so many souls'. It contrasted Mitchell's killing of Aborigines on all his expeditions with the experiences of Sturt and Hume and Hovell, claiming that he was 'dreadfully frightened of the blacks'. *Sydney Gazette*, 14 January 1837.

[54] The minutes of the Council's investigations, together with Mitchell's statements, the instructions to him and evidence from members of the party were published at Mitchell's request in the *Government Gazette*, Supplement, 21 January 1837, pp. 59-74. The following quotations are also from this source.

the deaths of Captains Barker and Logan, the Fraser affair, and the murder of two of Finch's men and Cunningham during his own expeditions, Mitchell asked: 'How much more critical was my position when sent into the heart of a savage region, far out of reach of all support and with a few armed convicts as my only means of defence?' If he had been content to rest his case at this point, the Council might have let him off lightly enough but he evidently felt compelled to issue a final challenge:

> I still look back on that eventful day with entire satisfaction, and a sense of gratitude to God for such a deliverance from impending danger, in a cause in which I considered myself the humble instrument in His hands, for the common benefit of the civilised and savage portions of our race.

This attempt not only to justify his action but to assert its merit evidently proved too much for Bourke and the Council. Mitchell was sternly reminded of the paragraph in his instructions requiring extreme forbearance in relations with the Aborigines and he was told that insufficient efforts had been made to obtain the goodwill of the Lake Victoria Aborigines and to conciliate those seeking revenge after the incident of the previous expedition.

After reading the minutes of the Council's investigation, Glenelg observed with some charity that the Surveyor-General's conduct, 'if not entirely discreet, was far less open to censure than might have been inferred from his report of it'.[55] At the same time, however, he felt that a public inquiry would have been preferable:

> An impressive lesson . . . might thus have been given of the importance attached by the Government to the Life of a Native, and the exculpation of Major Mitchell would have been more satisfactory both to the Public at large and to himself.[56]

In future, he instructed, an official inquest was to be held into the death of any Aborigine killed by government officers or by men under their command. Bourke was also to refer all the documents relating to the case to his legal advisers to see if there was any doubt about the lawfulness of Mitchell's action.[57]

[55] Glenelg to Bourke, 26 July 1837, *HRA*, XIX, p. 49.
[56] Ibid., p. 49.
[57] Attorney-General J. H. Plunkett subsequently advised Gipps in March 1838 that it was unnecessary to take further steps in the case. Plunkett to Deas Thomson, 27 March 1838, enclosed with Gipps' despatch to Glenelg, 18 April 1838, *CO*, 201/272, Reel 311, pp. 347-9.

Another precedent established during Bourke's governorship was the effective decision that no account was to be taken of the Aborigines' claim to their own land. So vast was the colony of New South Wales, so scanty its Aboriginal population and so apparently tenuous their occupancy of territory that the question had never arisen. But in 1835 John Batman and the fourteen members of the Geelong and Dutigalla Association (later known as the Port Phillip Association) decided that by obtaining the cession of land from Aborigines at Port Phillip they might successfully pursue a claim with the British government. Batman, who had been employed for some years in 'catching' the Aborigines of Van Diemen's Land, accordingly sailed for Port Phillip in May 1835 with seven of his 'Sydney blacks' and on 6 June at Merri Creek concluded two agreements[58] with eight Aborigines, three brothers described as 'principal chiefs' and five others as 'chiefs' of 'a certain Native Tribe called Dutigallar'. In return for a payment of twenty pairs of blankets, thirty tomahawks,

[58] Copies of these can be found in James Bonwick, *John Batman, Founder of Victoria*, Melbourne 1868, pp. 68-71; the originals are in the possession of the La Trobe Library, Melbourne. The two treaties were prepared for Batman by the lawyer, Joseph Tice Gellibrand, another member of the Port Phillip Association who was killed by Aborigines while on an exploring expedition in the Otway Ranges near Geelong in 1837. The principle of transfer involved was *feoffment*, an archaic form but more simple than the usual lease and release and more suited to such a transaction. *Feoffment* had to take place on the land itself with the handing over of a piece of soil or twig as a symbol of the whole. Accordingly, as Batman told Arthur in his letter of 25 June 1835, each of the eight Aborigines gave him some soil and, in return for the mark of the 'Sydney blacks', 'their own private mark' which was then attached to the treaties as the 'signature of the country and tribe'. He also said that they 'appeared most fully to comprehend my proposals' and marked trees as boundaries of the land involved. Batman and Gellibrand were no doubt aware of earlier land treaties with the American Indians and they went to some lengths to obtain such legitimization as was possible, the former describing the Aborigines to Arthur as 'the real owners of the soil'. Batman had been brought up among Aborigines at Parramatta, possibly to the extent of being initiated, and must have known (as J. H. Wedge did) that there were no 'chiefs' and that there was no conception of selling tribal lands. John Pascoe Fawkner claimed that the treaties could not have been explained to the Aborigines because the 'Sydney blacks' could neither read English nor speak the language of the Dutigallar. However, Fawkner had earlier told Batman that unless he had the assistance of one of his 'Sydney blacks' in making a similar agreement, he would have to send to Sydney for some. The treaties were also ridiculed by others but a correspondent to Launceston's *Cornwall Chronicle* of 13 June 1835 regretted that a similar device had not been used to conciliate the Van Diemen's Land Aborigines during first settlement.

one hundred knives, fifty pairs of scissors, thirty looking-glasses, two hundred handkerchiefs, one hundred pounds of flour and six shirts, together with an undertaking to pay a 'yearly rent or tribute' in similar items,[59] Batman claimed to have received 500,000 acres at Port Phillip, the second agreement securing him a further 100,000 acres at Geelong. All this land he then transferred to the Association.

While indicating that there was no prospect of favourable consideration, Governor Arthur promised to transmit the Association's claim to London. But Bourke, seeing it as a threat to his entire land policy, moved to nip the scheme in the bud. In August 1835 he issued a proclamation that

> every such treaty, bargain and contract with the Aboriginal Natives . . . for the possession, title or claim to any Lands, lying . . . within the limits of the Government of the Colony of New South Wales . . . is void and of no effect against the rights of the Crown . . .[60]

Forwarding this to Glenelg, he explained that he had acted in order to protect rights of the Crown which might be damaged by the 'alleged treaty'. At the same time, however, he observed that Batman and his associates had rested their claim for recognition of the treaty not upon any title which it might have conveyed but on 'the merits of their Undertaking'.[61]

Undeterred by this setback, the Association decided to put its case directly to Glenelg through George Mercer, its British representative. While mentioning several advantages which the scheme would have for the British government, Mercer made a strong appeal to the Secretary of State's well-known concern for the Aborigines. The treaty, he said, had established good relations with the Aborigines, but if it were broken by the white man, 'reliance on him will be at an end; and the country, if ever, occupied hereafter by the extermination of the aboriginal proprietors alone'.[62] If Glenelg was impressed by this argument, he was still not prepared to make any special offer to the Association and in his despatch approving

---

[59] This was to consist of 100 pairs of blankets, 100 knives, 100 tomahawks, 50 suits of clothing, 50 looking glasses, 50 pairs of scissors and 5 tons of flour.
[60] Proclamation dated 26 August 1835, *HRA*, XVIII, pp. 811-2.
[61] Bourke to Glenelg, 10 October 1835, *HRA*, XVIII, p. 153.
[62] Mercer to Glenelg, 26 January 1836, Enclosure No. I, Glenelg to Bourke, 13 April 1836, ibid., p. 382.

Bourke's action and enclosing the correspondence with Mercer he gave his own view:

> Although many circumstances have contributed to render me anxious that the Aborigines should be placed under a zealous and effective protection, and that their Rights should be studiously defended, I yet believe we should consult very ill for the real welfare of that hapless and unfortunate Race by recognising in them any right to alienate to private adventurers the Land of the Colony . . .[63]

More important, however, was the challenge which the treaty would present to the Crown's own position in New South Wales: 'such a concession would subvert the foundation on which all Property rights in New South Wales at present rest'.[64]

Batman and his associates had not based their claim on the legality of the two agreements and the right of the Aborigines to alienate land. At best it had been a tawdry gesture to a handful of Aborigines at Port Phillip, a device whose real purpose was to facilitate the acquisition of vast tracts of land from the Crown on terms substantially more favourable than the current upset price of land. Ironically enough, however, this same gesture with its promise of tribute in perpetuity might well have provided the basis for Aboriginal claims in later times if Bourke or Glenelg had given it any recognition. As it was, the question of whether the Aborigines possessed any right to land had been arbitrarily dismissed.

A custom which Bourke inherited was the annual Parramatta feast[65] established by Macquarie in December 1814 as a means of conciliating the Aborigines and reviewing the progress of the Native Institution. By December 1832, however, attendance was dwindling, the Native Institution had been abandoned and intoxicated Aborigines had become something of a nuisance in Parramatta town where they stayed on after the event. Bourke observed that 'The Clothing given at the feast is usually bartered for rum before the Natives leave Parramatta'[66] and that it would make more sense to hold the feast at the beginning of winter when the distribution

[63] Glenelg to Bourke, 13 April 1836, ibid., p. 379.
[64] Ibid., p. 379.
[65] A brief history of the feast can be found in Reece, 'Feasts and Blankets', *Archaeology and Physical Anthropology in Oceania*, II, No. 3, October 1967, pp. 190-206.
[66] Bourke's Minute, 24 March 1833, *CSIL*, 4/6666.3, 33/1471.

of clothing issued on the occasion would be more valued by the Aborigines. The feast due in December 1832 was consequently postponed until May of the following year and magistrates and settlers were asked to inform Aborigines that blankets would not be issued at Parramatta but sent instead to police offices and stations for distribution on 10 May. Attendance at the feast dwindled still further when it became known that blankets were no longer being given out and Bourke, finding the custom 'productive of some disorder and much inconvenience', finally abolished it in April 1835.[67]

Informing magistrates of his decision, the governor also announced that in future the annual distribution of blankets would be continued in the interior 'as an opportunity of obtaining an influence with the Natives which . . . may lead to their permanent advantage, whilst it will promote the convenience and security of settlers and their property'.[68] This would also keep the Aborigines in 'their Districts' and away from the towns to which they were increasingly being attracted. Parcels of blankets were sent by the Colonial Storekeeper to magistrates, Crown Lands Commissioners and settlers who were required by the Colonial Secretary to supply annual returns[69] of all adult male Aborigines in their district, including information on probable age, number of wives and children, tribe and 'Place or District of usual Resort'. These were intended as a source of information for the government as well as a guide for the Storekeeper who had to ensure that the correct number of blankets was delivered by 1 May. In theory, preference was to be given to Aborigines who had performed useful service such as tracking convict 'bolters' and to those too old or ill to fend for themselves, but in practice a blanket was handed out to every Aborigine who turned up at the local police office or authorized station on the designated day. The news spread rapidly among the Aborigines of the squatting districts as well as within the Nineteen Counties and by 1837 the annual donation was costing the colonial government £903. While some Aborigines were registered under

---

[67] GG, 1 April 1835, p. 175. Similar feasts were held by Governor Gawler at Adelaide in late 1838 and by the Protectors at Melbourne in early 1839.

[68] Ibid.

[69] These returns, although by no means comprehensive or even very accurate, provide the only statistical information available on the Aborigines for the period 1833-46. A collection of returns can be found in NSWA, 4/6666.3 and 4/1133.3.

different names[70] at various police offices,[71] some settlers falsified their returns and either sold the blankets or gave them to their assigned servants.[72] Nevertheless, the annual 'gift' took on considerable economic significance, especially in areas where the traditional possum skin rugs were no longer easily obtainable. More importantly, perhaps, the blanket became for many Aborigines a symbol of a special relationship with the governor and the 'big white boss' beyond the seas.

Bourke's final innovation in his policy towards the Aborigines arose from his belief that conflicts between Aborigines and whites arose largely from the stockmen's alleged habit of 'kidnapping' Aboriginal women and holding them against their will. In August 1837 he received a letter from Henry Bingham, police magistrate at Cassilis, drawing attention to

> the prevailing habit of many of the servants at the distant stations taking and keeping by *force* the black native women, the Wives of the Natives, and making use of the *Arms* injudiciously left with them and not by any means required, except at the "extreme stations", to threaten the Blacks if they endeavour to take them back, and I have no hesitation in giving it as my opinion that this leads in many cases to the lives of innocent parties falling a sacrifice to their lawless proceeding. In the recent murder of Mr Purcell's stockkeeper at Calloway Creek, he was found murdered at the hut of Mr Marsden's of Yarragany Creek and Mr Marsden's stockkeeper badly wounded by a spear —all having arisen from the highly improper conduct of Mr Marsden's hut-keeper at *that station* keeping by force and threat a black woman.[73]

[70] From Wellington Valley the Rev. William Watson warned that unless care was taken, the lists would contain three times the actual numbers of Aborigines:

> All the Adult Male Natives have at least three names—one received at his birth, a second when he is initiated into the Order of Young Men, and the third when he arrives at maturity. Moreover, casual occurrences frequently occasion the acquisition of a new name. A native who some time ago was wounded in the back by a musket ball received the name Birrah Ball (Black Ball).

(Watson to McLeay, 29 July 1835, *CSIL*, 4/6666.3, 35/1068.) In addition, many Aborigines were given English names.

[71] George Mackenzie of Williams River to McLeay, 27 May 1833, *CSIL*, 4/6666.3, 33/3775.

[72] Anonymous Minute, unregistered letter *c.* 1835, *CSIL*, 4/6666.3.

[73] N.S.W. Executive Council, Minutes, Appendix no. 8, p. 350, *NSWA*, 4/1445.

Shortly afterwards Bourke issued a notice requiring Crown Lands Commissioners to report the names of any persons in the squatting districts who were forcibly detaining Aboriginal women. Anyone involved in 'so abominable and unchristian a proceeding' was to have his squatting licence immediately cancelled and to be prosecuted under the 1836 Act as an illegal occupant of Crown land.[74]

THE INFLUENCE OF THE EVANGELICALS

Even before the abolition of slavery in British colonies came into effect in August 1834 the small but influential group of Evangelical philanthropists known to contemporaries as 'Exeter Hall' or, less accurately, the 'Clapham Sect',[75] were turning their attention to other problems. Interest in the welfare of native races had been stimulated by reports of serious clashes between blacks and whites in both Cape Colony and Van Diemen's Land and of the rapid destruction wrought by introduced European diseases in these and other British colonies. The publication of Bannister's *Humane Policy* in 1830 and official correspondence relating to 'military operations lately carried on against the Aboriginal Inhabitants of Van Diemen's Land'[76] in the following year marked the beginning of a demand for further information about Australia.

By 1834 Thomas Buxton,[77] one of the leading figures in the anti-slavery movement, was sufficiently interested in the welfare of the

---

[74] *GG*, 20 September 1837, p. 652.
[75] The 'Clapham Sect' was Sydney Smith's facetious name for an informal group of Evangelical Anglicans of substantial means and philanthropic inclinations living on the edge of Clapham Common and worshipping in its parish church during the incumbency of James Venn (1792-1813). Centred on the Wilberforce, Teignmouth, Stephen and Thornton families, the group joined with Evangelical Dissenters and humanitarians in providing the driving force for the anti-slavery movement and were also connected with the Church Missionary Society, the British and Foreign Bible Society and other organizations. By 1830 the group had been superseded by the various philanthropic bodies, organized by Evangelical Anglicans and Dissenters, which met at Exeter Hall in the Strand—a building which became the symbol of a broader-based philanthropic movement. For an inside view, see James Stephen, 'The Clapham Sect' in his *Essays in Ecclesiastical Biography*, 2nd edn, London 1872, pp. 523-84.
[76] *PP*, 1831, Vol. XIX, No. 259.
[77] Thomas Fowell Buxton, Bart. (1786-1845) was early associated with the Quakers through his mother and through the Gurney family of Norwich. A distinguished graduate of Trinity College, Dublin, he married Hannah

Kaffirs and other native races to press for an official inquiry into the situation in all British colonies. Hearing of this, J. D. Lang, who was then in London, wrote to Buxton describing in eloquent terms the plight of the Aborigines of New South Wales and offering a number of recommendations for their protection and 'improvement'. He claimed that they now numbered only 10,000 and were rapidly diminishing in the older parts of the colony due to infanticide, intemperance and disease. Stressing that the Aborigines bitterly resented the whites taking over their hunting grounds and driving away their game, Lang went on to describe what they had received in return:

> What equivalent has been afforded them in exchange for their fields and their forests? Why, the very worst features of English civilization have reappeared in their territory. They have been transformed into a race of paupers, and taught to beg their bread where they formerly earned it. Their native habits of temperance have been succeeded by scenes of beastly intoxication Their tongues had been taught to frame horrid imprecations in a language which they imperfectly understand. Their bodies have been wasted by strange and incurable diseases. Their impatience of injuries has been tried with the most wanton and brutal aggressions, and in moments of frenzy they have sometimes been stimulated to deeds of indiscriminate and murderous revenge.[78]

In July 1834 Buxton moved an address from the House of Commons requesting that the Crown should establish an inquiry into the condition of the aboriginal inhabitants of all British colonies. In his speech he observed that civilization through the agency of British colonization had proved a curse rather than a blessing to

---

Gurney, the sister of Elizabeth Fry, and entered a brewing firm in Spitalfields. There he became interested in various charitable undertakings and in 1816 was instrumental in raising money for famine relief in the district. He also became involved in prison reform, publishing an influential book on the subject in 1818 and serving on two committees after entering Parliament in that year. Already active in the African Institution, he was chosen by Wilberforce in 1824 to succeed him as the head of the anti-slavery party in the House of Commons. Following an energetic campaign and an influential resolution produced by Buxton in 1831, a bill abolishing slavery in British colonies was passed in 1833. Not content with this, Buxton continued to campaign against slavery and was involved in The Society for the Extinction of the Slave Trade and the Civilization of Africa, sponsor of the Niger expedition whose failure led to Buxton's retirement from public life. *DNB.*, Vol. III, pp. 559-61 and Charles Buxton, *Memoirs of Sir Thomas Fowell Buxton* . . . , 6th edn, London 1855.

[78] *PD*, Series 3, Vol. XXIV, 1834, pp. 1061-2.

these peoples whose numbers had declined through the introduction of 'British brandy and gunpowder'.[79]

August saw the publication of papers relating to the natives of Canada, New South Wales, Van Diemen's Land and British Guiana[80] and in July 1835 Buxton finally secured the establishment of a Select Committee of the House of Commons to consider how justice and Christianity could be brought to the indigenous peoples of all British colonies. Supporting his motion, Buxton read extracts describing extensive depopulation in a number of colonies and for his remarks on New South Wales and Van Diemen's Land he relied on information supplied by Lang. He pointed out that in Van Diemen's Land, which had only been settled since 1803, 'scarcely one' of its Aboriginal inhabitants remained and the rapid disappearance of the tribes around Sydney indicated that the process of extinction was continuing on the mainland. Of one tribe which had formerly numbered 500 there remained only two or three men and a few women and children who complained that the whites had 'rooted them out of the soil'.[81] While emphasizing the injustice of dispossessing native peoples, Buxton claimed that proper behaviour on the part of the whites would always produce corresponding good behaviour on the part of the natives.

Buxton had already begun to organize the British and Foreign Aborigines' Protection Society which was formally established in 1836 with Buxton as chairman and a committee which included a fair sprinkling of MPs and Evangelicals. In one of its earliest pamphlets the Society revealed its preoccupation with the ruinous effects of colonization on indigenous peoples:

> Among these multitudinous tribes our imported diseases produce frightful ravages; our ardent spirits deprave and consume their population; our unjust laws exclude them from enjoying that first element of well-ordered societies—judicial protection, as well as from the possibility of a timely incorporation with Colonial communities; which, in addition to all these evils, our neglect of suitable methods of improving them, prevents their adopting the civilised manners and customs to which they are inclined.[82]

[79] Ibid., p. 106.
[80] PP, 1834, Vol. XLIV, No. 617.
[81] PD, Series 3, Vol. XXIX, 1835, p. 551.
[82] 'Appeal of the British and Foreign Aborigines' Protection Society . . .', Aborigines Papers, ML, MS.A610, p. 185.

The Society was by no means against the extension of colonies but it was concerned that future modes of colonization should be directed with more wisdom and humanity than before. To this end it announced its intention of publishing documents relating to the problem, holding meetings to advocate aboriginal rights, lobbying government departments and presenting petitions to the Crown and Parliament.

A Committee of the House of Commons was appointed in due course and its members, including Sir Rufane Donkin and Sir George Grey who also belonged to the Aborigines' Protection Society, were able to interview a number of key witnesses before the end of 1836. Among these were Broughton and Bannister who, together with Dandeson Coates, John Beecham and William Ellis of the Church Missionary Society, emphasized the need to separate the Aborigines from the whites. The influence of Broughton's evidence can be gauged from the fact that it was quoted extensively by Buxton in the final Report. Lang's 1834 letter was also tabled, as was one from the Quaker James Backhouse[83] emphasizing the imminent extinction of the Aborigines. Sir George Arthur submitted his views on the success of conciliation and collection in Van Diemen's Land and Lang and Bannister provided detailed proposals for a system of protectorships.

The writing of the Report was entrusted to Buxton who, according to his nephew, regarded it as 'a sort of manual' for the future treatment of indigenous peoples:

> The object of the report was to prove, first, the destructive cruelty to which the native tribes had generally been subjected: and, secondly, that, wherever they had received equitable and humane treatment,

---

[83] The two Quaker missionaries James Backhouse (1794-1869) and George Washington Walker (1800-59) visited the Australian colonies 1832-8, reporting to Arthur and Bourke on penal establishments and the Aborigines. They inspected Flinders Island and the missions at Lake Macquarie, Wellington Valley and Port Phillip and promoted the establishment of Aboriginal protection committees in Sydney, Adelaide and Perth. Copies of their reports were sent to London Friends and the Colonial Office and these, together with the published *Extracts* from Backhouse's letters, were no doubt influential in the abolition of transportation and the introduction of a new policy towards the Aborigines. Backhouse's *Narrative of a Visit to the Australian Colonies*, London 1843, contains some useful descriptions of the Aborigines and the mission establishments. *ADB*, Vol. I, pp. 45-6; Vol. II, pp. 562-3.

they had increased in numbers, acquired the arts of civilized life, and accepted the blessings of religion.[84]

In a letter written while he was engaged on the work, Buxton noted:

the next few months are very important, as in them the Aborigines' Report will be settled. Most earnestly I pray that it may stop the oppressor, and open the door to the admission of multitudes of heathens to the fold of Christ.[85]

Before being tabled in the House, the Report was given a careful revision by Grey.

At no time had Buxton made any attempt to obtain the opinion of other interested groups on the situation in New South Wales. No representative of the squatting interest was called to inform his Committee of the special problems of the pastoral frontier. Nor was there anyone to point out the impracticability of segregation due to the pressure for new pasture lands and the Aborigines' own desire for European goods. And so Buxton produced a Report which the squatting interest could easily caricature as an Exeter Hall 'job'.

Not surprisingly, the 1837 Report[86] found that the British colonization of South Africa, the Australian colonies and North America had brought disastrous consequences for their indigenous inhabitants and urged the British government to assume moral responsibility for their physical and spiritual well-being. This was based on the belief that indigenous inhabitants of every country possessed an 'incontrovertible right' to the soil:

A plain and sacred right, however, which seems not to have been understood. Europeans have entered their borders uninvited, and ... have not only acted as if they were undoubted lords of the soil, but have punished the natives as aggressors if they have evinced a disposition to live in their own country.

'If they have been found upon their own property, they have been treated as thieves and robbers. They are driven back into the interior as if they were dogs or kangaroos.'[87]

---

[84] Charles Buxton, *Memoirs of Sir Thomas Fowell Buxton*, p. 349.
[85] Ibid., p. 349.
[86] This actually consisted of two reports: the 1836 'Report from the Select Committee on Aborigines (British Settlements;) . . .', *PP*, 1836, VII, No. 538, and the 1837 'Report from the Select Committee on Aborigines (British Settlements) . . .', *PP*, 1837, Vol. VII, No. 425. The term '1837 Report' is used to cover both of these, but each quotation is cited according to the Parliamentary papers from which it has been taken.
[87] *PP*, 1837, Vol. VII, No. 425, pp. 5-6.

It was also held that colonial legislatures could not be entrusted with the responsibility since the interests which they represented necessarily clashed with those of the natives.

The Committee rejected the idea of 'attachment', insisting that the preservation and welfare of uncivilized races demanded that 'their relations with their more cultivated neighbours should be diminished rather than multiplied'.[88] The Report and its Recommendations echoed Buxton's theme of extinction when it warned that

> the first distinct apprehension of the reality and magnitude of the evil has not been acquired until it was ascertained that some uncivilized nation had ceased to exist.[89]

Although the Committee was unwilling to impose rules for the government of races in various stages of civilization, it felt that the 'uncertainty and vacillation' of previous policy was far more dangerous. Accordingly, a number of general recommendations were made which were to have a profound effect on British policy towards indigenous peoples.

The responsibility for protection, religious instruction and education was to devolve on Her Majesty's Executive, although the cost was to be borne by the colonial treasuries; new territories were not to be acquired without the Executive's permission and settlers were forbidden to purchase land from natives within Crown territories; treaties of any kind were forbidden since the parties would be negotiating on terms of such disparity that they would be 'rather the preparatives and the apology for disputes than securities of peace';[90] natives had been taught to consider as praiseworthy actions which whites considered as capital offences, and accordingly those who violated British law were to be treated with 'the utmost indulgence compatible with a due regard for the lives and properties of others'.[91] However, since settlers were often exposed to outrages in areas where there was no established civil government, the natives were to be encouraged to surrender their own offenders to justice; the sale of spirits to natives was forbidden and labour

[88] Ibid., p. 80.
[89] Ibid., p. 84.
[90] Ibid., p. 80.
[91] Ibid.

contracts limited to twelve months; and finally, missionaries were to be chosen for their ability to implement schemes of social and political 'improvement' as well as the fulfilment of their spiritual duties.

Specific recommendations were made for the duties of Protectors of Aborigines to be appointed in the Australian colonies. After gaining personal knowledge of the Aborigines and their language, the Protectors were to encourage whichever 'industry' was most suited to their habits and disposition. However, as long as agriculture was distasteful to them they were to be 'provided with the means of pursuing the choice without molestation'[92] on land set aside for that purpose. The education of children was to be left to missionaries.

The Protectors were also to act as coroners in any case where Aborigines were killed by whites and were to compile special laws for the use of the local governments. As Buxton put it:

> To require from the ignorant hordes of savages living in Eastern or Western Australia the observance of our laws would be absurd, and to punish their non-observance of them by severe penalties would be palpably unjust.[93]

On the other hand, they were to prosecute all crimes committed against Aborigines and arrange legal defence for them if they were indicted for offences against whites. They were also to make regular reports and recommendations to the local government which were then to be forwarded to the Colonial Office.

One further recommendation is of interest. The Protectors were to discourage the use of Aborigines as police in tracking escaped convicts in the outlying districts. It was pointed out that much of the antagonism towards the Aborigines in Van Diemen's Land had stemmed from this. Furthermore, it was thought that they would become the victims of their own zeal in such a service.

The Report created negligible public interest in England but the Minutes of Evidence provided Exeter Hall with enough ammunition for a broadside of books, pamphlets and articles emphasizing the evils which had accompanied British colonization. William Howitt's *Colonization and Christianity* claimed that the penal

[92] Ibid., p. 83.
[93] Ibid., p. 84.

colony system, invented by Columbus, had produced in New South Wales and Van Diemen's Land 'a contagion . . . sufficient to curse and demoralise all this portion of the world'.[94] Saxe Bannister joined in the cry with *British Colonization and Coloured Tribes*[95] and annotated editions of the Minutes of Evidence were published for the Aborigines' Protection Society, the Church Missionary Society and the Quakers. In the same year a special sub-committee of the Aborigines' Protection Society produced its own detailed report on the Australian Aborigines[96] and Standish Motte, a Quaker barrister, was commissioned to draft legislation protecting the rights and interests of all indigenous peoples of British colonies.[97] Representations were later made to the Colonial Office on the admissibility of Aboriginal evidence in courts of law.

Although the Committee and its recommendations aroused no general interest, the Colonial Office was sympathetic. James Stephen,[98] permanent under-secretary of the department from 1836 until 1847, came from a family which had been closely connected with the anti-slavery movement. His own humanitarian outlook had been strengthened by his friendship with William Wilberforce and his wife was the daughter of the Rev. John Venn of Clapham, one of the prominent members of the 'Clapham Sect'. In 1813 Stephen had been appointed legal adviser to the Colonial Office and in 1825 became salaried legal counsellor to the Colonial Office and the Board of Trade, in which positions he became closely acquainted with the problem of the legal status of native peoples in British colonies. One of the most influential connections of Exeter Hall, his effect on policy was unabating. In the words of Sir Henry Taylor, 'he, more than any other man, virtually governed the Colonial empire'.[99] Although not always sympathetic towards missionaries,

---

94 London 1838, p. 470.
95 London 1838.
96 *Report of the Sub-Committee on Australia with Notes*, London 1838.
97 *Outline of a System of Legislation, for Securing Protection to the Aboriginal Inhabitants of all Countries Colonized by Great Britain*, London 1840.
98 See Paul Knaplund, *James Stephen and the British Colonial System 1813-1847*, Madison 1953; S. C. McCulloch, 'James Stephen and the Problems of New South Wales, 1838-1846', *Pacific Historical Review*, XXVI, 1957, pp. 353-64; and *DNB*, Vol. LIV, pp. 163-4. His own *Essays in Ecclesiastical Biography* provide a good insight into Stephen's character.
99 *Autobiography of Sir Henry Taylor 1800-1875*, 2 vols, London 1885, Vol. II, p. 301.

he was a deeply religious man and displayed a sincere, if pessimistic, concern for the spiritual and material welfare of native peoples.

Lord Glenelg, Secretary of State for Colonies from 1835 until 1839, was also connected with the 'Clapham Sect' through his father[100] and was committed to the protection and evangelization of colonial peoples. His attitude to the Aborigines was demonstrated soon after his appointment in 1835 when he told Sir Richard Bourke that 'the moral improvement of that unfortunate race is an object, among the first, which demands the attention of the Colonial and Home Governments'.[101] There can be little doubt that he was disturbed by the evidence given before Buxton's Committee. Even while the composition of the Committee was still being discussed, Buxton's cry of 'justice for the Aborigines' was having some impact. In February 1836, for example, the Letters Patent issued to the South Australian Colonization Commissioners contained the well-intentioned but quite impracticable provision that settlers should not interfere with the rights of Aborigines already occupying land.

One of the direct results of the 1837 Report was a greater concern within the Colonial Office for the legal status of native peoples. In an important despatch of July 1837, Glenelg emphasized that since Bourke's Commission asserted Her Majesty's sovereignty over every part of the continent, excepting the colonies of Western and Southern Australia, all the natives inhabiting this territory 'must be considered as subjects of the Queen, and as within H.M.'s Allegiance'. He continued:

> to regard them as Aliens with whom a War can exist, and against whom H.M.'s Troops may exercise belligerent right, is to deny that protection to which they derive the highest possible claim from the Sovereignty which has been assumed over the whole of their Ancient Possessions.[102]

Certain exceptions were to be made, however, as in the case of Major Mitchell's encounter with the Aborigines of the Murray.

---

[100] Charles Grant (1746-1823) was a prominent member of the 'Clapham Sect'. He was a founding vice-president of the British and Foreign Bible Society, a promoter of the Church Missionary Society and an active member of the Society for the Propagation of the Gospel. *DNB*, VIII, pp. 379-80.

[101] Glenelg to Bourke, 30 November 1835, *HRA*, XVIII, p. 207.

[102] Glenelg to Bourke, 26 July 1837, *HRA*, XIX, p. 48.

K

While Glenelg thought that incidents of this nature were extremely regrettable, he admitted that in some cases they were unavoidable and 'in extreme Exigencies of that nature, Public Officers are not to be governed altogether by Ordinary rules'.[103] But in future an official inquest was to be held into the death of any Aborigine killed by government officers or by people under their command.

In January 1838 Glenelg wrote to Gipps enclosing a copy of the 1837 Report and informing him that Her Majesty's Government had 'directed their anxious attention to the adoption of some plan for the better protection and civilization of the Native Tribes within the limits of your Government'.[104] It had been decided that in the first instance five Protectors of Aborigines would be appointed—a Chief Protector to be based at Port Phillip ('the most convenient point from whence he could traverse the surrounding country') and four Assistant Protectors, two of whom would 'occupy' the area to the north-east and the others the north-west as far as the South Australian border. Glenelg revealed that he intended appointing Robinson, whose work at Flinders Island had 'shewn him eminently suited for such an Office', as Chief Protector and would direct Franklin to inform Robinson and send him to Sydney if he accepted. Robinson, however, had already made it clear that he would not leave Flinders Island unless he was able to take all the Van Diemen's Land Aborigines with him and although transfer to the mainland had Arthur's blessing, Franklin had indicated a number of objections. Glenelg felt that if Franklin was satisfied after his forthcoming visit to Flinders Island that the Aborigines there could be removed without danger to themselves and with their own consent, 'important advantages might be anticipated from the formation in New Holland of an Aboriginal Settlement comparitively so far advanced in civilization'. Nevertheless, the Secretary of State urged Gipps to communicate with Franklin and gave him the somewhat unnecessary advice to act 'with the utmost Caution and Circumspection'. Robinson was to be induced to accept the office irrespective of the Flinders Island question.

Relying on Gipps' 'local knowledge and experience' to remedy omissions, Glenelg then proceeded to set out the general principles

---

[103] Ibid., p. 48.
[104] Glenelg to Gipps, 31 January 1838, *HRA*, XIX, p. 252. The following quotations are also from this despatch.

to be followed: the Chief Protector and his four Assistants were to attach themselves 'as closely and constantly as possible' to the tribes in the districts to be allocated to them, and to accompany them in their wanderings until they could be persuaded to develop more settled habits (in this happy event they were to be instructed in agriculture and the construction of permanent homes and anything else which conduced to their 'civilization and social improvement'); as magistrates, they were to guard the rights and interests of the Aborigines, protecting them from encroachments on their 'property' and acts of cruelty and injustice; Aboriginal children were to be educated and instructed in the elements of Christianity, thus preparing the way for missionary-teachers; and finally, the Protectors were to distribute food and clothing and collect details of numbers and 'all important particulars in regard to them'. Noting that the plan was to be financed entirely from colonial revenue, Glenelg was of the optimistic opinion that Gipps' Legislative Council would concur in the importance of the object and the obligation that rested on the colonists, so that no further argument would be necessary to induce 'a cheerful co-operation on their part'. Although they were directly responsible to the Secretary of State, the Protectors' passages, expenses and salaries were to be met by the sorely-pressed Treasury of New South Wales. Evidently Glenelg accepted the 1837 Committee's argument that

> When it is remembered that unsettled land has been sold by the Government of New South Wales, yielding in a single year returns to the local Treasury exceeding 100,000 1., and that in the recollection of many living men every part of this territory was the undisputed property of the Aborigines, it is demanding little indeed that no expenditure should be withheld for the maintenance of missionaries . . . and protectors.[105]

Glenelg's 'plan' was a vague compromise based on the suggestions of a committee largely influenced by the Evangelicals and their idea of segregation and it should have been obvious from the beginning that the duties of the Protectors were impossibly onerous and in some ways irreconcilable. However, Glenelg probably had no idea of the number of Aborigines in the Port Phillip district and the vast areas over which the Protectors would have to 'itinerate'

[105] *PP*, 1837, Vol. VII, No. 425, p. 82.

with the tribes while at the same time fulfilling their other functions. The entire 'plan' inevitably bore signs of ignorance of the situation in New South Wales and preoccupation with the preservation of the Aborigines from threatened extinction. Glenelg's motives were unexceptionable but his narrow conception of the 'Aboriginal problem' was bound to create difficulties.

Glenelg's successors were also more or less committed to the same line. Normanby, Russell and Stanley were all sympathetically disposed towards the Aborigines and Normanby continued Glenelg's policy by fully approving Gipps' action in the Myall Creek case.[106] During the Gipps administration the Aborigines' Protection Society continued to exert pressure on the Colonial Office, especially in the matter of legal status, and it was partly on their prompting that Normanby wrote to Gipps in 1839 suggesting that he should prepare legislation securing the admissibility of Aboriginal evidence in courts of law.[107] In 1840 Russell also followed the recommendations of the 1837 Report by calling for annual reports on the condition of the Aborigines and allowing an expenditure of not more than fifteen per cent of the Land Fund (revenue raised from the sale of Crown lands) on their 'protection'.[108] However, he was fatalistic about the outcome of contact between whites and Aborigines:

> Between the native, who is weakened by intoxicating liquors, and the European who has all the strength of superior Civilization and is free from all its restraints, the unequal contest is generally of no long duration; the Natives decline, diminish, and finally disappear.[109]

It was only after receiving the extremely unfavourable reports for 1841 that Stanley authorized Gipps to discontinue financial assistance to the missions and the Protectorate.[110] At the same time, he could not

> acquiesce in the theory that they are incapable of improvement, and that their extinction, before the advance of the white settler, is a necessity which it is impossible to controul.[111]

[106] Normanby to Gipps, 17 July 1839, *HRA*, XX, pp. 242-3.
[107] Normanby to Gipps, 31 August 1839, ibid., pp. 302-3.
[108] Russell to Gipps, 25 August 1840, Ibid., p. 776.
[109] Ibid., p. 775.
[110] Stanley to Gipps, 20 December 1842, *HRA*, XXII, p. 439.
[111] Ibid., p. 439.

Stanley still approved of the allocation of fifteen per cent of the Land Fund 'for the benefit, civilization and protection of the Aborigines'.[112]

However, the most important permanent influence in the Colonial Office, James Stephen, shared Russell's pessimism about the chances of survival. On Gipps' first despatch reporting the Nunn case he commented:

> The causes and the consequences of this state of things are clear and irremediable, nor do I suppose that it is possible to discover any method by which the impending catastrophe, namely, the elimination of the Black Race, can be averted.[113]

Gipps' final report on the investigation only strengthened this pessimism:

> The tendency of these collisions with the blacks is unhappily too clear for doubt. They will ere long cease to be remembered amongst the races of the earth.[114]

However, Stephen's vision of a mono-racial society in Australia would probably have prevented any positive evaluation of the future of the Aborigines, even if their numbers had not been rapidly declining. When Gipps informed him in July 1841 that the squatters were agitating for the importation of Indian coolie labour at the expense of the Land Fund, he wrote:

> There is not on the globe a social interest more momentous, if we look forward for five or six generations, than that of reserving the continent of New Holland as a place where the English race shall be spread from sea to sea unmixed with any lower caste.[115]

[112] Ibid., p. 281. Stanley to Gipps, 15 September 1842, ibid., p. 281.
[113] CO, 201/272, p. 414.
[114] CO, 201/286, p. 294.
[115] CO, 201/310. Quoted by P. Knaplund, 'Sir James Stephen on a White Australia', The Victorian Historical Magazine, XII, No. 4, June 1928, p. 241.

CHAPTER FOUR

The Myall Creek Trials

From time immemorial it had been the custom for influential settlers to head parties like this, against the
blacks. All former governors had sanctioned this method
of proceeding, by immediate reprisals; and some of these
men had thus been initiated into it. They were hanged
for doing what they had been taught was perfectly lawful by their masters; and some of the masters magistrates of the territory.

ALEXANDER HARRIS

To tell how hands in friendship pledged
Piled high the fatal pire;
To tell—to tell of the gloomy ridge!
And the *stockmen's human fire.*

ELIZA DUNLOP

Like Sir George Arthur in Van Diemen's Land, Sir George Gipps
had to deal with a bloody climax in relations between settlers and
Aborigines. But unlike Arthur, he was obliged to pursue a policy
which stressed that the Aborigines were British subjects with rights
which were to be strictly upheld. As already indicated, this policy
had been secured by a small band of British and colonial philanthropists preoccupied with the likely extinction of the Aborigines
and largely ignorant of the problems of the pastoral frontier. Nor
were Gipps and his Port Phillip subordinate, Superintendent Charles
La Trobe, any better equipped than their predecessors to deal with
these problems. Both had spent some time in the West Indies:
Gipps was stationed there between 1824 and 1829 as an army
engineer and La Trobe was sent there in 1837 to report on negro
education.[1] Indeed, it was probably these reports which won La

---

[1] La Trobe's reports on British Guiana and Trinidad can be found in *PP*,
1839, XXXIV, No. 35.

Trobe the approval of the Colonial Office and the position of Superintendent of the Port Phillip District of New South Wales.[2] At any rate, both men were acquainted to some extent with the situation arising from the liberation of negro slaves in the West Indian colonies.

However, their knowledge of the Australian Aborigines was limited and there was little in the way of information and administrative experience to be garnered from their predecessors. Since Gipps' personal papers appear to have been lost, it is difficult to say what informed his own policy towards the Aborigines. He placed considerable credence on the published journals of his Surveyor-General, Sir Thomas Mitchell,[3] and took note of Captain George Grey's Report[4] although he seems to have ignored Grey's informative journals of exploration. Nor is it clear that he read the documents collected by Judge Burton.[5] La Trobe attempted to learn something about the Aborigines from first-hand observations but it is difficult to say how much useful information he obtained during his various journeys in the Port Phillip district.[6]

Gipps was very much the military engineer with an ordered mind and a passion for discipline and efficiency. Intolerant of inconsistencies, he was fair-minded but tough. Above all, he was an extremely hard worker with an immense capacity for detail. Lacking Arthur's moral concern, he found the 'indolence' of the Aborigines annoying and his attitudes seem to have been coloured more by this than by any other factor. Apart from his visit to Wellington Valley in 1840 he seems to have had no first-hand experience of the Aborigines.

The guiding principle of his whole administration (strengthened, no doubt, by Governor Sir George Gawler's recall from South Australia in 1841), was that Whitehall insisted above all on colonial governors maintaining their governments in a state of solvency.

2 A. Gross, *Charles Joseph La Trobe*, Melbourne 1956, p. 9.
3 During the Legislative Council debate on the Lee case in 1842, Gipps quoted extensively from Mitchell's *Three Expeditions*.
4 Grey's Report was the only plan for the civilization and Christianization of the Aborigines on which Gipps commented publicly.
5 *BP*, Supreme Court Papers, NSWA, No. 1161.
6 One important service performed by La Trobe was to ask pioneer settlers to record their memoirs of the early days. Letters written in response were preserved and some were later used by Bride in his *Letters from Victorian Pioneers*.

The unfortunate coincidence of his governorship with a period of severe economic recession and drought, together with a serious decline in revenue from land sales and increased expenditure on immigration, laid him open to charges of parsimony in the colony and extravagance in Whitehall.

La Trobe, a professional writer and son of a Moravian missionary, was a more compassionate man and his attitude to native races had been made clear earlier in his remarks on the disappearance of the North American Indians.[7] But his official position at Port Phillip carried very little real authority and he lacked the initiative and confidence with which to strengthen it. Saddled by Gipps with responsibility for the Port Phillip Protectorate, he gave Robinson a free hand and acted as little more than a channel of communication between the Chief Protector and the governor. His gentlemanly and trusting nature was something of a disadvantage when dealing with hard-headed squatters, but his greatest weakness was an inability to make decisions. His reports from Port Phillip were like the earlier ones on negro education: 'marked by a wordiness which somehow avoided expressions of opinion',[8] and he seems always to have avoided any recommendation of a positive course of action. According to Lang, La Trobe himself had no illusions about his position and ability:

> At a public meeting in Melbourne, this gentleman modestly described himself as a person whose highest ambition was to play 'second fiddle' to Sir George Gipps. At all events, he was quite incapable of playing a first fiddle anywhere . . .[9]

One squatter probably spoke for many of his fellows when he described the Superintendent as 'a person of very little authority or influence'.[10]

In his attempts to enforce Lord Glenelg's ruling on the status of the Aborigines as British subjects, Gipps encountered insurmountable difficulties and aroused fierce opposition from the squatting

---

[7] *The Rambler in North America: 1832-3*, 2nd ed, 2 vols, London 1836, Vol. I, pp. 165-70.

[8] Gross, *Charles Joseph La Trobe*, p. 8.

[9] *An Historical and Statistical Account of New South Wales*, 4th ed, 2 vols, London 1875, Vol. I, p. 287.

[10] G. Mackaness (ed.), *The Correspondence of John Cotton, Victorian Pioneer 1842-1849*, 3 Pts, Sydney 1953, Pt 1, p. 22.

interest. It is significant that the meeting of the Executive Council which learnt for the first time of the Protectorate also had to deal with the first reports of the Myall Creek murders. Gipps also thought it wise to postpone the announcement of the Protectorate and the publication of a notice on the treatment of the Aborigines which he had based on Glenelg's despatch of 26 July 1837.

The demands of the squatting interest were most clearly expressed in a number of petitions presented to Gipps between 1838 and 1842. A precedent had been established in 1837 when Bourke answered a request from 46 squatters in the Geelong district for a Police Magistrate and a detachment of Mounted Police,[11] but a series of Aboriginal attacks along the route from the Murray River to Port Phillip, including the Faithfull massacre in April 1838, raised the larger problem of protecting squatters and their servants overlanding sheep and cattle and depasturing them in remote areas. According to a petition presented to Gipps by a delegation of squatters headed by Philip Parker King in June 1838,[12] many had been forced to abandon their stations, in some cases leaving their flocks and herds to what were described as marauding tribes threatening the land link between Yass and Port Phillip. The petitioners argued that by encouraging immigration the British and colonial governments had contracted the responsibility of providing protection for the property and persons of settlers against Aboriginal depredations. If the government shirked this responsibility, the squatters would assume the right to protect themselves and their neighbours by force of arms. Claiming to be unaware of any aggressive actions by whites which could have excited the Aborigines to commit depredations and murders, they insisted that it was only through an acquaintance with the white man's power and determination to punish aggression that 'unprincipled savages' would become peaceable and 'civilized'. Finally, the petition sounded a threatening note:

> If adequate action is not afforded by the government, the settlers will undoubtedly take measures to protect themselves, as it is not to be

11 GD, ML, MS. A1267-14.
12 The Australian, 22 June 1838. Gipps pointed out to Glenelg that the petitioners had taken the constitutionally unorthodox step of addressing their document to the Governor-in-Council. Gipps to Glenelg, 21 July 1838, HRA, XIX, p. 509.

supposed that they will remain quietly looking on whilst their property is being destroyed and their servants murdered.[13]

In his despatch forwarding this petition to Glenelg, Gipps explained that at an interview prior to its presentation the principal signatories had asked him to levy war on the Aborigines, or, alternatively, to sanction the formation of a militia to be supplied with arms and munitions from government stores.[14] Some months later *The Australian* published a report of a conversation between Gipps and a 'wealthy grazier' from the southern district which was probably based on his meeting with King:

Settler — I have called upon your Excellency for the purpose of representing the dreadful state of the southern district in consequence of the repeated aggressions of the aborigines.

Sir George — What do you require? The aborigines are subject to the laws of the country, which I apprehend are sufficient to protect every one, both whites and blacks.

Settler — It is impossible to apprehend the natives; and when they are apprehended they cannot be tried for their offences, inasmuch as no person can interpret their language. An armed force is the only remedy that can effectually protect our interests.

Sir George — It is a question of great difficulty. It cannot be expected that every person who wanders into the interior in search of pasture for his flocks and herds is to be protected by an armed force. The government cannot interfere, Sir, in the way you require.

Settler — Then, your Excellency, although I for one shall regret the result, still, for our own protection, and for the protection of the lives of our servants, and flocks, and herds, we must take the law into our own hands.

Sir George — Very well, Sir, you can do as you like; but you will remember that if either you or your servants commit any murders upon the aborigines, or if you abet them in doing so, and either you or they are tried for it and found guilty, so sure as my name is George Gipps, *so sure shall you or they be hanged!*[15]

In his instructions to the officer sent to investigate the Faithfull massacre, Gipps had expressed surprise that Faithfull's party, who were armed, had not defended themselves.[16] But in his public reply

13 *The Australian*, 22 June 1838.
14 Gipps to Glenelg, 21 July 1838, *HRA*, XIX, p. 509.
15 22 November 1838.
16 *BP*, No. 60.

to the petition he emphasized that he had been instructed by Her Majesty's government to treat the Aborigines as Her subjects and it was therefore impossible to levy war or to sanction 'indiscriminate retaliation', *despite earlier precedents*.[17] He was prepared to increase the military force at Melbourne, giving the police magistrate there discretionary power to send parties or soldiers into the interior, and went as far as planning a chain of military posts between Yass and Port Phillip. However, he emphasized that it was impossible to give protection to every squatter in search of new pastures.

Repeating this point to Glenelg, Gipps made a clear statement of his attitude to the racial problems arising from pastoral expansion, an attitude which was to remain unchanged during the period of his governorship:

> If Proprietors, for the sake of obtaining better pasturage for their increasing flocks, will venture with them to such a distance from protection, they must be considered to run the same risk as men would do, who were to drive their sheep into a Country infested with wolves, with this difference however that, if they were really wolves, the Government would encourage the shepherds to combine and destroy them, whilst all we can now do is to raise, in the name of Justice and humanity, a voice in favour of our poor savage fellow creatures, too feeble to be heard at such a distance.[18]

However, later petitions from Liverpool Plains in September 1838,[19] Geelong in September 1839[20] and February 1840,[21] and Port Fairy in February 1842,[22] continued to ask for police protection and effective administration of the law.

THE TRIALS

The sharpest differences between Gipps and the squatters over the Aborigines arose from the Myall Creek case—the prosecution of the men who had killed twenty-eight Aborigines at Henry Dangar's Myall Creek Station on the Liverpool Plains in June 1838. The conviction and execution of seven of the men after an earlier acquittal created a tremendous furore in the colony where it was regarded

17 *The Australian*, 29 June 1838.
18 Gipps to Glenelg, 21 July 1838, *HRA*, XIX, pp. 509-10.
19 *The Colonist*, 22 September 1838.
20 *Port Phillip Gazette*, 7 September 1839.
21 *GD*, ML, MS. A1222, pp. 793-4.
22 *Port Phillip Gazette*, 30 March 1842.

as an extraordinary and unprecedented thing that a white man should have been hanged for killing a 'black'.[23]

In many ways the Myall Creek case was something of an accident. Had it not been for the humanity displayed by the two overseers William Hobbs and Thomas Foster and the initiative taken by Frederick Foot, the incident would no doubt have passed unreported. Like the other massacres which took place in the Liverpool Plains during early settlement, it would now be nothing more than a vague tradition. A great deal of the credit was also due to Edward Day, the magistrate from Muswellbrook who travelled 150 miles to the Myall Creek district where he spent most of July and August 1838 taking evidence and locating eleven of the twelve men who had been involved. A number of obstacles were placed in the path of his investigations by hostile squatters and overseers[24] and there was probably collusion in the escape of John Fleming,[25] the young native-born overseer who had played an important part in

---

[23] It has already been noted that Macquarie authorized the execution of a convict for the murder of an Aboriginal constable at Newcastle but this incident appears to have been forgotten by the 1830s. The most recent prosecution had taken place in 1827 when Lieut. Lowe was acquitted on a charge of murdering an Aborigine at Maitland.

[24] In a letter to the author dated 21 May 1973, Mr Len Payne gave this account of Day's problems:

Day was received everywhere outside Myall Creek & Newton's very coldly from the first. As he moved west this increased to barely concealed hostility. The length of his stay (47 days) astonished everybody; feeling became very incensed, shepherds etc hid, near an area called Mungi-Bundi [and] it is told that a herd of cattle (Longhorns) was deliberately stampeded in the troopers' direction (by whites *not* blacks) which was made an alibi for several shots to be fired. A settler named Smith of Mogil Mogil is said to have had a direct altercation with Day himself in which words to the effect of 'that's if you ever get them there' are interpreted as a veiled threat of some action which might be taken to free the arrested men.

[25] According to local tradition, Fleming escaped from Day's troopers on a horse from Dangar's lower station. This was later found behind a hotel in Maitland, suggesting that he had joined a ship. What became of Fleming is not known, although it has been claimed that he went to Tasmania where no attempt was made to arrest him and that he returned to the mainland some years later. See C. H. Chomley, *Tales of Old Times* . . . , Melbourne 1883, p. 88, and A. L. Haydon, *The Trooper Police of Australia* . . ., London 1911, p. 302. A reward of £50 offered for Fleming's capture, *GG*, 12 September 1838, pp. 81-4, was described by *The Sydney Herald* as an insult to the native-born, being not much more than the £10 offered for the apprehension of convict 'bolters'.

the massacre and the destruction of the bodies. Again, the success-ful prosecution depended very much on the evidence of George Anderson, the Myall Creek hutkeeper who might well have decided that it was more in the interests of his personal safety to remain silent, and on the zeal and tenacity of Attorney-General Plunkett.[26]

In October 1838, a month before the first trial, the Sydney press reported the formation of an organization of Hunter River and Liverpool Plains landholders and squatters, known as the Hunter River Black Association,[27] whose avowed aim was to raise money for the legal defence of the eleven accused. Thanks to the energy of its chairman Robert Scott, a sum of £300 was collected at a meet-ing at Patrick's Plains, the subscribers including Henry Dangar and John Larnach[28] who, like Scott, had stations on the Liverpool Plains. Three of the colony's foremost barristers, William a'Beckett, William Foster and Richard Windeyer were retained as counsel and Scott went to the trouble of visiting the men in prison where he 'ad-vised them not to split among themselves, saying that there was no direct evidence against them, and that, if they were only true to each other, they could not be convicted'.[29] At the same time, Scott took care to arrange an interview with Gipps to explain his actions.

[26] John Hubert Plunkett (1802-69) of County Roscommon, Ireland, graduated from Dublin's Trinity College in 1824 and was called to the Irish and English bars. Appointed Solicitor-General of New South Wales as a result of his services to Daniel O'Connell, he arrived in Sydney in 1832 and suc-ceeded John Kinchela as Attorney-General in February 1836, which office he held until retirement in 1856. He was a member of the Executive Coun-cil from 1843 to 1856. Plunkett achieved a number of humanitarian reforms in New South Wales, especially in his revision of the Magistrate's Act and the extension of the law to protect convicts and expirees. Chief architect of the 1836 Church Act which effectively disestablished the Church of England and placed the main Christian sects on an equal legal footing, he was also a benefactor of Catholic charities and gave assistance to Caroline Chisholm and the Irish Sisters of Charity. By 1838 his opposition to the assignment system had already earned the enmity of the squatters and his energetic prosecution of the Myall Creek murderers led them to demand his resigna-tion. See John N. Molony, *An Architect of Freedom: John Hubert Plunkett in New South Wales 1832-1869*, Canberra 1973.

[27] This was a semi-clandestine organization about which little information can be found. However, its principals had earlier assisted soldiers and police in expeditions against the Aborigines in the Hunter River district. They had also agitated for greater convict discipline.

[28] Larnach was the son-in-law of the notorious 'Major' James Mudie whose 'Castle Forbes' estate on the Hunter River had been the scene of a convict uprising in 1833.

[29] Gipps to Glenelg, 20 December 1838, *HRA*, XIX, p. 705.

In a number of editorials *The Sydney Herald* and the *Commercial Journal* stirred up public opinion to demand an acquittal. The colonists were told by the *Herald* that they should resist the imposition of a policy dictated by Exeter Hall:

> If they cannot do it by *direct*, they can do it by *indirect* means. Much may be done by means of passive *resistance*. The Colonists must do their duty in the jury-box—they must refuse all protection or countenance to public robbers of whatever grade—and they must sustain each other in every effort to rout the Glenelg minions.[30]

On the morning before the trial the *Herald* issued another open challenge:

> We say to the Colonists, since the Government makes no adequate exertion to protect yourselves; and if the ferocious savages endeavour to plunder and destroy your property, or to murder yourselves, your families, or your servants, do to them *as you would do to any white robbers* or murderers—SHOOT THEM DEAD, if you can.[31]

Altogether, the trial aroused sensational interest and there was a general desire to see the men acquitted, whether they were guilty or not.[32] Attorney-General Plunkett was extremely concerned about the comments published in the *Herald* and told the jury he hoped that no 'bloody article that appeared in a newspaper' would influence their verdict. 'Murder is regarded as the greatest crime in all nations', he said, 'but here is a case which shews that there are gradations even in murder'.[33]

Despite the evidence that twenty-eight Aborigines had been killed and their bodies burnt at Myall Creek, the difficulty of identifying the remains meant that the men could only be charged with the murder of 'Daddy', 'or of an Aboriginal black to the Attorney-General unknown'. Numerous witnesses were called, including Hobbs, Foster, Anderson and other assigned servants who had seen the armed party, but it could not be established beyond doubt that the huge headless and armless body which Hobbs had seen was that of 'Daddy'.

---

[30] 15 October 1838.
[31] 14 November 1838.
[32] *The Colonist*, 10 November 1838.
[33] *The Australian*, 17 November 1838. In an obvious reference to the Black Association, Plunkett said: 'if there be men who have joined together for the purpose of defending men such as these, the object of that society is to encourage bloodshed and crime of every description'.

The jury was very much in sympathy with the prisoners and one of its members is said to have remarked after the trial:

> I look on the blacks as a set of monkies, and the earlier they are exterminated from the face of the earth the better. I would never consent to hang a white man for a black one. I knew well they were guilty of the murder, but I for one would never see a white man suffer for shooting a black.[34]

Its verdict of not guilty, which was reached after only fifteen minutes, was certainly one of the most popular decisions ever delivered in the Supreme Court and it was with some difficulty that Judge James Dowling prevented the overflowing audience from cheering. For once the squatters 'joined heart and hand with the prison population'.[35] However, the mood of victory in the court room was upset when Plunkett succeeded in having all the men remanded so that a fresh indictment could be prepared. Seven—Kilmaister, Hawkins, Johnston, Foley, Oates, Parry and Russell—were later charged on twenty counts with the murder of the child Charley, 'or of an Aboriginal child to the Attorney-General unknown'.

The Sydney newspapers declined to comment on the verdict since the men were on remand, but on 20 November *The Australian* delivered a blasting attack on the Black Association whose object seemed to be 'to protect the stockkeepers and shepherds in the elimination of the blacks'. If this were true, the newspaper continued, the organization should immediately be disbanded and its members deprived of their assigned servants and brought to court. Two days later it took up the same theme, this time remarking on the somewhat incongruous situation where squatters, including magistrates, were rallying to the cause of accused convicts:

> Our Hunter's River Pluto-*cracy* seem especially inclined to distinguish themselves in this holy and benevolent fraternity . . . those of the

---

34 *The Australian*, 8 December 1838.
35 *The Monitor*, 19 November 1838. Reports of the first trial can be found in *The Australian* of 17 November 1838 and the *Sydney Gazette* of 20 November 1838. The latter was republished in Glasgow in 1839 as a pamphlet entitled *Australia. A full and particular account of the Trial of Eleven Men, for the most horrible and cold-blooded Murder, and afterwards Burning! of twenty-eight individuals, men, women and children, without any provocation; being one of the blackest stains that ever disgraced the pages of British history*. . . . The evidence of the chief prosecution witness, George Anderson, was quoted by Roger Therry in his *Reminiscences of Thirty Years' Residence in New South Wales and Victoria*, London 1863 (reprinted Sydney 1973), pp. 274-7.

grand *élite* who so perseveringly sounded the tocsin of Insubordina-
tion and Convict Discipline are now found throwing their protecting
aegis over assigned servants!

It also took the opportunity of publishing a report of Gipps' conversation with King a few months earlier in the hope that it might
'serve to enlighten our insubordinate friends on the Hunter'.

Apprehensive that the *Herald* would once again sway the jury,
Plunkett attempted to obtain a court order forbidding any further
comment on the case. However, Judge Burton[36] refused this request,
telling Plunkett that he should have followed the British Attorney-
General's practice of applying for the suspension of publication of

---

[36] William Westbrooke Burton (1794-1888) was the son of Sir Edmond Burton,
solicitor and Town Clerk of Daventry, Northamptonshire, and a clergyman's
daughter. Having received his early education at Daventry Grammar School,
he entered the Royal Navy as a midshipman in 1807 and visited a number
of places including China and the West Indies. Following the family tradition, he was called to the Bar in 1824 and served as Recorder for Daventry
1826-27. In 1827 he accepted Lord Bathurst's offer of a Puisne Judgeship
on the Bench at Cape of Good Hope where he served until 1832. In that
year he was appointed to the Supreme Court of N.S.W. and arrived in the
colony. One of his earliest duties was to visit the penal settlement of Norfolk
Island for the trial of prisoners who had been involved in an unsuccessful
rebellion there. As a result, 11 men were hanged. Burton had learned at
first hand of the evils of the convict system. In November 1835 his views
on the increase of crime in the colony created a sensation. While dwelling
on the convict system, he also mentioned a number of other factors including

the occupation of the waste lands of the Colony by unauthorised and
improper persons, both bond and free, who, commencing with nothing, or
very small capital, soon after acquire a degree of wealth which must lead
every reasonable man to the conclusion they do not get it honestly.

While winning the approbation of Lang and Marsden, Burton's remarks
were rejected by the squatting interest. However, they influenced the establishment of the 1837 Select Committee on Transportation and its decision
to abolish transportation and the assignment system. In his book, *The State
of Religion and Education in New South Wales*, London 1840, Burton
referred to the findings of the Committee and reiterated that the convict
system had not only been inefficient in deterring crime but had actually
further corrupted those undergoing punishment. Burton corresponded with
Threlkeld on the Aborigines and collected a large amount of material dealing with former policy and with the culture and capacities of the Aborigines. Experience in N.S.W. evidently persuaded him to prepare special
legislation for the protection of Aborigines but this appears to have been
counter to Gipps' ideas. The material he collected is now in Supreme Court
Papers, *NSWA*, No. 1161 and Threlkeld's 'Memoranda' prepared for Burton
in late 1838 is held separately in Supreme Court Papers, *NSWA*, No. 1123.
K. G. Allars, 'Sir William Westbrooke Burton', *JRAHS*, XXXVII, Pt. V,
1951, pp. 257-94, and *ADB*, Vol. I, pp. 184-6.

a trial which had not yet been terminated.[37] Besides, he said,
'however wicked persons might attempt by their writings, to sway
the course of justice, he would never admit that the moral state of
the course of justice could be perverted by any thing that was
said out of the doors of the Court'.[38] Consequently the *Herald* was
left to continue its campaign unhampered. On 26 November, the
day before the second trial was due to begin, it published a report
that Aborigines had driven away cattle on the Gwydir. This was
yet another opportunity to warn the government:

> How long are the settlers to endure outrages such as are here de-
> tailed? . . . We say the Government *must* interfere, or the settlers
> WILL set the Government at *defiance* by taking the law into their
> own hands—by executing *summary justice*. To this it *will* come at
> last, in spite of all the ranters that ever lived.

The trial[39] was plagued with difficulties, not the least being the
unwillingness of Sydney's citizens to serve on the jury. Out of a
panel of 48, only 28 turned up and Plunkett believed that those
eligible for service had been 'waited upon' by representatives of the
squatting interest to ascertain their attitude to the case. Many were
actually intimidated into staying away[40] and there seems to have
been an attempt both to discredit Hobbs and to prevent him from
giving evidence again. When the jury was finally sworn in, a'Beckett
handed in a paper on behalf of the prisoners pleading a *demurrer*
(not sufficient in law for the accused to plead to) to the first five
counts, *autrefois acquit* (previously acquitted on the same charge)
to the second five and 'not guilty' to the final ten. Burton over-
ruled the *demurrer*, although he asked the jury to decide if the

---

[37] *The Australian*, 27 November 1838.
[38] Ibid.
[39] A report of the second trial can be found in *The Australian* of 29 November,
1 and 6 December 1838. The most useful collection of material on the two
trials is contained in a sessional paper of the House of Commons: 'Despatches Relative to the Massacre of various Aborigines of Australia, in the
Year 1838 and respecting the Trial of their murderers', *PP*, 1839, XXIV,
No. 526. This consists of Dowling's notes on the first trial; Burton's report
on the second trial, the *demurrer* and the plea of *autrefois acquit*; and
Burton's final report to the Executive Council and its Minute of 7 December 1838. The British paper and the MSS. on which it is based can be
found at *CO*, 201/277. Dowling's original notes on the first trial can be
found at NSWA, 2/3341, pp. 85-149, and those of Burton on the second
at 2/2439, pp. 28-107.
[40] The *Sydney Morning Herald*, 29 June 1849.

L

offence on which the men were now indicted was the one for which they had already been tried and acquitted. After an hour the jury had not reached a decision and Burton had to instruct it once again on the point at issue.

This time the twelve decided in favour of the Crown and the trial was scheduled for 29 November. Meanwhile the *Herald* continued its strident campaign. On 28 November it virtually instructed the jurymen to bring in a verdict of not guilty.

> Will they not say to each other—'Before we hang white men for killing blacks, let us see that black men are hanged for killing white men. Let us . . . have no maudlin sympathy—if hanging is the order of the day, let all be hanged; let the black aggressor suffer as well as the white aggressor . . .' This is the principle upon which they *will* act, if they understand the meaning of the oath which is administered to them . . .

In his address to the jury, Plunkett said he had no doubt that 'great prejudice existed in the public mind' over the case. He hoped, however, that the jury would cast this aside and return a verdict which would 'satisfy their consciences, and the justice of the country'.[41] He explained that it would now be possible for the seven accused to put the other four men in the witness box in order to establish their own innocence. If they did not avail themselves of this opportunity, it would be 'presumptive proof of their guilt'.

The evidence given at the second trial was substantially the same which had been heard earlier and there was only one new witness, an assigned servant to Dr Newton. However, Day revealed that as Kilmaister was leaving the room after the initial questioning at Myall Creek, he had remarked that he was more surprised at Kilmaister than at any of the others because of his great intimacy with the Aborigines. 'If you knew what they threatened to do to me, you would not be surprised', the stockman had replied and Plunkett seized upon this as proof that Kilmaister, at least, was 'actuated by malice, in the share he took in the matter'.

One of the features of the trial was Plunkett's cross-examination of Henry Dangar who gave Kilmaister an excellent character[42] but

---

[41] This and following quotations are from *The Australian*, 1 December 1838.
[42] Three other squatters employing accused men—George Bowman, John Cobb and T. Simpson Hall—and the overseer of Archibald Bell's station, Jolliffe, gave them good characters.

would not believe Anderson on his oath 'on account of his being greatly addicted to telling lies, and on account of his general bad character'. Very little could be adduced to support this opinion and Dangar's explanation for dismissing Hobbs from his service[43] was similarly unconvincing. 'He has not given me satisfaction in the care of my property', Dangar told the court, although he had re-marked to Day in September that he was 'well pleased' with his overseer. The examination also gave Plunkett the opportunity of questioning Dangar on the discreditable circumstances of his effective dismissal from the Survey Department by Darling in 1827. Finally, after two and a half hours of summing up by Judge Burton, the jury retired for forty-five minutes and as the men's names were called the foreman, George Sewell, gave a verdict of not guilty. However, another juryman, William Knight, immediately rose to explain that it was really one of guilty on the first five charges and not guilty on the remaining fifteen.

On 5 December the defence again used the argument that the men had been convicted on a charge for which they had already been tried and acquitted, but Burton's earlier rejection of the *demurrer* and the jury's decision on *autrefois acquit* were upheld by Chief Justice Sir Francis Forbes. Although ten of the jurymen made a strong recommendation for mercy, Burton proceeded to the death sentence. In one of the most devastating judgments ever handed down in a colonial court, he dwelt at length on the barbarity of the crime and the circumstances in which it was committed:

> Prisoners at the bar, you have been found guilty . . . of the murder of men, women and children, and the law of the land says, whoever is guilty of murder shall suffer death, and this sentence it is imperative in all Courts which are called on to try such cases, to pass. This is not a law of mere human convenience which may be adopted or rejected at pleasure, according to the conventional usages of society, but is founded on the law of God, given at the earliest period of scripture history when there were only a few people on the face of the earth;

---

[43] This happened within a few days of Dangar's arrival at Myall Creek in September. Hobbs had evidently been hired in October 1836 and his contract was coming up for renewal. Dangar's obvious bias and his behaviour in the witness box caused Burton to make some highly critical remarks in his summing-up. Referring at the close of the trial to the reflections cast on Hobbs, Burton said he 'left the Court without a stain on his character, which was raised, instead of being lowered, by the just part he had taken in the case'.

and from these few are descended all the people that are now in existence, men of all kindred, men of all languages, men of all colour. The law was given in imperative terms, whosoever sheds man's blood, by man shall his blood be shed, and I doubt whether this law can be varied from, at any rate there will be a great national guilt incurred by those who dare to depart from it. No civilised country has a right to vary the construction of this law in order to declare to what objects it shall be applied, for the terms of the law are express and cannot be misunderstood. The circumstances of the murder of which you have been found guilty are of such singular atrocity that I am persuaded that you long ago must have expected what the result would be. This is not the case where a single individual has met his death by violent means; this is not the case, as has too often stained indelibly the annals of this Colony, where death has ensued from a drunken quarrel; this is not the case, when, as this session [of] the Court has been pained to hear, the blood of a human being and the intoxicating liquor were mingled on the same floor; this is not the case where the life or property of an individual has been attacked, ever so weakly, and arms have been resorted to. No such extenuating circumstances as these, if any consider them extenuating, have taken place. This is not the case of the murder of one individual, but of many—men, women, and children, old men and babes hanging at their mothers' breasts, to the number in all, according to the evidence, probably of thirty individuals, whose bodies on one occasion were murdered—poor defenceless human beings. A party of blacks were seated around their fires, which they had just made up for the night—they were resting secure in the protection of one of you—they were totally unsuspecting—when they were suddenly surrounded by a band of armed men, of whom you, the prisoners of the bar, were half, and all of whom were equally guilty. The blacks fled for the hut of one of you for safety, but that hut proved the mesh of their destruction. In that hut, into which they had fled depending for security—in that hut, amid the tears, the sighs, the sobs, and the groans of the unhappy victims, you bound them, one by one, with cords—the father, the mother, and the child—you led them away a small distance from the hut, where, one and all, with the exception of one woman, met one common destruction. I am not stating these facts for the purpose of aggravating the painful feelings which you must naturally feel after being convicted of this offence, but in order to pourtray to the bystanders the nature of your offence in an alarming light, in order that they may see what offence it is for which you are about to offer up your lives. I cannot expect that any words of mine can reach your hearts, but I hope that the grace of God may reach them, for nothing else can reach those hardened hearts which could surround that fatal [party], and slay the fathers, mothers, and the infants. Extraordinary pains were taken by someone, either by yourselves or persons interested in the concealment of this affair, to keep it from coming to light. You burnt the bodies for the purpose of concealment, but it pleased God to send a witness to the spot before they were entirely consumed. Afterwards some one removed even the remains that were left. The place was swept, varnished, so that no vestige might remain; but the crime had been witnessed in heaven, and could not be concealed. The hundreds of birds of prey that were floating about were witnesses enough to the whole neighbourhood that a carcass was lying there, which would attract even the least interested to the spot, to see whether his own ox or his ass were lying there. But notwithstanding all the efforts that were made, the rib-bone and jaw-bone of a child, and some teeth, were found on the spot. But there is a yet more striking proof of your guilt; for it pleased God in his Providence the day before this crime was committed to send rain on earth, through which your tracks from Newton's to Dangar's, and from Dangar's to the fatal spot, were easily traced. From the hut to the spot where the deed was committed there were the traces of horsemen on each side and the naked feet of the blacks in the middle, while from the spot there were no traces of the blacks returning. This affords the strongest corroboration of the evidence of the man Anderson. This offence was not committed without premeditation, for it was proved that the party were collecting down the river some days before the murder. They were met down the river by Burroughs, preparing pouches, and putting straps to swords, doubtless for this purpose. On the Saturday they called at Newton's asking for the blacks, of course intending to do something with them. On Sunday evening, after spending the day in looking for them, you took them away from the station, thus closing that hallowed day by a scene of murder, and doubly exposing yourselves to Divine vengeance. I do not think that Christian men, men speaking the English language could have brought themselves to the commitment of this crime unless they had reason to suppose they would be screened from the effects of it. You might have flattered yourselves that you would have been protected and screened, many did seek to conceal it, none endeavoured to bring it to light, but unhappy men, what you did was seen by God. I do not make these remarks for the purpose of increasing your pain; and I would not for a moment delay passing sentence upon you, but to make the bystanders know what the law is, and what the Judges will do on such occasions, and that is their duty. Whether few persons or many are concerned, whether one or twenty, whether black or white, the law will be equally upheld. You are objects of great commisseration, and while I do my duty as a judge, I cannot conceal my feelings as a man, and therefore I say, that I feel deeply for the situation in which you are placed, whatever may have been the motives by which you were stimulated, and I trust that they were none other than those mentioned in the indictment,—that you had not the fear of God before your eyes, but were moved and seduced by the instigations of the devil. If they were not your only motives,—if you did act at the instigation of others, I trust that it may be brought to light. I cannot but look at you with commisseration; you were all transported to this Colony, although some of you have since become free; you were removed from a Christian country and placed in a dangerous and tempting situation; you were entirely removed from the benefit of the ordinances of religion; you were one hundred and fifty miles from the nearest Police station on which you could rely for protection —by which you could have been controlled. I cannot but deplore that you should have been placed in such a situation;—that such circumstances should have existed, and above all,—that you should have committed such a crime. But this commisseration must not interfere with the stern duty, which, as a Judge, the law enforces on me, which is to order that you, and each of you, be removed to the place whence you came, and thence to a place of public execution, and that at such time as His Excellency the Governor shall appoint you be hanged by the neck until your bodies be dead, and may the Lord have mercy on your souls.[44]

Following this peroration, Plunkett succeeded in having the four other men[45] remanded until the next sessions so that there would be enough time to get hold of Davey and prepare him to take a Bible oath in the witness box.[46] There was no doubt in the minds of his contemporaries that the Attorney-General had been the moving force in bringing the original case to court and in securing a second trial.

With the conspicuous exception of the *Herald*, the Sydney newspapers were satisfied with the verdict. 'As of the guilt of the prisoners convicted of having committed this wholesale murder', said the *Sydney Gazette* on 4 December, 'no reasonable man could have any doubt after hearing or perusing the evidence produced on the first trial'. Indeed, it tended to support Burton's earlier doubts about the willingness of civil juries to convict in capital cases, doubts which had not been shared by Plunkett. There was also a demand that the 'instigators' should be prosecuted as well. 'There are others, we think, more stained with moral guilt than they', remarked *The Australian* on 6 December, and on the day of the executions (18 December) it took up the same theme in stronger terms.

For the *prime movers*, abettors and subsequent comforters in the

---

44 *The Sydney Herald*, 7 December 1838.
45 Blake, Toulouse, Palliser and Lamb.
46 There is no record of Plunkett's attempts to locate Davey although Threlkeld's report that the Aboriginal stockman was 'put out of the way' after the arrests has already been noted.

aboriginal massacre, we have only to say, that we consider the death of these seven men and their murdered victims to lie at their doors.

The government was also asked when it was going to hold legal inquiries into the two earlier incidents where parties of police had killed Aborigines. A letter from a Hunter River correspondent published by *The Australian* on 15 December drew attention to Major Nunn's expedition and on 4 December the *Sydney Gazette* referred to the 'official slaughtering of blacks at Port Macquarie' which it had reported shortly after Gipps' arrival in the colony. It went on to criticize the government for failing to enforce the law equally on both races:

> the original cause of all these atrocities is traceable to the neglect of the Executive in not making due provision for the equal administration of justice between the black man and the white man. The law, it is true, makes no difference; but what is the use of a law it is impossible to put into force. While the black man escapes with impunity from the law of the land, for the crime he has committed on the white man, so long will the feeling prevail . . . that justice is not equally administered; and while such an impression gains ground among the ignorant and uneducated men, it is not the fear of the gallows that will restrain such outbreaks as the present; nor does it require the foresight of a prophet to foretell that the weak and defenceless blacks will always be the severest sufferers.

The *Herald*'s first response to the verdict and sentence was a lightly-veiled warning to Gipps and the Executive Council not to go ahead with the executions:

> We tell the Executive Authorities that the now *proved* inequality of the laws . . . will create a spirit of retaliation, will incite an actual war of extermination . . . We say . . . to the Executive Authorities— '*pause* before you become the instrument of inflicting evils on blacks and whites which are frightful to contemplate.'[47]

When this did not succeed, it published a rumour based on 'what appears to be indisputable evidence' that at least three of the men under sentence of death were nowhere near Myall Creek on the day of the massacre and had been mistaken for three men still at large.[48] The Solicitor-General immediately wrote requesting the

[47] 10 December 1838.
[48] 14 December 1838. This was probably based on the fact that John Flem ing, one of the supposed ring-leaders, had escaped.

source of this information and the *Herald* had to reply rather lamely that the responsibility for investigating its claim lay solely with the government. It had spared no effort in its opposition to the trials and its appeals to the jurymen for an acquittal had been quite blatant. Another judge might well have indicted its editor for gross interference with the course of justice.

Petitions for mercy signed by eleven members of the first jury, ten members of the second jury and 490 citizens of Sydney, Parramatta and Windsor were turned down flatly by Gipps. However, he was anxious enough about the 'excitement' created by the trials and the sentences to order that no-one was to be allowed within the prison yard without a special pass and that the area around the gallows should be cleared. An unusually large crowd assembled on the rocks behind the prison early on the morning of 18 December but the executions took place at 9 a.m. without incident. The *Sydney Gazette* reported that before the men assembled on the platform they 'appeared to be devout and attentive to the religious consolations of their pastors' and embraced each other as the hangman arranged the ropes:

> It was expected that some of them would have addressed the bystanders, but they appeared too intent on their devotions to think of anything but the life to come. Several of the culprits joined hands, and prayed audibly for forgiveness to their Maker, when the drop fell and launched them into eternity.[49]

REACTIONS

In a despatch written the day after the executions, Gipps told Glenelg that 'until after their first trial, they [the seven men] never thought . . . that their lives were even in jeopardy'.[50] Further evidence of this came to light two days later when the head gaoler, Henry Keck, informed the Sheriff that

> frequently, during their confinement here, they each and all, at different times, acknowledged to me their guilt, but implied that it was done, solely in defence of their Masters' property, that they were not aware, that in destroying the Aborigines, they were violating the Law, or that it would take cognizance of their having done so as it had,

[49] 20 December 1838.
[50] Gipps to Glenelg, 19 December 1838, *HRA*, XIX, p. 704.

(according to their belief) been so frequently done in the Colony before.[51]

On the same day the *Herald* went so far as to warn Gipps that the English press, acted upon by influential colonists, had forced the recall of Brisbane and Bourke and was already taking notice of the 'just remonstrances' of the colonists against his administration. Referring to Gipps' meeting with Robert Scott, it pointed out that the Hunter River landholders had driven Bourke out of the colony and that they would rise again to the trumpet call:

> We much fear that the emigrant land and stockholders of the Colony —the *Colonists*, in fact—and we, as an organ, will have to go over pretty nearly the same work again.

There are no reports of popular reactions to the hangings except for the *Sydney Gazette*'s mention of 'ill-suppressed murmurings of the rabble . . . relative to the alleged hardship of hanging so many white men for the murder of a *few black cannibals*'.[52] However, one incident is revealing. On the day after the trial George Sewell was told by his publican friends Thomas Douglas and Edward Borton while drinking at Douglas' house that he was a 'b——y rogue for finding the prisoners guilty' and that Knight 'ought to have had his brains knocked out' for getting up in court. They 'would have sat for a month before they would have found a white man guilty of killing a parcel of cannibals'.[53] Plunkett attempted to have the two publicans indicted for contempt of court but Burton ruled that while their remarks were highly objectionable, they could not be accused of intimidating jurymen since the case had already been decided. This reverse afforded the *Herald* a convenient opportunity to lambast Plunkett, whom it described as 'not fit to exercise the extensive powers with which he is invested'. More importantly, it questioned the second jury's verdict:

> Are people, whatever may be their rank in life, to be thus muzzled? Are they to be told that after a case has been decided they are not to offer an opinion adverse to the conduct of the Jury . . .?—not to say, if they think it, that the Judge was partial, or took an erroneous view of the law; and that the Jury were . . . a parcel of fools or something worse?[54]

[51] Keck to Thomas McQuoid, 21 December 1838, *CO*, 201/284, p. 93.
[52] 20 December 1838.
[53] *The Australian*, 6 and 11 December 1838.
[54] 14 December 1838.

Not surprisingly, the *Herald* also raged against Plunkett's intention of putting Davey in the witness box:

> Will a young savage, who must be instructed as a parrot would be instructed, be admitted to give evidence in a case of life and death? Does any rational man suppose that such evidence be anything but one-sided? . . . By what process is he to be suddenly turned from his fear of 'Debil-Debil' into a rational creature understanding the responsibility he incurs in invoking the God of the Christians to attest the truth of what he may utter in the witness box? Is he to be tutored by some canting hypocrite, as a black cockatoo would be tutored, and be placed in the witness box to repeat what he has been so taught—at the peril of four men's lives? . . . We trust that, should any such witness be pushed into the witness box, that the Counsel for the defence will probe his competency to the quick, and not permit the possibility of four men's lives being frittered away upon the statements . . . of a young black savage, possessing no more idea of ultimate responsibility . . . than a baboon.[55]

The Attorney-General had postponed indicting the four other Myall Creek men the second time in the hope of finding Davey and obtaining an *approver*, i.e. having one of them turn Queen's evidence. But Davey could not be located, the men (as originally advised by Scott) did not 'split' and Plunkett finally told Gipps in February 1839 that they would have to be discharged. Gipps had already reported to Glenelg that Scott's name had been removed from the list of magistrates due to his actions prior to and during the first trial which had 'contributed, I have no doubt, to produce a verdict . . . directly against the evidence'.[56] Scott's advice to the men had prevented an *approver* and consequently 'it was not possible to get at the different shades of guilt, which attached to the different prisoners, or to ascertain who were the first instigators . . . and who might have come into it reluctantly'.[57] Gipps was convinced that although the men who had been hanged were all guilty, one of the four others 'was the most guilty of the whole'.[58] While accepting Plunkett's recommendation to release them, he told Glenelg that he did this 'not so much moved by any doubt of their guilt, as by the hope that the law might be considered as

[55] 24 December 1838.
[56] Gipps to Glenelg, 20 December 1838, *HRA*, XIX, p. 705.
[57] Ibid., pp. 705-6.
[58] Ibid., p. 706.

sufficiently vindicated by the executions which had already taken place'.[59]

The immediate effect of the trials and executions was the undermining of confidence of squatters and their servants who had previously killed Aborigines or had come very close to doing so. Although the *Sydney Gazette, The Monitor* and *The Colonist* expressed horror at the grisly details revealed in the evidence, *The Sydney Herald* was much more in touch with popular opinion in its shock and indignation that white men should pay with their lives for killing 'blacks'—especially since settlers, soldiers and police had been doing so with official encouragement for the past thirty years. In a memorandum to Robert Scott in January 1839, George Bowman referred to the punitive expeditions to the Hawkesbury in 1816-17 and to Bathurst in 1824 when 'The Military did not attempt to take the Blacks and make Prisoners of them but shot all they fell in with and received great praise from the Government for so doing'.[60] And Alexander Harris wrote that the men had been observing a custom which had been sanctioned by the government since the very foundation of the colony. The squatting interest generally regarded the conviction of the men in the second trial as 'a mere trick' and their execution as nothing less than 'legal murder'.

Another serious charge was that the government was showing partiality towards the Aborigines in the administration of justice. As the *Herald* put it:

> Let there be a rumour of an outrage committed on a black, and the Government is eager enough to interfere, and invoke the vengeance of the law against the aggressors. Not so, however, in the case of cannibalizing murders of whites by blacks.[62]

The squatters regarded Myall Creek as the inevitable result of the government's failure to provide adequate protection in the squatting districts. Despite the inconvenient fact that the Aborigines killed were mostly women and children who had no connection with attacks on sheep and cattle down river, the Myall Creek men were represented as faithful servants protecting their masters' property. Harris and many others took the view that the seven had

[59] Gipps to Glenelg, 26 February 1839, *HRA*, XX, p. 40.
[60] Bowman to Scott, 5 January 1839, *BP*, No. 102.
[61] *Settlers and Convicts*, p. 220.
[62] 18 December 1838.

been sacrificed to the 'protection' theory and that 'the law was in effect punishing men for remedying its own neglect'.[63]

After the trials, greater pains were taken by whites to conceal or destroy the bodies of Aborigines they had killed and prosecutions became almost impossible. Reports of poisoning from a number of districts were also difficult to prove in a court of law. For their part, the squatters claimed that Aborigines had been poisoned by eating the entrails of sheep which had died from the arsenic dressing used to cure scab.[64] Because of the paucity of legal evidence, this was the explanation which the authorities themselves were obliged to 'swallow'.

Many squatters believed that the hanging of the seven whites was interpreted by the Aborigines as an open mandate for renewed depredations and acts of revenge. One wrote to *The Colonist* from the Liverpool Plains in February 1839 that

> The blacks know [that the whites are unable to protect themselves] and accordingly they have within the last few weeks declared that they are protected by the 'Cabon Guberner', and by 'Bugery Mr. Day' in waging a war of extermination not only against the sheep and cattle, but also against the white men on the Big River.[65]

Others claimed that Aborigines in the older settled parts of the district who had previously been 'tame' were now being reinforced by 'myalls' or 'wild blacks' from outlying parts in nightly raids on stock.

It has already been noted[66] that following the arrest of the Myall Creek men, there was a definite attempt on the part of the squatting interest to represent Aborigines as less than human—and an equally vigorous response from Evangelicals and others emphasizing their essential humanity. When the full details of the massacre became available, the Evangelicals were filled with horror and righteous indignation. For them the massacre symbolized the colonists' his-

---

[63] *Settlers and Convicts*, p. 220.
[64] C. Hodgkinson, *Australia from Port Macquarie to Moreton Bay; . . .* , London 1845, p. 114. There are at least two good reasons for rejecting this hypothesis: firstly, the Aborigines would not eat animals which they had not killed or seen slaughtered; secondly, some of the stations where poisoning was reported were stocking only cattle at the time. However, it is true that they did like to eat entrails.
[65] *The Colonist*, 13 February 1839, letter from 'Stat Umbra'.
[66] See Ch. 2.

tory of injustice towards the Aborigines. In October 1838 the Rev. John Saunders described this to his Baptist congregation in Sydney as 'national guilt'[67] and a month later J. D. Lang held up the treatment of Aborigines and convicts as the two 'public or national sins' of New South Wales. In a thundering sermon, which might well be compared with another preached by the Dominican Antonio de Montesinos more than three hundred years earlier to the settlers of Hispaniola on their cruelty to the Indians,[68] Lang described the harsh drought then affecting most of the colony as Divine retribution for 'blood-guiltiness'.

Nor was it difficult for him to find an Old Testament parallel in the three years of drought following Saul's destruction of the Gibeonites, 'a miserable tribe of ancient Aboriginal inhabitants of the land of Israel' who had been condemned by the Almighty 'to utter extermination because of their flagrant, their abominable and their heaven-defying iniquities'.[69] If God had so punished the house of Saul for the slaughter of those who were foredoomed, he asked, how much greater would His vengeance be on the colonists for the destruction of those against whom no curse had been recorded?

> let us ask ourselves seriously . . . whether . . . we can lay our hands upon our hearts, and plead *not guilty* concerning the Gibeonites, I mean the wretched Aboriginal inhabitants of this land? . . . Not only have we despoiled them of their land, and given them in exchange European vice and European disease in every foul and fatal form, but the blood of hundreds, nay of thousands . . . who have fallen from time to time in their native forests, when waging unequal warfare with their civilized aggressors, still stains the hands of many of the inhabitants of the land!

Lang dismissed the plea of those who, having had little or no contact with the Aborigines, felt that they had not contracted guilt: 'when God visits a nation for its national sins, the sword of justice falls indiscriminately on all the families of the nation'. Just as the children of Israel suffered for the deeds of the house of Saul, so the people of New South Wales would suffer for the crimes of the squatters and their convict servants. The destruction of the Aborigines had been made possible by

[67] *The Colonist*, 17, 20 and 24 October 1838.
[68] Lewis Hanke, *The Spanish Struggle for Justice in the Conquest of America*, Philadelphia 1949, pp. 17-18.
[69] *National Sins*, p. 13. The following quotations are from the same source.

the low standard of public opinion that has been created by general consent in this colony, in reference to the ri[ghts] of the Aborigines . . . and for the creation of this . . . every individual member of this community is personally responsible.

Furthermore, he assured his congregation, the Lord of Sabaoth had already heard the cry of their wrongs and 'When he maketh inquisition for blood, he remembereth them'. Two days later rain fell on Sydney, but the resulting humidity brought on an epidemic of influenza which carried off many of the aged and the very young. Lang returned triumphantly to his theme: '[God] has been pleased to pour into that cup of mercy a few drops from the vial of his indignation and wrath'.

Others, like Eliza Dunlop, Irish Catholic wife of the Wollombi magistrate, were stirred to literary efforts. In December 1838 *The Australian* published Mrs Dunlop's poem 'The Aboriginal Mother' in which a woman survivor of Myall Creek vowed 'To shew their God how treacherously/The stranger men destroy.'[70] And Henry Parkes, no friend of the squatters since his early labours in Sir John Jamison's[71] vineyards near Parramatta, repeated the theme of 'white savagism' when he recalled David Collins' description of the two Aboriginal boys murdered near Windsor in 1796:

> Loud talk ye of the savages
> As they were beasts of prey!—
> But men of English birth have done
> More savage things than they.

[70] 13 December 1838. Later set to music by Isaac Nathan and dedicated to Lady Gipps. (*The Sydney Morning Herald*, 27 August 1842.) Mrs Dunlop and her daughter Rachel, who later married David Milson, took a keen interest in the Aborigines of the Wollombi area and studied their language. Mrs Dunlop's MS. collection, 'The Vase, comprising songs for music and poems', ML, MS.B1541, contains notes on 'Native Poetry' as well as other poems on Aboriginal themes. Mrs Milson's 'Kamilaroi vocabulary and aboriginal songs; . . .', ML, MS.A1668, contains translations of two interesting Aboriginal songs recording their reactions to the whites. See Roy H. Goddard, 'Aboriginal Poets as Historians', *Mankind*, Vol. I, No. 10, October 1934, pp. 243-6 and *The Life and Times of James Milson*, Melbourne 1955. Myall Creek also inspired Charles Harpur's poem 'An Aboriginal Mother's Lament' written about ten years after the event.

[71] Jamison's 'Baan Baa' station on the Namoi River was one of the first on the Liverpool Plains and according to Threlkeld was known as a 'murdering station' because of the treatment of Aborigines there. Another 'murdering station' was Cobb's.

Attributing Aboriginal depredations to the justified resentment felt by a dispossessed and uncompensated race, Parkes painted a grim picture of the survivors,

> . . . in desert corners driven
> Crouch tamely in disgrace,
> Till hunted by the fire-arm'd men
> From every hiding-place![72]

The Myall Creek case had the effect of temporarily rallying colonial philanthropists into some semblance of unity. In October 1838 two well-attended public meetings in Sydney resulted in the formation of the Australian Aborigines' Protection Society[73] with Lang, Saunders and Threlkeld as some of the leading lights. At the first meeting on 16 October a number of speakers told an overflowing audience at the Mechanics' Institute hall that the Myall Creek affair emphasized the urgent need to protect Aborigines from the wanton brutality of whites. Robinson spoke for no less than three hours on his experiences in Van Diemen's Land and Saunders launched a blistering attack on the *Herald's* attitude to the Myall Creek trials—which resulted in the newspaper suing him for libel.

In spite of the initial enthusiasm, the Society does not appear to have survived more than two or three months at the most. It could not match the influence of its active British parent on the Colonial Office and there were few opportunities for organized activity in the colony. Nor could the small band of colonial philanthropists maintain the new organization in addition to the various missionary aid groups already existing. Once the horror of Myall Creek had been dissipated by the execution of seven of the culprits and by the passage of time, there was very little momentum to sustain the more broadly-based Society with its call for inter-denominational cooperation. Furthermore, failure to criticize Major Nunn's expedition and the Port Macquarie affair weakened its position in the public eye by identifying it with the colonial government.

---

[72] *The Weekly Register*, 27 July 1844. The poem was probably written some years before being published.
[73] A copy of its constitution is preserved in the Ferguson Collection and a list of its Committee of Management can be found in *The Colonist*, 3 October 1838. The Society was established as a branch of the British and Foreign Aborigines' Protection Society.

Nevertheless, the denominational organizations continued to invoke Myall Creek as proof of the need for constant vigilance. At the second annual meeting of the Society in Aid of the German Mission in January 1839, Lang and Saunders warned of the need to guard against the repetition of Myall Creek.[74] Sections of the Sydney press also came forward to champion the rights of the Aborigines. Edward Hall of *The Monitor* and *The Australian* and William Duncan of *The Morning Chronicle* and *The Weekly Register* took a keen interest in Aboriginal welfare from this time and some of Hall's articles were reprinted in British periodicals.

RIGHTS OF THE ABORIGINES

One significant offshoot of the controversy aroused by Myall Creek was a debate over Aboriginal rights and land rights in general. Sustained by opposition to the Port Phillip Protectorate and by the Lee case in 1842, it provided an occasion to discuss the whole question of squatting tenure. Although slight by comparison with the protracted discussions in Spain during the early sixteenth century over the status and treatment of Indians in Hispaniola and Cuba[75] and the later discussion in North America,[76] the debate was a unique reflection of how the better educated section of the squatting interest saw the colonization of New South Wales in the grand scheme of things. Moreover, the process of dispossession and destruction of the Aborigines was more marked and dramatic during this period than at any other time in colonial history and there were some philanthropists who found it necessary to answer the moral questions which this process inevitably raised.

The principal legal question was whether the Aborigines possessed a prior right to the land which had been proclaimed the property of the British Crown by right of discovery, and which the squatters were now claiming as theirs by right of preoccupancy.

On one side were the Evangelicals who argued that since the

---

[74] *The Colonist*, 9 January 1839.
[75] See Hawke, *The Spanish Struggle for Justice*.
[76] Wilcomb E. Washburn, *Red Man's Land/White Man's Law: A Study of the Past and Present Status of the American Indian*, New York 1971, and 'The Moral and Legal Justifications for Dispossessing the Indians' in J. M. Smith (ed.), *Seventeenth Century America: Essays in Colonial History*, North Carolina 1959, pp. 15-32. See also, A. K. Weinberg, *Manifest Destiny: A Study of Nationalist Expansionism in American History*, Baltimore 1935.

whites had taken away the Aborigines' land (and hence their livelihood) and had introduced European vices and disease, they were
morally bound to make compensation in the form of material
assistance and spiritual guidance. It was assumed that the 'majority
of the intruders on native soils have acted directly in opposition . . .
to every law, human and divine'[77] and that the white settlers of
New South Wales were largely responsible for the moral degeneracy
and rapid extinction of the Aborigines. In a series of articles published in *The Colonist* in 1835,[78] for example, J. D. Lang had
elaborated on his view that the one antidote to this 'moral pestil-
ence' was Christianity. The settlers and the government, he claimed,
were under an obligation to support all missionary endeavours
among the Aborigines—all, that is, except those of the Roman
Catholic Church. Lang recognized the prior occupancy of the
Aborigines and on several occasions wrote of the Aborigines' individual and collective sense of ownership and their bitterness
at being dispossessed by the whites. However, he still subscribed
to the Lockeian view that 'he who put land to its most productive
use had the best claim to it'. A contributor to the *Australian and
New Zealand Monthly Magazine* in 1842 found it deplorable that
the whites had considered themselves exempt from any form of
obligation to the Aborigines, but believed that civilization was sufficient reward. He regarded it as the responsibility of the whites

> to subvert . . . the aborigines from their useless lives, and to train
> them . . . to the knowledge of the advantages resulting from an ac-
> quaintance with the more useful arts and sciences; likewise to make
> them understand the value of living under the protection of that form
> of government which guarantees a full protection of their persons,
> privileges and properties; and lastly, an intermingling of the races by
> marriage should be promoted, by which means a more effectual
> guarantee is afforded for a reformation than by all the others com-
> bined.[79]

Another version of the case for compensation was put forward
by the Rev. John Saunders in his sermon of 14 October 1838[80]
describing the whites' injustice to the Aborigines as 'national guilt'.
Emphasizing that 'each tribe had its distinct locality and each

[77] *Australian and New Zealand Monthly Magazine*, No. 5, 1842, p. 292.
[78] 5, 12 and 19 November 1835.
[79] No. 5, 1842, p. 292.
[80] Reported in *The Colonist*, 17, 20 and 24 October 1838.

M

superior person in the tribe a portion of this district', Saunders said that the whites had not only taken away the Aborigines' land and destroyed their game but had brutalized them through intoxication, fraud and theft and had even bribed them to shed each other's blood by way of public entertainment. Finally, they had avenged the deaths of whites by killing one hundred Aborigines for every white killed. Taking his text from *Isaiah*, Saunders warned that the only means of avoiding Divine retribution for this national sin was to make full restitution: 'It is our duty', he said, 'to recompense the Aborigines to the extent that we have injured them'.

In an editorial of 12 December 1838 headed 'The Lords of the Soil', *The Colonist* accepted Saunders' charge of 'national guilt', believing that the right of civilized countries to take possession of barbarian ones rested on the principle that the invaders should give '*a full equivalent*'. However, that equivalent was to be determined by 'circumstances':

> In some cases, as in that of the intelligent New Zealanders, price may be a matter of bargain between the native and the foreigner; but in others, such as the benighted New Hollanders, whose mental imbecility disqualifies them for entering into a formal compact, the only equivalent that can be rendered is a benevolent care for the amelioration of his condition.

The Evangelical position, for all its rhetoric, was significantly more compromising than that of Bishop Broughton whose outburst during the 1842 Legislative Council debate on the Lee case must have raised some eyebrows:

> The aboriginal natives of the colony, so far as they may choose to use it, have an equal, nay a superior right to white men, to subdue and replenish the soil, and anyone who goes among the Aborigines, and interferes with their natural right of procuring the necessaries of existence, is an aggressor . . .[81]

The position of the British and colonial governments had always been that New South Wales was a Crown possession by right of discovery. John Batman's attempt in 1835 to promote a claim to land at Port Phillip by means of two treaties with the Aborigines had been rejected out of hand, even though these had not been represented by Batman as conferring any title. Lord Glenelg with

[81] *The Sydney Morning Herald*, 24 August 1842.

all his avowed sympathy for the Aborigines believed not only that a recognition of the Aborigines' right to alienate land would undermine the whole position of the Crown, but that it would not be in the Aborigines' best interests to possess such a right. The 1837 Report, however, exerted an important influence on Colonial Office policy, pointing out, among other things, that the native inhabitants of British colonies possessed an 'incontrovertible right' to the soil. This 'incontrovertible right' was evidently not regarded by the committee as investing the Aborigines with any effective *legal* title. Besides, they had recommended that treaties should be discouraged since natives always had the weaker bargaining position. But it formed part of an argument designed to persuade the British government to assume responsibility for the material and spiritual welfare of all indigenous peoples. As already indicated, this subsequently provided the rationale for the establishment of the Port Phillip Protectorate and for Russell's authorization of fifteen per cent of the Land Fund to finance 'protection'.

On the other side the squatting interest asserted their right not only to the land which they were using, but to land as yet untouched by pastoral expansion. They resented the Crown's progressive attempts to reassert its title to all unalienated land, especially through the 1839 and 1842 Acts, and were incensed by an increase in the upset price of land to £1 per acre and the new squatting regulations introduced by Gipps in 1844. To them, the appointment of Protectors responsible only to the British government was a further argument for colonial control of the Civil List and the revenue derived from Crown Land sales. In their view, the 'waste' or unalienated land of New South Wales belong to the 'colonists' (i.e. themselves), and the British government and its colonial agent (the governor) had no right to dispose of this land and its proceeds.

The squatters' case rested on three arguments, the first being that the Aborigines had made no use of the land and had therefore foregone any claim to preoccupancy. In the words of John Cotton of 'Doogallook' on the Goulburn River, they were 'unprofitable occupants of a fine country and ought to be dispossessed'.[82] There was no question that the Aborigines had come to New South Wales

---

82 Mackaness, *Correspondence of John Cotton*, Pt. 3, p. 9.

before anyone else but 'the mere priority of arrival' was not seen as conferring any paramount right. Captain Phillip, argued *The Sydney Herald* in a series of articles in early 1841 occasioned by the resumption of land for Protector Parker's new station on the River Loddon, had as much right to come to New South Wales by sea as the Aborigines had by land and was just as much directed by Providence as was their arrangement into tribes living in different localities.

The 'lords of the soil', as the Aborigines were sarcastically described in the squatting press, had never really 'occupied' the land at all but had wandered over it as if it were a common:

> their ownership, their right, was nothing more than that of the Emu or the Kangaroo. They bestowed no labour upon the land and that— and *that only*—it is which gives property in it.[83]

Unlike the North American Indians, they were not divided into nations with fixed localities, cultivating the ground and understanding the right of property. Consequently, the British nation had taken possession of 'a vast waste' which it now had the right to dispose. The whites, however, had through their labour won the right of preoccupancy:

> the mere fact of a certain tribe or number of tribes of the black aborigines having, in their wanderings, arrived first. . . . gives them no priority of right,—no paramount right to the soil of Botany Bay or Port Phillip, so long as they add nothing thereto in the way of improvement. The whites, by their improvements, though they arrived second in point of time, have acquired a right to the soil where they have improved it, which is good in law, equity, and common sense, against the whole fraternity of prior black wanderers.[84]

The Aborigines, it was agreed, could have acquired similar rights by developing the natural resources of New South Wales but instead they had forfeited their opportunity through laziness and prodigality. As John Cotton explained to a relative in England:

> The worthless, idle aborigine has been driven back from the land that he knew not how to make use of, and valued not, to make room for a more noble race of beings, who are capable of estimating the value of this fine country. Is it not right that it should be so? Imagine an illiterate country boor to be possessed of a noble palace fitted with

[83] *The Sydney Herald*, 7 November 1838.
[84] 16 March 1841.

valuable pictures, books and works of art, and surrounded by a princely domain; imagine that this boor, instead of inhabiting his palace and instructing himself by reading the books or learning to read them, and admiring the beautiful works of art around him, should take up his residence in a mountain hut smoking his pipe in idleness all the day; would you not think it right that such a person should be dispossessed of that which he did not know how to enjoy or appreciate? It would be no use to him as he did not know the value of his possession.[85]

The squatters argued that they had developed the resources of New South Wales, bringing wealth and happiness to tens of thousands of people who would otherwise have been doomed to squalid poverty in Britain. In support of their position they cited the opinions of the famous jurists Sir William Blackstone and Emerich de Vattel, but the most frequently invoked authority was John Locke's statement that

> the labour of a man's body, and the work of his hands, we may say are properly his. Whatsoever . . . he removes out of the state that nature hath provided and left it in, he hath mixed his labour with, and joined it to something that is his own, and thereby makes it his property.[86]

This suggested the convenient proposition that a squatter who had 'converted' or 'improved' vast tracts of 'waste' land in New South Wales into sheep and cattle runs had thereby acquired a 'natural' claim to ownership.

A leading article in the *Herald* of 7 November 1838 asserted that the pastoralists had not only won the right to the land they were using, but had improved the value of adjacent land and were thereby entitled to control its disposal and the expenditure of revenue raised from its lease or sale. This revenue, it said, belonged to the people who had given a Civil List and not, as Russell and Gipps claimed, to the Crown:

> We assert . . . that every shilling of the land revenue of this Colony which has been appropriated by the mere order of the Secretary Of State . . . has been illegally appropriated.

The Crown was 'merely a trustee' for unoccupied lands on behalf of the 'colonists'.

---

[85] Mackaness, *Correspondence of John Cotton*, Pt. 3, p. 9.
[86] Quoted by *The Sydney Herald*, 5 December 1839.

The final argument advanced by the squatting interest was that the British settlers, by virtue of their Christianity and their superior civilization, were performing the role to which God and History had destined them.

> The British people found a portion of the globe in a state of waste—they took possession of it; and they had a perfect right to do so; under the Divine authority, by which man was commanded to go forth and people and *till* the land.[87]

The Australian of 17 October 1839 cited the precedent of the Norman Conquest which, although initially disastrous, had infused the honest and virtuous councils of the Saxons with 'a spirit of acuteness and enterprise'. The whole of Greek and Jewish, as well as English history, was invoked to show that the settlers of New South Wales were carrying out a 'heaven-commissioned task' in colonizing a new country. Each period of ancient and modern history demonstrated the 'eternal truth . . . that power is the herald and pioneer of human enlightenment and happiness'.

The most thorough-going refutation of Aboriginal rights was made by the lawyer Richard Windeyer who had defended the Myall Creek men in court. Windeyer indicated an interest in Aboriginal welfare by joining the Aborigines' Protection Society and by later calling for a special committee on the condition of the Aborigines. But at the Society's first meeting he went to some pains to make the point that the Aborigines possessed no title to land.[88] And at a public lecture in 1844 he argued that since the Aborigines could not be said to have had either laws or personal property in land when the whites arrived, they could not even claim the rights of a conquered nation. Caricaturing the customs of the Aborigines as little more than a collection of bestial perversions, including polygamy and cannibalistic infanticide, he concluded that they were 'almost in that state of nature conceived by Hobbes . . . in which all having a right to everything, a consequence is the war of all against all'.[89] Indeed, he went so far as to deny that they possessed a society at all. Pointing out that the tribe was not a

---

[87] *The Sydney Herald*, 7 November 1838. James Macarthur used this argument during the debate on the Lee case in 1842. *The Sydney Morning Herald*, 24 August 1842.
[88] *The Australian*, 18 October 1838.
[89] 'On the Rights of the Aborigines of Australia', ML, MS.A1400, p. 23.

political unit, he cited Sir James Mackintosh's pronouncement that 'no society has ever subsisted or ever could subsist without being protected by government and bound together by Laws'.[90]

Windeyer's view of the history of human civilization was that property rights were always preceded by personal rights—and yet the Aborigines seemed to him to lack even these:

> the fact is that they have no laws properly so called, that the condemnation of the Breton Law by Edward 3rd's Parliament at Kilkenny as a 'lewd custom' may both in the ancient and modern sense of the language be applied to their practices without a particle of injustice.[91]

Consequently, the taking up of land by squatters in New South Wales was not an invasion of the rights of the Aborigines since the latter possessed no rights to speak of. It was yet another illustration of that 'grand, fundamental law . . . that those who have should take the power and those should keep who can'. Nor would Windeyer even concede that the Aborigines had any special rights to the kangaroos which, unlike the sheep and cattle in the squatting districts, had been given to mankind in common. 'What have they done to make them theirs more than ours?', he asked.

The squatters in Windeyer's audience rapped their benches in approbation but a few days later William Duncan in *The Morning Chronicle* attacked the lecture as yet another example of what he regarded as the transparent hypocrisy of the squatting interest. Blackstone, wrote Duncan, was a 'pander to power'. And if cultivation alone endowed land rights, what was to prevent Admiral du Petit Thoire, who had recently been active in Tahiti, or even the Dutch, from taking over the 10,000 or so square miles of land leased by Dr Alexander Imlay on the south coast of New South Wales, of which not one acre was tilled? And would Sir Robert Peel uphold Windeyer's legal opinion if the Prussians established an agricultural settlement on the northern coast? In fact, said Duncan, the Aborigines had been robbed of their land by the 'right' of *vi et armis capere* as practised by Alexander, Mahmoud and Lord Ellenborough, but in each of these cases the conqueror had incurred and had recognized a moral responsibility for the welfare

[90] Ibid., p. 29.
[91] Ibid., p. 27.

of the conquered. It was not sufficient to take away the Aborigines' land and hand them Bibles.[92]

The debate on Aboriginal rights was more than a mere exercise in polemics. For those concerned with Aboriginal welfare, it was part of the effort to arouse a sense of moral responsibility in the colonists. For the squatting interest, it was closely associated with their own special preoccupation with land tenure and colonial control of land policy and the Land Fund. A Hunter River correspondent to the *Herald* attacked the British government's stand in the matter as being hypocritical:

> If as the *canters* of the present day maintain, the blacks have *an original right* in the soil, *let the government be honest and buy it of them*: but if they continue to drive them back as they do the kangaroos, and sell and lease us the land, let us not have our lives put in jeopardy by these savages, disputing with us for the lands which the government has sold or leased to us.[93]

But the most realistic view of the clash of interests between Aborigines and whites was stated by Alexander Harris:

> if we want a league of peace on equal grounds, really there is no road to it but that we give up their land and forsake their country: for this and this only is the source of the aggravation.[94]

[92] *The Morning Chronicle*, 22 June 1844.
[93] 22 April 1839.
[94] *Settlers and Convicts*, p. 222.

CHAPTER FIVE

Gipps and the Aborigines

I have heard tales and some things I have seen that
would form as dark a page as ever you read in a book of
history, but I thank God I have never participated in
them. If I could remedy these things, I would speak
loudly though it cost me all I am worth in the world,
but as I cannot, I will keep aloof and know nothing
and say nothing.

HENRY MEYRICK

. . . from the difficulty and uncertainty of bringing . . .
[Aborigines] to justice, there is a disposition, engen-
dered in the minds of the less principled portion of the
White Population, to take the law into their own
hands. . .

SIR GEORGE GIPPS

THE RULE OF LAW

The enormity of the Myall Creek affair and reports of further strife
in the Liverpool Plains and Portland Bay areas prompted Gipps to
seek a more effective enforcement of law in the squatting districts.
The new Crown Lands Bill[1] which he presented to an extraordinary session of the Legislative Council in February 1839 provided
for the establishment of a special force of Border Police[2] to be
attached to the Crown Lands Commissioners. 'The law as it respects
Aborigines', he told Glenelg when forwarding the Bill, 'required
neither improvement, nor alteration; the means only were required

---

[1] 2 Vict., No. 27: 'An Act further to restrain the unauthorised occupation of
Crown Lands, and to provide the means of defraying the expense of a
Border Police', GG, 6 April 1839, pp. 393-9.
[2] This was by no means Gipps' own idea. Sadleir had made such a suggestion
in 1837 and it had been repeated in the Hunter River Black Association's
petition of September 1838. The Colonist, 22 September 1838.

of putting the Law into execution'.[3] However, while pointing out that the legislation made no mention of protecting the Aborigines, Gipps emphasized that its main purpose was to put an end to the atrocities being committed by both races in the squatting districts. The Commissioners, for example, were empowered to withhold squatting licences on grounds including 'any malicious injury or offence committed upon or against any aboriginal native'. Anticipating Colonial Office criticism that by facilitating occupation of the squatting districts and providing security for cattle and sheep he was encouraging dispersion of the white population and lessening inducement to purchase land within the limits of location, Gipps added:

> it is too late to calculate the evils of dispersion . . . All the power of Government, aided even by a Military force ten times greater than that which is maintained in the Colony, would not suffice to bring back within the limits of our twenty counties the Flocks and Herds, which now stray hundreds of miles beyond them; and therefore the only question is whether we will abandon all control over these distant regions, and have the occupiers of them unrestrained in their lawless aggressions upon each other and upon the Aborigines, or make such efforts, as are in our power, to preserve order amongst all classes.[4]

In his speech to the Council, Gipps had explained that since the Border Police would be protecting squatters and their property, licence-holders were to pay half the cost of its equipment and maintenance in the form of a poll tax on sheep, cattle and horses.

It was only after the establishment of the Border Police that Gipps had sufficient confidence to publish in full the original notice on the Aborigines which he had drafted in April of the previous year after receiving Glenelg's instructions. This statement left no doubt about his determination to enforce Glenelg's policy on the legal status of Aborigines:

> As human beings partaking of our common nature—as the Aboriginal possessors of the soil from which the wealth of this country has been principally derived—and as the subjects of the Queen, whose authority extends over every part of New Holland—the Natives of this Colony have an equal right with the people of European origin to the protection and assurance of the Law of England.

[3] Gipps to Glenelg, 6 April 1839, *HRA*, XX, p. 91.
[4] Ibid., pp. 91-2.

To allow either to injure or oppress the other, or to permit the stronger to regard the weaker party as aliens with whom a war can exist, and against whom they may exercise belligerent rights, is not less inconsistent with the spirit of that Law than it is at variance with the dictates of justice and humanity.[5]

The first case to be considered after Myall Creek was Major Nunn's clash with the Aborigines of the Namoi and Gwydir rivers which had taken place in January 1838. Day had been instructed to take depositions from Nunn and his men, but before this could be arranged reports were received of the attack on William Faithfull's party at the Broken River and all available Mounted Police were sent to the Port Phillip District. Shortly afterwards the reports from Myall Creek took Day to the Liverpool Plains for seven weeks and he was then subpoenaed as a witness at the two trials. Consequently it was not until April 1839 that the first depositions were taken from Nunn and his men.

Plunkett, however, pointed out that the depositions could not be allowed as evidence against them.[6] Moreover, the Executive Council was of the opinion that the Aborigines had been the 'aggressors' and that the lapse of time and the difficulty of reassembling the witnesses would render an investigation almost impossible. A bizarre feature of the case was that Major Nunn and one of his officers were magistrates and should by rights have conducted an immediate inquest on the bodies of the Aborigines for whose deaths they and their men had been responsible.

The Executive Council decided that there was no point in pressing the investigation, feeling bound to

draw the widest distinction between the case of those murderers of men, women, and children, without personal provocation and in cold blood, and that of Officers and men repelling an attack made upon them, while acting under orders in execution of their duty.[7]

Few colonists would have respected this distinction, especially since it had long been common practice for parties of settlers and their servants to assist soldiers or police in 'dispersing' Aborigines from the vicinity of stations and towns. A number of stockmen from stations on the Liverpool Plains had accompanied Major

[5] GG, 21 May 1839, p. 606.
[6] Enclosure, Gipps to Glenelg, 22 July 1839, HRA, XX, p. 257.
[7] Ibid., p. 247.

Nunn's party, as had the then Crown Lands Commissioner for Liverpool Plains, Alexander Paterson. Besides, the Council's overriding concern was more practical than its utterances indicated. In a private despatch to Glenelg in April 1838 Gipps had expressed its apprehension that 'mischief' might ensue if offence were given to officers and men of the Mounted Police, most of whom were volunteers from regiments serving in the colony and at liberty to resign from police duties at any time.[8]

Nor was Plunkett so assiduous in prosecuting cases involving government officers. In his report to Gipps in March 1838 on the possible unlawfulness of Mitchell's action on the Darling, he had emphasized that none of the witnesses before the Executive Council inquiry could be certain that any Aborigines had been killed and that an inquest or any prosecution for homicide could not have been held unless a dead body was found. Believing that a fresh investigation could not produce any clearer result and would only 'raise a prejudice against an absent and highly meritorious Public Officer', the Attorney-General then recommended that it was unnecessary to take any further steps in the case.[9]

Together with his pronouncement on the legal status of Aborigines, Gipps also republished in May 1839 Bourke's order forbidding forcible detention of Aboriginal women in the squatting districts.[10] In one leading article *The Sydney Herald* asked:

> How dares the [British] Government presume thus to lecture the colonists of New South Wales on their duties towards the blacks?

And in another:

> We repeat, that this official notification is an insult to the settlers . . . the rest of this notice . . . is on a par with many other effusions emanating ostensibly from Sir George Gipps; and will serve to demonstrate in aftertimes the wisdom of his whiggish patrons, who inflict upon the colonists their drawling philanthropy and mawkish sentimentality.[11]

Gipps had already increased his unpopularity with local and British investors of the Australian Agricultural Company in 1838

---

[8] Gipps to Glenelg, 27 April 1838, Transcripts of Missing Despatches 1833-8, ML, MS.A1267⁵, pp. 938-9.
[9] Plunkett to Deas Thomson, 27 March 1838, enclosed with Gipps' despatch to Glenelg, 18 April 1838, *CO*, 201/272, Reel 311, pp. 347-9.
[10] *GG*, May 1839, p. 606.
[11] 10 June; 5 July 1839.

by insisting that Bourke's order was to be strictly observed by the Company on its three pastoral holdings, two of which were on the Liverpool Plains beyond the limits of location. For some years the Company had been complaining of insufficient convicts being made available to them as assigned servants. J. S. Brownrigg repeated to Glenelg the complaint of former Colonial Commissioner Dumaresq that those received contained 'an undue and unfair proportion of the worst and most depraved characters from the Iron Gangs'[12] and demanded police assistance to maintain law and order on its remote stations which altogether employed 200 men. The Company had also made strenuous objections when Gipps, irritated by the Company's coal monopoly and the high price of 8s. per ton which it was thereby able to secure, began to investigate the possibilities of establishing government mines. Consequently the Company reacted violently to Gipps' warning that all their convicts would be withdrawn if rumours of assigned servants living and travelling with Aboriginal women were substantiated. In the colony, Acting Commissioner J. E. Ebsworth regretted that Gipps had not provided specific examples,[13] and in London former Commissioner Brownrigg claimed that not even the most glaring revelations of convict immorality on the Company's establishments would justify the ruinous action that Gipps had threatened.[14]

While the *Herald* was scornful of the order regarding Aboriginal women, the *Port Phillip Gazette* rejected Gipps' argument that since the squatters would derive most benefit from the Border Police, they should pay half the cost. Its editorial of 17 April 1839 claimed that all colonists would benefit from the pacification of the Aborigines and should therefore contribute to the upkeep of an institution which ensured protection for the wool industry, the staple export upon which the wealth, indeed the very existence of the colony, depended.

Gipps' second major step was to press for the admissibility of Aboriginal evidence in courts of law. One of the aspects of the Myall Creek trials which had attracted his attention was the difficulty of calling as a witness the Aboriginal stockman Davey who had seen the massacre and could probably have testified to

---

12 Brownrigg to Glenelg, 22 December 1838, Enclosure No. 2, Glenelg to Gipps, 12 January 1839, *HRA*, XIX, p. 746.
13 Ebsworth to Deas Thomson, 7 July 1838, ibid., p. 748.
14 Brownrigg to Glenelg, 22 December 1838, ibid., p. 747.

the degree of culpability of each of the eleven men. In order to remedy this anomaly, and in anticipation of a request from the Marquess of Normanby[15] who had succeeded Glenelg, Gipps in September 1839 introduced in the Legislative Council a Bill[16] designed to raise the evidence of Aborigines taken without a Bible oath to the level of *approvers*. This meant that evidence from Aboriginal witnesses could be accepted by a court if it was supported by corroborative evidence from other sources. The squatting interest was strongly opposed to the Bill and *The Australian*, whose editorial policy had swung to support for the squatting interest after a change in ownership, deprecated the Council's attempt to 'palm such a law on Her Majesty's subjects',[17] maintaining that it could not be reconciled with English law which rejected unsworn evidence. However, after being passed by the Council and forwarded to London it was disallowed by the Crown law officers as 'contrary to British laws'.[18]

The question was revived in 1843 when the British Parliament passed an Act[19] which removed all doubts that natives of British colonies were British subjects and admitted their unsworn evidence at the level of *approvers*. Informing Gipps of this, Stanley encouraged him to revive the 1839 Bill[20] but when it was re-introduced in the Legislative Council in June 1844, representatives of the squatting interest realized that if passed, it would have the force of the Imperial Act. Consequently they mounted a fierce debate and expressed sentiments which William Duncan thought would 'reflect little credit on the council or the colony.'[21] These revealed very clearly that the Myall Creek episode had not been forgotten: Wentworth and Windeyer revived the old catch-cry of

---

15 Normanby to Gipps, 31 August 1839, *HRA*, XX, pp. 302-5.
16 3 Vict., No. 16: 'An Act to allow the Aboriginal Natives of New South Wales to be received as Competent Witnesses in Criminal Cases', *GG*, 26 October 1839, p. 1197.
17 21 September 1839.
18 Russell to Gipps, 11 August 1840, *HRA*, XX, p. 756. A similar Bill devised by Governor John Hutt in Western Australia in 1841 was disallowed on the same grounds. G. R. Mellor, *British Imperial Trusteeship 1783-1850*, London 1951, p. 305.
19 5 Vict., cap. 22: 'An Act to authorize the Legislatures of certain of Her Majesty's Colonies to pass Laws for the admission in certain cases of unsworn testimony in Civil and Criminal proceedings.' *V&P*, 1849, I, p. 990. The legislation was largely influenced by Standish Motte's suggestions.
20 Stanley to Gipps, 6 July 1843, *HRA*, XXIII, p. 9.
21 *The Weekly Register*, 22 June 1844.

'judicial murder' which was again to be used in 1849 to defeat similar legislation.[22]

Wentworth compared Aboriginal evidence with 'the chatterings of the ourang-outang' and Major Mitchell insisted that 'the whole study of their lives was, how they should best conceal the workings of their minds from the eye of the observer'.[23] But the most interesting speech was made by Robert Lowe[24] whose motives in this instance were probably quite disinterested. For him, the Bible oath was indispensable to the administration of justice because belief in the existence of God and 'a future state of punishments and rewards' was the best test of a good conscience. However, an Aborigine, who was by definition without religious beliefs, would not possess the conscience to discern right from wrong. Lowe's speech showed that a highly-educated and enlightened Englishman could harbour prejudices as strong as those of men from less cultivated backgrounds:

> We could not pretend to much knowledge of the character of the aborigines; but believing them . . . a race of untutored savages, he must protest against leaving evidence so questionable to a jury at all. Only picture their examination. See the wild savage of the woods standing amid the hum and press of civilised men: among them, but not of them. See the trembling prisoner in vain endeavouring to gather his future fate from the stolid apathy or malignant scowl of those scarce human lineaments. Hear his evidence given through an interpreter, in a language . . . which . . . is destitute of abstract ideas, and of those nicely defined terms which distinguish the almost imperceptible limits of guilt and misfortune. See him become at once the supreme arbiter of life and death: a life of whose end and author he is alike ignorant, a death of whose fearful secrets he knows nothing—see him ready, from savage waywardness, from puerile petulance, or from a bribe so paltry that the meanest wretch whoever perjured himself for hire would spurn with contempt and disgust such a crime for such a

[22] A full report of this interesting debate can be found in *The Sydney Morning Herald*, 29 June 1849.

[23] *The Sydney Morning Herald*, 20 June 1844.

[24] Robert Lowe (1811-92), later Viscount Sherbrooke, arrived in Sydney in 1842 where he established a practice as a barrister in the Supreme Court. Elected to the Legislative Council in 1843, he at first sided with Gipps with whom he was personally acquainted but fell out with him over the 1844 squatting regulations which he regarded as unconstitutional. He was probably the most influential opponent of the 1844 Evidence Bill and spoke against similar legislation again in 1849. See R. L. Knight, *Illiberal Liberal: Robert Lowe in New South Wales, 1842-1850*, Melbourne 1966, and *ADB*, Vol. II, pp. 134-7.

price—see him ready to trample on a being of whose unspeakable importance to accountable agents he has never heard, and by false witness to hurry a fellow-creature into the presence of that God whose very name is a stranger to his language—see him, finally, after the last act of the tragedy is over, standing on the steps of the court, and, with his national talent for mimicry, representing to the admiring crowd the verdict of the foreman, the sentence of the judge, and the thrilling appeal of the prisoner for mercy: see all this, and then turn from the sickening mockery, and say, *Great is the Majesty of British Justice!*[25]

Supporters of the Bill, such at Roger Therry, saw it as a means of giving the Aborigines a degree of protection a little superior to that enjoyed by the beasts of the field: 'to place them on a footing somewhat superior to the ourang-outang, to the level of which animal . . . [Wentworth] had degraded them'. For William Bland, a pedantic insistence on the Bible oath was a 'legal fiction'. He claimed to have seen in English witnesses boxes 'men so deeply imbued in crime that it would be farcical to suppose that they could be actuated by any religious motives . . .'. But this support was of little avail against the squatting interest which easily succeeded in having the Bill thrown out.[26]

Of the Sydney and Melbourne press, only *The Morning Chronicle* and *The Weekly Register* lamented the failure of Gipps' efforts. For the squatting interest and the vast majority of colonists, the admission of Aboriginal evidence meant that more white men would be hanged. Consequently the Bill's defeat was a source of considerable relief. In August 1845 Stanley urged Gipps to make another attempt[27] but he replied that there was now no chance of its being accepted by the Council.[28]

Another measure to increase the efficiency of justice, this time in relation to the Aborigines, was defeated by petty jealousies among those entrusted with the responsibility of administering the law.

25 *The Sydney Morning Herald*, 20 June 1844. The following quotations are also from this source.
26 In the same year the Legislative Council of South Australia, despite opposition from the *South Australian Register*, passed an Aboriginal Evidence Ordinance with provisions similar to those in Gipps' unsuccessful Bill. See Hassell, *Relations between the Settlers and Aborigines in South Australia*, p. 90.
27 Stanley to Gipps, 31 August 1845, HRA, XXIV, p. 500.
28 A further attempt was narrowly defeated in 1849 and it was not until 1876 that the Legislative Assembly of N.S.W. passed an Act providing for the acceptance of Aboriginal evidence given under an affirmation.

In the early part of December 1840 Gipps was hoping to introduce a Bill which would enable a judge of the Supreme Court to hold an immediate assizes in Melbourne without the formality of being appointed Resident Justice. This, he told La Trobe,[29] was chiefly designed to dispose more speedily of a number of cases involving offences committed by Aborigines in the Port Phillip district. However, the judges of the Supreme Court could not agree and Gipps was reluctantly obliged to discard the plan.[30]

Gipps also made a vain attempt to reduce conflicts by prohibiting settlement in areas where Aborigines were known to be numerous, and in so doing precipitated his long battle with the squatting interest. In June 1840 Francis Allman, Commissioner for the Wellington Valley district, told Gipps of rumours that Aborigines had been driven away from water-holes on the Bogan River and was directed to make an investigation. He later reported that he could not confirm the rumours, but that there was a 'great want of water' in the district and that it would be advisable not to issue licences for depasturing more than twenty miles beyond Mount Harris. Gipps agreed to this[31] and Allman subsequently refused to renew the licence of William Lee, a Bathurst squatter whose convict overseer had taken stock beyond the limit in September 1841 and whose party had been involved in a serious clash with the Aborigines of the Bogan.

Seeing this as an opportunity to attack the 1839 Crown Lands Act, the squatting interest took up Lee's case at a public meeting in Bathurst on 29 July 1842. Three weeks later, James Macarthur presented in the Legislative Council a petition from Bathurst squatters asking that the Act should be amended to allow the establishment of a panel of 'disinterested gentlemen' who would investigate all complaints against licence-holders. Describing the non-renewal of Lee's licence as an 'act of extreme injustice' and an example of the arbitrary powers vested in the Commissioners, Macarthur went on to emphasize the need for a firm policy towards the

---

[29] Gipps to La Trobe, early December 1840, *GL Corr*, H7014.
[30] Gipps to La Trobe, 12 December 1840, ibid., H7015.
[31] In 1842 Gipps also prohibited the issue of depasturing and timber licences for the northern part of the Moreton Bay district, known as the 'Bunya Bunya country', when he learnt that large numbers of Aborigines collected there to eat the fruit of the Bunya pine, *araucaria bidwilli*. *GG*, 19 April 1842, p. 587.

N

Aborigines. In reply, Gipps accused Lee of moral responsibility for the incident and quoted a passage from Mitchell's *Three Expeditions* describing the Aborigines' strong proprietorial attachment to water-holes in the locality occupied by Lee's men. In his belief

> the attack originated in the blacks being driven from their water-holes, and if that was the case, where was the treachery of the attack. They were called upon to make the attack by self-preservation, and their cause was as noble a one as any for which armed warrior ever drew sword.[32]

Gipps also remarked that the petitioners had expressed concern for the 'lives of horned cattle, and even of sucking calves', but had said nothing about the Aborigines killed as a consequence of Lee's disregard for the Mount Harris line. More importantly, he regarded the petition as an attempt to test the strength of the squatting interest against that of the government, particularly in the administration of Crown lands, and announced his determination to take a firm stand.

Not surprizingly, the squatting press was quick to respond. Describing Gipps as 'the systematic foe and persecutor of the squatting interest', *The Australian* announced that it was 'high time that some determined stand should be made by the staple growing interest, against the systematically dealt discouragements of the present Governor'.[33] The incident had provided a useful focus for opposition to Gipps' attempts to enforce stricter controls on squatting and it marked the beginning of a process of organized agitation which broke Gipps and ultimately led to security of tenure for the squatting interest.[34]

The expansion of settlement along the Macquarie and Bogan Rivers meant that the Wellington Valley mission was no longer isolated from contact with whites; indeed, it became a busy crossroads. In 1838 the missionaries James Günther and William Watson told Gipps of the disastrous consequences of establishing a police office and a township in their area. The presence of whites had already reduced the number of Aborigines under their supervision to less than thirty. In response to requests from the Church Mis-

---

[32] *The Australian*, 26 August 1842.
[33] Ibid.
[34] Campbell, ' "Squatting" in New South Wales', p. 104.

sionary Society in London and its committee in the colony, Gipps removed the projected township of Wellington to a site seven miles from the mission station but held as little hope for the mission's future as did the neighbouring squatters who opposed the removal[35] and later impounded Watson's cattle.[36]

The 'inconveniences' of Wellington Valley caused Gipps to view with disapproval any further schemes for Aboriginal reserves. But early in 1840 a second petition from the squatters of the Geelong district, headed by Dr Alexander Thomson,[37] asked that reserves be set aside for the Protectors in the Port Phillip district.[38] It explained that although Protector Sievewright has succeeded in collecting large numbers of Aborigines near Purrumbete, there was no permanent provision made for them and they were raiding nearby stations. Consequently Gipps instructed La Trobe three months later to authorize a reserve for each Protector.[39] This was to consist of a permanent nucleus of one square mile to be used for agricultural purposes and a further temporary reserve of five miles' radius for hunting and food-gathering. But conflicts became more frequent in the Portland Bay district and in 1841 Gipps told Lord John Russell that they were due to the superiority of the pastures there and the consequent rapidity of occupation by squatters and dispossession of the Aborigines.[40]

The Border Police had already shown themselves unable to bring law and order to the squatting districts. Recruited from 'well-

---

35 For the controversy over Wellington Valley, see *HRA*, XX, pp. 607-27.
36 Watson to Surveyor-General, 12 February 1842, Rev. William Watson Papers, ML, Uncat. MSS, set 331.
37 Alexander Thomson (1800-66), doctor of medicine and catechist of the Presbyterian Church, settled in Tasmania in 1831 but moved to Port Phillip in 1836 where he was appointed medical officer by Captain Lonsdale. Thomson was not a member of the Port Phillip Association but acted as its catechist and medical officer and was one of the witnesses to John Batman's 1836 'treaty' with the Aborigines. He later took up 'Barwon Falls' near Geelong, as well as a number of other stations, and became one of the spokesmen for the squatting interest. Although he assisted the Rev. Francis Tuckfield in the establishment of the Buntingdale Aboriginal mission, he organized a number of petitions for police protection against Aboriginal depredations. In 1843 he was elected to the Legislative Council as one of the five Port Phillip representatives, and was one of the most outspoken advocates of Port Phillip separation. *ADB*, Vol. II, pp. 522-3.
38 *GD*, ML, MS. A1222, pp. 793-4.
39 Ibid., pp. 813-4.
40 Gipps to Russell, 8 February 1841, *HRA*, XXI, p. 210.

behaved' convicts and transported ex-soldiers, they made common cause with convicts and ex-convicts whom they were supposed to keep in order. More importantly, their numbers were absurdly inadequate to perform any useful function as a buffer between the two races in areas where conflicts were a problem. In the Liverpool Plains district, for example, whose area of 300 square miles was populated by an estimated 2000-3000 Aborigines in 1838, Commissioner Mayne had at his disposal only ten mounted troopers.[41] When called upon by squatters to 'disperse' Aborigines from the vicinity of their stations, Mayne found this difficult to reconcile with his responsibilities as an *ex officio* Protector. Squatters in the New England and Portland Bay districts complained that the Border Police were never on the spot to prevent Aboriginal depredations and by the time they arrived it was usually too late to detect and arrest the culprits. Besides, the Aborigines took care not to attack stock or property in the Commissioner's neighbourhood.[42]

Nevertheless some of the Commissioners and their troopers could be as ruthless as squatters and their men in 'dispersing' Aborigines. In 1841 the Commissioner for New England, G. J. McDonald, found a large party of Aborigines camped on a tributary of the Clarence River near Grafton. According to one description:

> A cordon was formed during the night, hemming the camp in with the river behind it. At a given signal at daybreak . . . the camp was rushed and men, women and children were shot down indiscriminately. Some took to the river, and were shot as they swam. There dead bodies subsequently floated down past the Settlement.[43]

This attack was in reprisal for a theft on 'Ramorhie' station which was subsequently traced to a white hutkeeper. Another 'dispersal' took place in the following year in the McLeay River district but on this occasion Commissioner Henry Oakes disappeared before the firing began.[44] His subsequent enquiries were conveniently addressed to persons who were also known to have been absent at

---

[41] 'Report of the Committee on Police and Gaols', *V&P*, 1839, II, pp. 20-5.
[42] 'Reminiscences of Mrs Susan Bundarra Young . . .', *JRAHS*, VIII, 1923, p. 399.
[43] 'The Bawden Lectures, Early Days in the Clarence District . . .', *Clarence River Historical Society Records*, II, 1938, p. 76.
[44] This was probably the punitive expedition against the 'Yarraharpny' tribe (inhabiting the coast between the McLeay and Nambucca Rivers) referred to by Henderson, *Excursions*, Vol. II, p. 116. Tindale, 'Distribution of Australian Aboriginal Tribes', makes no mention of this tribe.

the time. It appears that in March 1845 a party of Border Police commanded by Oakes' successor, Oliver Fry, fired without warning on a party of Aborigines near the Windeyer family's 'Deepwater' station at New England killing seven men, four women and five children.[45] Again, during the absence of Commissioner Allman his Border Police from Bathurst joined the squatters in a campaign against the Aborigines of the Bogan which resulted in the destruction of practically all the males of the tribe involved in the attack on William Lee's party.

Other Commissioners turned a blind eye to punitive expeditions sent out by squatters. At New England in 1844 McDonald reported the murder of a shepherd on the Irby brothers' 'Bolivia' station but neglected to mention the retaliatory raid organized by Edward Irby which culminated in a massacre of Aborigines at Bluff Rock.[46] In this case McDonald could hardly plead lack of information because one of the Windeyers, who assisted the Irbys, had sent a man specially to inform him. Some Commissioners, after all, were no more than failed or would-be squatters with an outlook which can not have been very sympathetic to the Aborigines.

In spite of the fact that the Commissioners and their Border Police usually intervened in the squatters' favour, there were many criticisms. During the debate on the annual estimates for the Border Police in August 1842—a time when there was a good deal of excitement over the Lee case—Hannibal Macarthur complained that instead of acting as a medium of intercourse between Aborigines and whites as a vanguard of the colony's expansion, they had 'settled down into mere tax-gatherers'.[47] Squatting witnesses and correspondents of the 1844 Committee on Crown Lands Grievances expressed almost universal dissatisfaction with the 'border crawlers', recommending that they should be replaced immediately by a strengthened force of Mounted Police recruited from military regiments and with responsibilities extending into the squatting districts.[48]

[45] Richard Craig to Deas Thomson, 1 July 1846, CSIL, 4/2719, 46/5747. See also, Walker, *Old New England*, Sydney 1966, p. 30.
[46] E. and L. Irby, *Memoirs of Edward and Leonard Irby*, pp. 59-61, 89-90. For a graphic description of the Bluff Rock incident by Thomas Keating, an employee of the Irby brothers, see Walker, *Old New England*, p. 29.
[47] *The Australian*, 24 August 1842.
[48] 'Report of the Committee on Crown Lands Grievances', V&P, 1844, Vol. II, p. 136.

Gipps was at first unwilling to enact special legislation for the Aborigines, believing that existing laws were adequate if properly enforced for both races. A wide-ranging Bill for the protection of the Aborigines prepared by Burton[49] in the early part of 1838 does not appear to have met with his favour, although it anticipated many of the recommendations later made by the Colonial Office. Nevertheless, by the end of his first year in the colony the growing problem of Aboriginal drunkenness, both in the towns and in the vicinity of mushrooming 'bush inns', had caused him to insert in the new Publicans' Act[50] a clause forbidding the sale or gift of liquor to Aborigines. After a number of armed attacks on stations in the Port Phillip district in 1840, the Legislative Council also enacted a Bill[51] forbidding Aborigines from using firearms, unless with the permission of a magistrate. The British authorities did not appreciate Gipps' problems and the Firearms Bill was disallowed on the grounds that it discriminated unfairly against the Aborigines.[52] The Port Phillip squatters, however, had welcomed this piece of legislation, seeing it as a prelude to a special set of laws for pacification and control by means of summary trial and punishment at the scene of any detected crime.

Shortly afterwards, the governor received a copy of Captain Grey's Report which, among other things, criticized the failure to apply English law equally to both races. Gipps gave the document very careful consideration[53] and made public his comments in July 1841. He rejected Grey's first criticism, claiming that for many years Aborigines had not been allowed to be governed by their own laws and had been considered equally amenable to English law for offences committed against white men and their fellows. With regard to the admissibility of Aboriginal evidence, he pointed out that although the 1839 Evidence Bill had been disallowed, the situation favoured the Aborigines as much as the whites because the former were almost invariably acquitted. Moreover, on Judge

---

[49] Burton's draft of the Bill with pencilled comments by an unnamed long-term resident of the colony and Burton's own corrections can be found in *BP*, No. 69. The Rev. Joseph Orton's comments and Burton's notes on them are at *BP*, No. 70.

[50] 2 Vict., No. 18, *GG*, 27 October 1838, pp. 904-5.

[51] 4 Vict., No. 8, *GG*, 29 August 1840, p. 837.

[52] Russell to Gipps, 26 August 1841, *HRA*, XXI, p. 485.

[53] Gipps to Russell, 7 April 1841, ibid., pp. 312-5.

Burton's recommendation the government had undertaken to provide counsel for the defence of any Aborigine brought to trial.

Gipps was more interested in Grey's remarks on employment and referred to a recent petition from Wellington Valley which recommended that settlers look to the Aborigines for a solution to their labour problems. Although he had dismissed as impracticable a system of rewards for settlers who employed Aboriginal labour, he emphasized that the most effective means of civilizing the Aborigines was to employ the adults as wage-labourers and to educate their children in establishments conducted by missionaries or Protectors. He told Russell:

> I consider that it is, by contact with white men, and by being placed as nearly as possible on a par with them, that the civilization of the Aborigines is most likely to be advanced.[54]

The employment problem had been exacerbated in 1838 when the British government, acting on the recommendation of the House of Commons Select Committee on Transportation, ceased to make convicts available for assignment to settlers in New South Wales. The squatting interest began to investigate the possibility of importing Indian or Chinese coolie labour to man their stations and Gipps, knowing that James Stephen was adamantly opposed to any such scheme, instructed the 1841 Committee on Immigration to examine the potential of Aboriginal labour in the pastoral industry. Accordingly, a questionnaire was sent to a number of major landholders, as well as to the Protectors who were known to have already achieved some success in employing Aborigines on their establishments. The replies[55] were extremely unfavourable, with the conspicuous exception of those from the Protectors which for some reason were not published in the report with all the others. While they testified to the usefulness of the Aborigines, the Protectors opposed their attachment to stations. William Thomas wrote:

> the settlers' object is Interest, if an Aborigine can arrive to the [position] to serve Man (and not God) appears the ne plus ultra—Further, [the best position they] could ever arrive to would be that of a hired labourer . . . I repeat my opinion, that to attach a Tribe

---

54 Ibid., p. 315.
55 'Report from the Committee on Immigration', V&P, 1841.

to the Settlers [will reduce them to a position] of Slavery, and accelerate their speedy extinction.[56]

Squatting correspondents admitted employing Aborigines as bark-cutters and sheep-washers or as assistants during the lambing and mustering seasons, but most complained that they were unreliable and lacked the capacity for sustained physical labour. They would no doubt have applauded Threlkeld's observation in his mission report for 1838 that

> the employing of them is more an act of benevolence than beneficial to the person who engages them, there being so many idlers attached, who expect supplies, and who if not connived at, draw away the whole party long ere the task is completed. Another serious drawback is, that time cannot be calculated on, in the completion of the work.[57]

In view of the current agitation for the importation of 'coolie' labour, the squatters were hardly likely to furnish evidence which might be used by Gipps and the Colonial Office to support the objection that the potential of Aboriginal labour had never been fully explored. It is probable that they were making much more use of the Aborigines than they were prepared to admit—the Australian Agricultural Company, for example, was in 1839 permanently employing twenty Aborigines as shepherds and stockmen and 'many others occasionally'.[58]

In his report as chairman of the Committee, Bishop Broughton indicated that the correspondents' pessimism was not entirely justified and that they could not expect Aborigines to be reliable and hard working if they failed to pay fixed wages. He added that as long as convict labour was available there had been a marked tendency to pass over the Aborigine or to deprecate his value as a worker. Broughton pointed out that the existing 'system' did not provide the Aborigine with sufficient incentive to resist the 'invitation of his fellows' or the impulse to wander off on his own accord. The 'casual provision' made for him by his white employer failed to create any sense of obligation or any alarm at the thought of losing his job, since he could be 'sure of being received back into that state of lax dependence and irregular servitude in which the

---

[56] Aborigines Papers, ML, MS.A611, p. 103. The MS. replies of the Protectors and other correspondents can be found here.

[57] 'Memoranda' in Gunson, *Australian Reminiscences and Papers of L. E. Threlkeld*, Vol. I, p. 144.

[58] 'Report of the Committee on Police and Gaols', *V&P*, 1839, Vol. II, p. 166.

greater part of his time is idled away'.[59] Nevertheless, Broughton was unwilling to set down rules for improvement since everything depended on the 'prudence and humanity' of the settlers themselves. He suggested that some progress might be made if settlers could agree to fix wages and boycott those Aborigines who had absconded from service, but this would only be possible in the Nineteen Counties where their numbers were already insufficient to meet the labour shortage.

One of the questions contained in the circular is of further interest. Like Bourke, Gipps had at least considered the possibility that once Aborigines were settled on the stations as a labour force, they might intermarry with the lower classes of whites. None of the Committee's correspondents had witnessed any development in this direction, although some reported the birth and frequent killing of numbers of half-caste children. Gipps did not have any information or plan which, with the resources at his disposal, might have reduced conflicts in the squatting districts as well as improving the wretched condition of Aborigines in the settled districts and placing them 'as nearly as possible on a par with white men.' He seems to have decided that the only thing to be done was to enforce existing laws as strictly as possible.

A number of cases had already demonstrated how difficult it was to do this for the remote squatting districts. The Nunn affair, the Faithfull massacre and Myall Creek highlighted the problems involved in investigating transgressions which took place hundreds of miles from the nearest police post and magistrates' bench.

After Myall Creek it became almost impossible to prosecute whites for the murder of Aborigines. It was usually very difficult to obtain evidence and even on the rare occasions when whites admitted killing Aborigines there was still no guarantee that they could be indicted. A good example was the shooting of more than thirty Aborigines on the Whyte brothers' 'Koonong Wootong' station in the Wannon River area of the Portland Bay district in March 1840. Informing Lord John Russell of the incident, an anonymous colonist wrote:

In this Colony, the Murder of a Native is punished severely if it can be proved against anyone. But the only effect of this Law is to make

[59] 'Report from the Committee on Immigration', V&P, 1841, p. 5. Broughton's MS. draft of the Report can also be found in Aborigines Papers.

the Settlers cautious of telling when they do shoot the Blacks. It is quite certain that numbers of them are shot. Their bodies are buried and nothing more is heard of the matter.

A short time ago, a party of 38 natives stole several hundred sheep from an outstation near Portland Bay. When the Proprietors' [shep]-herds, who lived at another place, heard of it, they set off in pursuit of the Blacks, and, out of the 38, murdered 36 and left their bodies collected in a heap. This is perfectly known in Melbourne, but it is extremely hard to get sufficient proof. . . .[60]

When Protector Sievewright was sent to investigate, the Whyte brothers admitted not only that they had been personally involved, but that as many as seventy Aborigines might have been killed. However, the depositions which they made to Sievewright could not be used as evidence against them.[61] Although Crown Prosecutor James Croke in Melbourne and Attorney-General Plunkett in Sydney frequently warned magistrates and Protectors against taking depositions from principals, it was probably difficult to obtain witnesses who were not either participants or were not intimidated by their employers.

Besides, many of the magistrates had a personal interest in ensuring that there were no more prosecutions of the Myall Creek kind. Richard Craig,[62] an ex-convict farmer who knew the Aborigines of the Clarence River district and spoke their language, applied to the local bench of magistrates in 1844 to subpoena two constables who claimed to have been witnesses at the shooting of sixteen Aborigines by Commissioner Fry's party of Border Police. In a moving letter to Deas Thomson, Craig said that he 'need not mention any other reason [for the refusal of his request] than the magistrates all being squatters . . .'.[63] The Aborigines had already killed several whites in retaliation and Craig asked Gipps to 'cause this crewil man [Fry] to be brought to justice for the murders of these unprotected people'.[64]

Justice was difficult to secure when not only magistrates but the Port Phillip Resident Justice himself would not co-operate. The clearest example of Gipps' difficulties was the unsuccessful prose-

---

[60] Enclosure, Russell to Gipps, 29 December 1840, HRA, XXI, p. 139.

[61] GD, ML, MS.A1226, pp. 285-8.

[62] See J. F. Stephens, The Runaway: The Life Story of Richard Craig, duplicated typescript, North Tamborine, Queensland 1962.

[63] Craig to Deas Thomson, 1 July 1844, CSIL, 4/2719, 46/5747.

[64] Ibid.

cution of three stockmen charged with murdering three Aboriginal women and a child on F. Smith and T. Osbrey's 'Caramut' station near Port Fairy in February 1842. La Trobe's attempts to bring the murderers to justice were impeded by Judge J. W. Willis,[65] as well as by the squatting interest.

In his address to the jury in the case of 'Bob' and 'Jack' (two of the Van Diemen's Land Aborigines brought from Flinders Island by Robinson) who were charged with murdering two whalers at Westernport, Willis had opined that 'the proprietor of a run . . . may take all lawful means to prevent either natives or others from entering or remaining on it'.[66] An infuriated Gipps told Stanley that

> The conduct of Mr Willis and his harangues from the Bench, openly accusing the Government of partiality in pursuing to justice the perpetrators of crimes committed on the Aborigines, and allowing those committed by them to pass with impunity, can only . . . be accounted for by a desire to gain popularity in the District by encouraging the vilest and most inhuman passions of the dispersed occupiers of Crown lands.[67]

La Trobe offered £50 reward and a conditional pardon for information leading to an arrest in the Port Fairy case and this was increased by Gipps to £100, together with an unconditional pardon. But some members of the raiding party had already left the colony and when in August 1843 Judge William Jeffcott, Willis' successor, was summing up at the trial of the three men who had been located,[68]

> The foreman of the Jury informed him that they would not trouble His Honor to read over the notice of evidence, as they had made up their minds to the verdict . . . The Jury then returned a verdict of Not Guilty against each of the prisoners, which was received with applause from a very numerous audience.[69]

Conveying the verdict and relevant papers to Stanley, Gipps wrote:

---

[65] John Walpole Willis (1793-1877) was always an embarrassment to Gipps and it was with some satisfaction that the governor had him removed to the Melbourne bench of the Supreme Court in January 1841. However, Willis continued to be troublesome and Gipps recommended his dismissal in June 1843.

[66] *PP*, 1844, XXXIV, No. 627, p. 199.

[67] Gipps to Stanley, 2 July 1843, *HRA*, XXIII, p. 4.

[68] Hall, Beswick and Betts.

[69] *Portland Mercury and Normanby Advertiser*, 23 August 1843. I am indebted to Dr Peter Corris for this reference.

It seems to me established beyond any doubt that three Aboriginal Women and Child were murdered by a party of white men, who left Mr Osprey's [sic] Hut with firearms . . . and that two at least of the persons, who have been acquitted, accompanied the party.[70]

In a private note to La Trobe he described Osbrey as 'an Accomplice after the fact' for not informing the authorities of what he knew of the matter.[71]

Willis had earlier annoyed Gipps by suggesting from the Bench that Aborigines were not amenable to colonial courts for offences committed *inter se*. In September 1841 an Aborigine named 'Borijon' had been brought to trial in Melbourne for the murder of another Aborigine on the town's outskirts. When counsel raised the question of the court's jurisdiction, Willis indicated his serious doubts about its competency and said that if the accused were found guilty, he would have to reserve the point. Forwarding a copy of his remarks to Gipps, he requested that the question be referred to the British Attorney-General and Solicitor-General.[72] Determined to settle the matter, Gipps decided to introduce a Bill in the Legislative Council establishing beyond all challenge the amenability of Aborigines to English law. However, Chief Justice Dowling advised that he and his brother judges were agreed that the question had already been settled by the decision in the 1836 Murral case and that there was no need for a declaratory law.[73] Stanley concurred in their opinion[74] and declined to refer the question but the damage had already been done. Willis's highly-publicized remarks had been received with enthusiasm by those in the colony who saw them as casting doubt on the law's power to prosecute whites for offences against the Aborigines.

If Gipps was frustrated by the difficulty of enforcing the law to protect Aborigines, the squatters of New South Wales, especially those of the Liverpool Plains and Portland Bay districts, were infuriated by the law's inability to prevent Aboriginal attacks on life and property, or even to punish those few culprits who were actually caught.[75] A return to an address from Dr Alexander Thom-

---

70 Gipps to Stanley, 11 September 1843, *HRA*, XXIII, p. 125.
71 Gipps to La Trobe, 9 September 1843, *GL Corr.*, H7194.
72 Willis to Gipps, 22 September 1841, Enclosure No. 3, Gipps to Stanley, 24 January 1842, *HRA*, XXI, p. 658.
73 Dowling to Gipps, 8 January 1842, Enclosure No. 2, ibid., pp. 656-8.
74 Stanley to Gipps, 2 July 1842, *HRA*, XXII, p. 133.
75 See Appendix I.

son in 1843 revealed that of sixty-one Aborigines indicted since 1837 for offences ranging from cattle spearing to murder, eight had been hanged, seven had been either imprisoned or transported, and the rest had either been discharged or had escaped from custody.[76] And yet this, as everyone knew, accounted for a very small proportion of offences actually committed by Aborigines upon whites and their property and hardly touched offences committed among themselves.

In early 1841 Gipps forwarded to Russell a copy of a document which had been submitted to La Trobe by a young squatter of influential connections. This set out very clearly the problems of law enforcement as seen by squatters in the remote areas:

The stockman probably may be 250 miles from Court, or perhaps 150 miles from the Commissioner. He sees his Cattle speared daily and driven off the run. He possibly may be out in the Bush for weeks looking for them, and in bringing them home, the same thing occurs again. His master then finds fault with him, because he cannot muster the Cattle. Possibly he may take a Black to Court where for want of Evidence he almost invariably is let go. Supposing he is committed— the Stock-keeper would have to leave his business to come down to prosecute, but as he only knows his own run he cannot be spared, else the cattle will run away, and before his return may be killed by other Blacks, and driven all over the Country. Driven to desperation, the Stock-keeper who is usually an Emancipist, and who considers killing Blacks no murder, having no religion and no fear of God, in many instances doubtless does put the Blacks to death, when he can get a chance.

The Blacks then kill the Whites and generally eat them, and then after that probably a great number are destroyed immediately in the vicinity. This leads to more murders of Whites, and more slaughters of Blacks, till they gradually disappear from the Country with the exception of a few miserable crawlers about the Huts.

I think that possibly if all respectable Stock-holders resident in those parts were made Magistrates over the Aborigines, with the power to flog with a limited number of lashes, Blacks for taking the cattle or sheep, and also in cases of murder of white men, to be allowed to try by a jury of white men hastily summoned, whether the Prisoners at the Bar were present at the Murder, or whether they belonged to the tribe that committed the murder, and there and then hang one, these atrocities would cease. The Stock-keeper would not then take vengeance himself on them, being certain that one Black at least would be hanged.

But as it is, the Blacks will disappear before the Settlers, and are

[76] See Appendix II.

fast doing so, and every successive murder of white men will thin their numbers.[77]

Distance from police and magistrates and the extreme improbability of conviction and punishment encouraged squatters and their servants to take the law into their own hands. The northern parts of the Liverpool Plains were 200 miles from the nearest Police Office at Invermein (Scone) and squatters on the lower Murray were 300 miles from Gundagai. Even in those areas where access to a magistrate was relatively easy, the machinery of the law was not suited to the speedy detection and arrest of Aborigines for thefts or murder. When a warrant for the arrest of an Aborigine was obtained, there was the very real difficulty of making the actual arrest. This is how a member of the Border Police described an attempt to serve a warrant on an Aborigine suspected of stealing sheep in the Westernport district in 1844:

> As soon as I came up I immediately recognised him as 'Jim Crow'. I spoke to him and desired him to lay down his weapons—spear— which he held in his hands ready to throw and said he would not but would 'kill all the white fellows' which he afterwards repeated, still holding his spear in the same threatening attitude. After a parley of about 20 minutes I heard Sergeant Daplin call out 'lads charge him', but which was not done as the party were in fear of their lives. In about half an hour afterwards (an hour or two before sundown) I heard Sergeant Daplin order the men to fire, which they did and I saw Jim Crow fall.[78]

In the squatting districts the law became a target for ridicule. One of many anecdotes from 'Major Nunn's campaign' reveals that official procedure in arresting Aborigines was as farcical as the official 'Requirement' read in Spanish to 'unpacified' Indians in South America.[79]

> The sergeant reported to the Major
> 'Blackfellow up a tree, sir'.
> 'Order him down', said the Major.
> 'I have done so', replied the sergeant.
> 'He won't come and we cannot climb the tree'.
> 'Go again', said the Major, 'order him down three times in Her Majesty's name'.
> 'And supposing Her Majesty don't fetch him', said the sergeant.

[77] GD, ML, MS.A1224, pp. 309-12.
[78] Deposition of Daniel Cameron, 10 November 1844, CSIL, 4/1076.
[79] Hanke, The Spanish Struggle for Justice, pp. 33-5.

'Then *bring him down*', grimly answered Major Munn [sic].
The sergeant advanced with carbine pointed.
'I say, you nigger, come down in the Queen's name'.
'Baal mumkull' (do not kill me), shrieked the aboriginal in abject
   terror, not understanding one word of English, and realising that
   he was in peril of his life.
Said the sergeant, 'I orders you again in the Queen's name to come
   down'.
Still piteous cries of 'Baal, Baal'.
'I orders you a third time in the Queen's name to come down', re-
   peated the sergeant. 'Then if you ain't a-going to obey Her
   Majesty's orders, I must obey mine'.
His hand was upon the trigger. A shot, a thud, and the 'big game'
   fell at his feet.[80]

One of Rolf Boldrewood's books contains an anecdote about 'a
special humourist' who forged a warrant for the alleged shooting
of an Aborigine and arranged to have it served on a neighbouring
squatter.[81]

Even when thefts could be traced, there was the difficulty of
establishing individual responsibility. Mayne pointed out that when
property was stolen, it was invariably distributed among all the
Aborigines of the group.[82] However, possession of articles of clothing and personal effects of a murdered white was considered by
many squatters and their servants as sufficient justification to shoot
an Aborigine on sight.[83]

Nor was it only on the Liverpool Plains that Aboriginal popula-
tions were deliberately and systematically exterminated. In 1846
Henry Meyrick wrote that not less than 450 Aborigines had been
killed in Gippsland:

No wild beast of the forest was ever hunted down with such un-
sparing perseverance as they are. Men, women and children are shot
wherever they can be met with. Some excuse might be found for
shooting the men by those who are daily getting their cattle speared,
but what can they urge in their excuse who shoot the women and
children I cannot conceive. I have protested against it at every
station I have been in Gippsland, in the strongest language, but these
things are kept very secret as the penalty would certainly be hanging.[84]

[80] Praed, *The Australian Life*, pp. 15-16.
[81] *Old Melbourne Memories*, p. 48.
[82] Mayne to Deas Thomson, 20 April 1846, *CSIL*, 4/2719, 46/5195.
[83] Bride, *Letters*, p. 30.
[84] *Life in the Bush*, p. 136.

THE PROTECTORATE AND THE MISSIONS

The story of the Port Phillip Aboriginal Protectorate is now well known[85] and it is only necessary here to indicate the difficulties which it created. Not only were Glenelg's instructions vague, but Gipps found it extremely difficult to obtain information as to how they might be embodied in a practical system. The Protectors, most of them of an Evangelical disposition, apparently assumed that they were being appointed primarily as missionaries. All had large families and found it impossible to make long journeys in search of or in the company of Aborigines while at the same time fulfilling their other duties as magistrates, special custodians of Aboriginal life and property and mediators in conflicts between Aborigines and whites. Difficulty in communications meant that there was often a delay of months between the despatch of a letter and the receipt of a reply. Robinson was conscientious but incredibly verbose and his reports had to be carefully summarized by La Trobe before they could be forwarded. Even then they were of little practical use to Gipps since the Chief Protector's ideas were moulded by his experience in Van Diemen's Land, where 'collecting the tribes' had been successfully completed. In the huge expanse of the Port Phillip district with its multiplicity of tribes it was simple-minded to the point of stupidity. But Robinson clung to his idea with all the determination that a self-educated mind and a sense of Divine calling could combine to produce.

Most importantly, the expense of the Protectorate was very embarrassing to Gipps at a time when revenue from Crown land sales was rapidly declining and an over-generous provision of immigration warrants was threatening his administration with financial ruin. He must also have been apprehensive that failure to support the Protectorate might result in pressure from 'Exeter Hall' for his recall. The irony of the situation was that he should have had to implement an impractical scheme of someone else's design, against his own better judgement, in the absence of useful information, and at a time when it was bound to arouse the ire of the squatting interest and the majority of public opinion.

Gipps did not record his initial reaction to the Protectorate but

---

85 Foxcroft, *Australian Native Policy*, pp. 55-77; N. M. Carlyon, 'G. A. Robinson—Chief Protector', B.A. hons thesis, University of Melbourne, 1960; Nelson, 'Early Attempts to Civilize the Aborigines of the Port Phillip District'.

he was acutely aware that the instruction had come at a singularly inopportune moment. At a meeting of the Executive Council on 6 April 1838 he produced a draft notice of Glenelg's plan but was forced to postpone its publication for more than a year because of public 'excitement' aroused by the Faithfull massacre and the Myall Creek trials. On 12 December he announced in the *Government Gazette* that Protectors[86] had been appointed, but the colonial press had already informed the public of this, as well as of the projected transfer of the Van Diemen's Land Aborigines from Flinders Island to Port Phillip.

Nor were Robinson's first contacts with Gipps auspicious for the Protectorate. Determined to take all the Flinders Island Aborigines to Port Phillip, as agreed to by the now relenting Franklin,[87] he stayed on in Sydney for three months in late 1838, badgering an increasingly impatient Gipps at every opportunity in the vain hope that he could wear the governor down.[88] No doubt Robinson was also piqued that Gipps had decided to limit the area of the Protectorate to the Port Phillip district when Glenelg's despatch appeared to indicate a responsibility for the entire colony of New South Wales.

Gipps had conscientiously appointed a committee of the Legislative Council to report on the condition of the Aborigines, the effects of their intercourse with the whites, and the results of all previous schemes of Christianization and civilization. His urgent request for information to give form to Glenelg's vague plan was not met by the committee which unhelpfully declared itself 'unable conscientiously to pronounce an opinion, or to recommend the adoption of any particular course'.[89] However, its members were unanimous in opposing the transfer of the eighty-four Aborigines from Flinders Island to Port Phillip[90] and consequently Deas Thomson notified John Montagu, the Colonial Secretary of Van Diemen's

[86] These were: James Dredge, Edward Stone Parker, Charles William Sievewright and William Thomas. Dredge was later replaced by William Le Souef and Sievewright by Dr J. Watton.

[87] Franklin had initially opposed the transfer but after visiting Flinders Island and meeting Robinson he even agreed to pay the cost. Franklin did not share Arthur's sympathy for Robinson and was relieved to get rid of him.

[88] Robinson Papers, ML, MS.A7033, Vol. 12, Pt. 4.

[89] 'Report from the Committee on the Aborigines Question', *V&P*, 1838, n.p.

[90] Threlkeld, who had read Robinson's reports from Flinders Island, was the only witness before the committee who supported relocation on the mainland and thought that it might be beneficial.

Land, that Gipps, exercising the discretion given him by Glenelg, could not 'undertake to bring them to the Colony against so decided an expression of opinion on the part of the Committee . . . and therefore regrets to say the plan must be (at any rate for the present) abandoned'.[91] Robinson was eventually allowed to take a family of Aborigines with him to Port Phillip as 'personal attendants', which he interpreted rather generously by taking sixteen.

The Port Phillip newspapers and *The Sydney Herald* indicated the opposition that Gipps would have had to face if Arthur and Robinson had prevailed. Many of the Port Phillip squatters and their servants had come from Van Diemen's Land and had no wish to renew acquaintance with their old enemies. In a leading article of 5 October 1838 the *Herald* labelled the projected transfer and the appointment of Protectors as 'another of the many *jobs* created for the purpose of plundering the public money of the Colonists'. Claiming that the whites needed more protection than the Aborigines, the editor played facetiously on the outlandish classical names that Robinson had given his protégés and asserted:

> The whole gang of black animals are not worth the money which the Colonists will have to pay for printing the very documents [the Report] upon which we have already wasted too much time.

Early criticism of the Protectorate emphasized that as an experiment in civilization and Christianization it was doomed to failure and, furthermore, that the British government had no right to impose upon the colonists the responsibility of financing it. In a letter headed 'Misappropriation of Public Money' a regular correspondent to *The Australian* pointed out that while the Aborigines had lost their natural virtues, they had remained immune to the benefits of civilization. There was something in their character which offered 'insuperable obstacles' to philanthropy. Reason dictated that they should be left alone since it was 'the nature of things that they should gradually become extinct by means of their degeneracy and degradation'.[92] The correspondent claimed, moreover, that the founders of the scheme must have been aware that it would benefit the Protectors alone and added ominously that if the colony had possessed its own representative assembly the scheme would never

---

[91] Deas Thomson to Montagu, 30 October 1838, enclosed with Franklin's despatch to Glenelg of 13 February 1839, *CO*, 280/105, pp. 178-9.
[92] 27 December 1838.

have been accepted, despite the strongest recommendations of the British Cabinet.

This criticism was temperate in comparison with other letters appearing in the Sydney and Melbourne press during the first years of the Protectorate, many of the most vitriolic coming from squatters in the Portland Bay and Liverpool Plains districts where racial conflicts were common during the period. Their argument was that they and not the Aborigines needed protection and that the very presence of Protectors was encouraging Aborigines to commit bolder 'depredations' in the belief that the Protectors would shield them from reprisals. At the same time there was a good deal of sarcasm about applying 'The Soothing System' to 'savages'.

Until Gipps directed La Trobe to authorize reserves of land in April 1840,[93] the Protectors had to keep in contact with the tribes in their allocated districts without any permanent base of operations. At first they succeeded in attracting large numbers of Aborigines to whom they distributed whatever supplies of flour and other food were available, but when these were exhausted the Aborigines either plundered nearby stations or drifted towards Melbourne. Squatters were always apprehensive of large gatherings and saw the Protectorate as encouraging this tendency. In early 1840, Dr Alexander Thomson and a number of other squatters from the Geelong district petitioned the Colonial Secretary against Protector Sievewright's collection of Aborigines in their vicinity which had already resulted in raids on stock and other property.[94] Others complained that the Protectors were unable to prevent Aborigines from congregating on the outskirts of Melbourne whose citizens considered them a public nuisance.

Gipps' decision to allocate reserves for the establishment of Protectorate stations was probably based on the recommendation of this petition but it aroused antagonism among those squatters who were already depasturing their stock on the land in question. When Protector Parker chose to re-locate his station in the vicinity of Mt Franklin, the local squatters were openly hostile[95] and *The Sydney Herald* assured them that they would be

[93] *GD*, ML, MS.A1222, pp. 813-4.
[94] Ibid., pp. 793-4.
[95] For example, see the letter from Horatio Willis to La Trobe, March 1842, *GD*, ML, MS.A1228, pp. 267-74.

fully justified, both in law and equity, in resisting the aggression of the minions of Government *vi et armis*, and forcibly ejecting and driving them off . . . even if the aggressors were headed in the outrage by Mr La Trobe himself.[96]

A similar outcry had followed the removal of five squatters from the area of 64,000 acres allocated for the Wesleyan Missionary Society's Buntingdale mission on the Barwon River near Geelong.

Shortly after his arrival at Port Phillip, La Trobe had told Gipps that his first impression of the Protectorate was unsatisfactory and that there was no possibility of improvement without radical change. However, he was not prepared to recommend any changes. His reports became increasingly unfavourable without providing Gipps with any real insight into the problems of the Protectorate and how to solve them.[97]

By February 1841 Gipps was expressing exasperation with the Protectorate. Of Robinson and his subordinates he told Russell:

> The Chief Protector, whatever may be his other merits . . . is afflicted with such a love of writing that much of his time must be spent in that way, which would be much better devoted to active employment, and his assistants are . . . even more inactive than he is . . .[98]

Robinson's verbosity infuriated Gipps still further when conflicts between Aborigines and whites flared up during 1841 and 1842. A report of a journey into the western part of the Port Phillip district in early 1841[99] to enquire into particularly serious conflicts there took up no less than 302 pages of foolscap, from which Gipps could glean very little. The document is an interesting source of information for the modern ethnologist but was of little use to Gipps and La Trobe whose main concern was that the Chief Protector and his assistants should prevent racial conflicts. When Robinson failed to visit the Ovens district in September 1842 to investigate the murder of a shepherd, La Trobe suspended his salary.

Meanwhile, Protector Dredge had resigned[100] and Protector Sieve-

---

96 10 February 1841.
97 Kiddle, *Men of Yesterday*, p. 126.
98 Gipps to Russell, 3 February 1841, *HRA*, XXI, pp. 210-1.
99 'A Report of an Expedition to the Aboriginal Tribes of the Western Interior . . . 1841', *The Victorian Historical Magazine*, XII, No. 3, March 1928, pp. 138-70.
100 For the reasons given by Dredge for his resignation and related correspondence, see *V&P*, 1843, pp. 477-82, and his *Brief Notices of the Aborigines of New South Wales*.

wright had not moved from the vicinity of Geelong. Indeed, Sieve-wright had been an embarrassment to the government from his very arrival. An *affaire* with the wife of one of his fellow Protectors on the voyage out did little to strengthen the new Department's *esprit de corps* and was also the subject of vulgar gossip. In June 1842, Gipps suspended him for 'general inefficiency' and for his failure to rid himself of charges against his moral character.[101] La Trobe's criticisms of the Protectors were now becoming so trenchant that Gipps at first thought it unwise to forward a particularly critical letter[102] to Lord Stanley who had succeeded Russell as Secretary of State for Colonies.

Both La Trobe and Gipps had been extremely cautious in their handling of the Protectors in the belief that the latter could wield powerful influence through important Evangelical connections in England. Referring to an inquiry into atrocities on the Murray River being conducted by a military officer rather than by Robin-son, Gipps advised La Trobe, in October 1840, to take care with the Protectors over the case:

> their representations we know in England will be credited (I do not mean by the Govt.—but by Persons perhaps more powerful than the Govt.) whilst the reports of all persons filling official stations here, will be received with suspicion or entirely disbelieved.[103]

And informing him in December that he had passed on a number of papers concerning offences against Aborigines to Plunkett since they were related more to the administration of justice than to the responsibilities of executive government, Gipps advised the Super-intendent not to allow the Protectors to trouble him with such matters, although it was 'necessary to do this with great caution, as they are evidently getting up a case for England'.[104]

The government-assisted missions at Lake Macquarie and Well-ington Valley were in a sad plight by 1840. Threlkeld's report for 1840[105] was so discouraging that Deas Thomson informed him in May 1841 that Gipps would not agree to remove the mission to Newcastle and that financial assistance would cease at the end of

[101] Gipps to Stanley, 9 September 1842, *HRA*, XXII, pp. 258-9.
[102] This can be found at *GD*, ML, MS.A1228, pp. 381-6.
[103] Gipps to La Trobe, 24 October 1840, *GL Corr*, H7012.
[104] Gipps to La Trobe, 12 December 1840, *GL Corr*, H7015.
[105] Gunson, *Reminiscences and Papers of L. E. Threlkeld*, Vol. I, pp. 165-8.

the year.[106] In his final report for 1841 Threlkeld wrote:

> It is . . . perfectly apparent that the termination of the Mission has
> arisen solely from the Aborigines becoming extinct in these districts,
> and the very few that remain elsewhere are so scattered, that it is
> impossible to congregate them for instruction, and when seen in the
> towns, they are generally unfit to engage in profitable conversation.[107]

He might also have repeated a more significant observation made by
Backhouse and Walker to the 1838 Committee on the Aborigines
Question that Aborigines at the various missions felt themselves
looked down upon by whites and 'naturally returned to their own
people, in whose estimation they felt themselves raised by the
superior knowledge they had acquired'.[108] Information from James
Günther at Wellington Valley and J. C. S. Handt at Moreton Bay
was similarly unfavourable and Gipps concluded that very little had
been achieved, although a visit to Wellington Valley in late 1840
appears to have convinced him that William Watson had been
more successful than any of the other missionaries.[109]

These and a number of other reports passed on by Gipps to the
Colonial Office during 1841 and 1842 led Stanley to question the
'wisdom or propriety' of continuing the missions and to conclude
that 'the failure of the system of Protectors has been . . . as complete as that of the Missions'.[110] However, while authorizing Gipps
to discontinue financial assistance to the missions, he indicated that
the Protectorate should be given more time to produce results.
Committed to the implementation of the 1837 Report, Stanley was
loath to abandon the only scheme which had been introduced since
the founding of the colony for the protection and welfare of the
Aborigines. Consequently Gipps withdrew support from the Wellington Valley and Buntingdale missions and continued to support
the Protectorate—but on a reduced scale. Although he did not
make Stanley's instructions public, the news somehow leaked out
and was seized upon by Dr Thomson. In the new Legislative Council in August 1843 he called for information on the Protectorate
and the enforcement of law, making it clear that he also intended

---

106 Deas Thomson to Threlkeld, ibid. Vol. I, p. 168.
107 Ibid. Vol. I, p. 168.
108 'Report of the Committee on the Aborigines Question', V&P, 1838, p. 26.
109 Rev. William Watson Papers, ML, Uncat.MSS, set 331.
110 Stanley to Gipps, 20 December 1842, HRA, XXII, p. 438.

to emphasize 'the utter mockery of subjecting the Aboriginal natives of New South Wales to the forms of a British trial by jury. (Loud cries of Hear.)'[111]

The failure of Protestant, government-assisted missions at Port Phillip, Wellington Valley and Lake Macquarie, together with controversy over French settlement of Tahiti provided further fuel for sectarian antagonism in the colony and highlighted the uneasy relationship between the Roman Catholic hierarchy and Gipps' administration.

Antagonism between Catholics and Protestants had been earlier expressed in what sometimes became vulgar competition for Aborigines' souls. Roman Catholic priests adopted a more liberal policy to Aboriginal baptism than was practised by Anglicans and Protestants.[112] The Rev. J. J. Therry, for example, is described as having baptized several Aborigines and the Rev. John Brady installed some in his orphanage at Windsor.[113]

In December 1827 an Aborigine called 'Tommy' who had been found guilty of the murder of a Bathurst stockman continued to protest his innocence until the gallows. A number of clergymen were present including two Catholic priests, one of whom proceeded to baptize him. J. D. Lang remonstrated with them on the 'gross impropriety' of this act, claiming that Tommy could not understand the nature of the rite and that his soul, being in 'a state of darkness and unbelief', could not benefit from it. All the more determined, Father Power replied: 'We baptize infants who do not understand the nature of baptism; he is in the same state', and immediately made the sign of the cross on Tommy's forehead with holy water brought for that purpose.[114]

The Church of England, on the other hand, was not so accommodating. Broughton disapproved of mixed marriages on the grounds that the Aborigines were unbelievers and when the Rev.

---

111 *The Australian*, 30 August 1843.
112 There is an interesting comparison here with the controversy in sixteenth-century Spanish America between those who baptized Indians in the thousands and those like Las Casas who emphasized that potential converts should receive prior instruction in the faith and be given time to make up their minds. See Hanke, *The Spanish Struggle for Justice*.
113 T. L. L. Suttor, *Hierarchy and Democracy in Australia, 1788-1870*, Melbourne 1965, p. 98.
114 This account is based on descriptions in the *Sydney Gazette*, 2 January 1828 and *The South-Asian Register*, No. 3, April 1828, pp. 278-9.

William Cowper requested permission to marry an Aboriginal woman and an employee of the Australian Agricultural Company at Stroud and to baptize their children, the Bishop allowed the baptisms but forbade the marriage, remarking on the 'spiritual illegality' of unions between white men and black women. He cited St Paul's advice to the Corinthians criticizing the wisdom of continuing a marriage between a believing husband or wife and an unbelieving partner and he recommended that the children of the illicit union be sent to the orphan schools at Liverpool or to George Langhorne's institution at Port Phillip.[115]

By 1843 the antipathy between Archbishop John Bede Polding and the Catholics on one side and Broughton, his clergy and the Protestant sects on the other had been exacerbated by a number of events. Polding was at loggerheads with Gipps who was sympathetic to Broughton and was implementing the policy of a Colonial Office unfavourably disposed towards Catholics. Since the passing of Bourke's Church Act[116] in 1836, Polding had been demanding proportional distribution of the £30,000 allocated annually by the government as a contribution to the stipends of colonial clergy. On 1 January 1844 he chaired a meeting in St Mary's Church and later presented Gipps with a resolution calling on the government for more financial assistance.

In the same year Polding received his appointment as Archbishop of Sydney, a title which aroused Broughton's deep indignation. In what appears to have been a fit of spiteful retaliation, he prevailed on Gipps to remove the Catholics from part of a government building which they had been using as a school for a number of years. Gipps had previously been annoyed by Polding's assumption that while on leave of absence with two other priests in 1841 they would all receive a full allowance from the government. In the same year, the Rev. Peter Young and a number of other Roman Catholic clergy arrived in the colony without the permission of the Secretary of State for Colonies.

Polding had been bitterly disappointed by the British Government's refusal to give financial assistance to his plan for a mission to the Aborigines. In 1840 he had travelled to Britain and then to

---

[115] Broughton to Cowper, 6 September 1841, Broughton Papers, Archdiocesan Office, Sydney.
[116] 7 Wm., No. 3.

Europe to recruit teachers and obtain support for a planned establishment at Stradbroke Island in Moreton Bay.[117] By August 1842 he had collected four members of the Passionist order from Rome and taken them to London before journeying to the scene of their labours. While there he had appealed to the Colonial Office for £200 to defray the cost of their passages, only to be told by Stanley that while Her Majesty's government would recommend the missionaries to Gipps' 'protection', they were not to be chargeable in any way on colonial revenue.[118]

Polding's resentment was expressed over an incident which took place shortly after his return to Sydney. In November 1843, four Aborigines whose death sentences for murder had been commuted by the Executive Council to transportation for life were transferred from Darlinghurst gaol to Cockatoo Island where it was intended they should be instructed in various skills with a view to their 'improvement' and ultimate release. Here they met another Aborigine called 'Frying Pan' who had for some weeks been receiving instruction from the Rev. Peter Young, Roman Catholic chaplain to the island. Within ten days of their admission his Anglican counterpart, the Rev. Dr Robert Steele, had complained to the island's Superintendent that the four Aborigines should have been under his care. No definite provision had been made for their religious instruction since it was thought that they could neither speak nor understand English. Consequently the Superintendent informed the visiting magistrate who in turn appealed to the Governor for instructions. Gipps apparently directed him to transfer the Aborigines to Steele and immediately Polding complained to Deas Thomson of unjustified interference by civil authority, claiming that 'Frying Pan' had been already prepared for baptism and that the others had submitted themselves voluntarily for instruction.[119] Through Deas Thomson, Gipps replied that since the Aborigines concerned were 'Her Majesty's Subjects, and under custody of the Civil power, they ought to be instructed in the Religion of Her Majesty, which is also the Religion of the Empire'.[120]

Polding's response to this has been described as 'the one great

[117] For the history of the Dunwich mission, see Thorpe, *First Catholic Mission*.
[118] Stanley to Gipps and Enclosure, 6 September 1842, *HRA*, XXII, pp. 249-50.
[119] Polding to Deas Thomson, 28 December 1843, Enclosure, Stanley to Gipps, 17 July 1844, *HRA*, XXIII, p. 678.
[120] Ibid., p. 678.

cri de couer of his correspondence'.[121] Essentially, his complaint
was that Gipps had exceeded the bounds of civil authority. While
approving of the commutation of sentence on the Aborigines, he
was quick to point out that no right had been thereby obtained to
the cure of their souls. Polding went on to develop Gipps' arguments
to what he saw as their logical conclusion:

> If the reasons alleged justify the decision in the case of these men, it
> will follow that all prisoners, White or Black, become the property of
> the State, Body and Soul; and with equal rights, chains may envelope
> the one and a form of faith be imposed on the other. It will follow
> . . . that all subjects to the Civil authority are bound to take their
> creed from the Civil Authority; it will follow that the persecutions
> which the ambitious or the usurping have inflicted on those subjects to
> their power under a pretext of zeal for religion are perfectly justifiable,
> and that even now and in this Colony all who may not be of the
> Religion of Her Majesty are to be thankful for that they are not
> taken from the Pastors of their choice and compelled to attend the
> Ministrations of the Individual whom the Governor for the time being
> may deem more fit to teach them the religion of the Queen.[122]

Although Gipps did not agree that these conclusions followed 'inevitably' from his decision, he declined to enter into any further
argument. No doubt he realized that Polding had seized on this
question to express the indignation aroused by a number of more
important grievances.

In the following year the French settlement of Tahiti precipitated public controversy over the relative merits of Protestant and
Catholic missions. When Lang, Threlkeld and Saunders called a
public meeting to protest against the annexation and to uphold the
sovereignty of Queen Pomaré, William Duncan retaliated in *The
Morning Chronicle* by attacking the entire record of British Protestant missionary activity in the South Seas. He alleged that while
Threlkeld and Lang had been speculating in coal-mining and
college-building, their 'sable flocks' were 'destroyed under the administration of English *panaceas*, rum and bibles, and syphilis, and
preachments, and strychnine, and hymns, and fusillades, and rifle
practice'.[123] Ridiculing Samuel Marsden as 'that apostle of the

121 Suttor, *Hierarchy and Democracy*, p. 97.
122 Polding to Deas Thomson, 12 January 1844, Enclosure, Stanley to Gipps,
    17 July 1844, *HRA*, XXIII, p. 679.
123 8 June 1844.

Southern Hemisphere', Duncan described the Protestants as 'preaching . . . the bible trumpet-tongued among the blackfellows'.[124] He attributed the Protestants' lack of success more to their concentration on the gospel than to their commercial and political activities, although it was 'utter folly' to expect Aborigines to be converted to Christianity by men with wives, children, stock, servants and corn stacks to occupy them. The system of 'bible only' was caricatured by Duncan as producing such absurdities as a translation for the American Indians entitled *Mamussee Wanneetupanatamwe up-biblum God Naneeswe Nukkone Testament Kah Wonk Wusku Testament*.[125] It seemed to him absurd that the Protestants should so strenuously defend the sovereignty of Queen Pomaré while neglecting the rights of the Aborigines of New South Wales.

GOVERNMENT AID TO THE ABORIGINES

The decline of conflicts in some squatting districts by 1844 meant that individual squatters could express humanitarian concern for the plight of Aborigines in the settled districts. At the same time there was an opportunity to attack Gipps in an unexpected quarter for the parsimony of his administration's assistance to Aborigines.

Gipps had inherited from Bourke the annual custom of giving a blanket to every Aborigine who turned up at a Police Office on 1 May. By 1838 blankets had assumed considerable importance to the Aborigines, not only for their practical value when declining numbers of marsupials in the settled districts made it difficult to obtain the traditional skin rugs, but because they were accepted by the Aborigines as a form of tribute for the land which had been taken from them. Furthermore, it was the only occasion when they were accorded recognition by officialdom and told of the goodwill of the 'Gubernor' and the White Queen across the sea.

The 'indiscriminate' system of blanket distribution inevitably met with Gipps' disapproval and in a circular to all magistrates shortly after his arrival he directed that blankets should only be given out as rewards for particular services rendered by Aborigines, such as assisting in the capture of convict 'bolters' and in rescuing people from shipwrecks.[126] Subsequently he reduced the number of blankets

[124] Ibid.
[125] *The Morning Chronicle*, 15 June 1844.
[126] Circular dated 22 May 1838, *CSIL*, 4/1133.3, 38/515.

issued from 2,485 in 1841 to 562 in 1844 when he announced that the issue would be discontinued, except in very special circumstances. In his opinion, the Aborigines would 'never be induced to work, whilst the practice of giving them blankets in reward for their idleness is persevered in'.[127]

Moreover, he remained inflexible in the face of undeniable evidence that the reduction in issue caused serious suffering and resentment among Aborigines of the settled districts. In May 1842, for example, Captain William Oldrey, Police Magistrate at Broulee, informed Deas Thomson that the unusually serious winter in the district had caused many deaths among Aborigines assembled in expectation of the issue:

> The poor creatures are now suffering from the intense cold . . . and frequently stand shivering before me, demanding "when the government send down blankets for blackfellow?"[128]

When the blankets, delayed by transport difficulties, finally arrived on 7 May there were only 170 for more than 300 applicants. Informing Deas Thomson of this, Oldrey also applied for compensation for medicines and medical treatment which he had authorized. Gipps refused to send more blankets or to meet the medical expenses, claiming that he was in no position to answer the numerous calls for expenditure from all parts of the colony, 'and certainly from no part of it in greater number or in greater variety of shapes than from . . . Broulee'.[129] However, the 'erroneous' principle of 'indiscriminate' distribution retained by Oldrey weighed even more heavily with Gipps. Oldrey's belief that every Aborigine was entitled to a blanket would have been sufficient reason for the Governor's refusal to comply with the request, 'even had I the means of doing so'.[130] The Newcastle agent later noted that a number of women and children died due to the absence of warm clothing between May and October[131] and David Dunlop at Wollombi believed that the supply should be resumed

127 Gipps' Minute dated 13 April 1842 on a letter from Major J. Bowler to Deas Thomson, 4 April 1842, *CSIL*, 4/1133.3, 42/2667.
128 Oldrey to Deas Thomson, 2 May 1842, *CSIL*, 4/1133.3, 42/4201.
129 Gipps' Minute, ibid.
130 Gipps' Minute, ibid.
131 Letter from J. H. Crummer, 'Replies to a Circular Letter from the Select Committee on the Condition of the Aborigines. . . .', Appendix to the 'Report from the Select Committee on the Condition of the Aborigines . . .', *V&P*, 1845, p. 972.

for although of small real utility to creatures of improvident habits, yet if the lives of a few infants be saved, and their wretched mothers comforted by the warmth of a blanket, such should be a consideration to the government far above all paltry saving of so many shillings or pounds.[132]

At the same time there was evidence that blankets were as important to Aborigines' morale as to their material comfort. Henry Bingham at Tumut noted that the distribution 'shews them that the Government have some regard for them, which is very gratifying to them'[133] and others described the Aborigines as looking upon it as their *right*. For those who were sympathetic towards the Aborigines, the question assumed some importance. Polding, who attributed Aboriginal depopulation to a sense of injustice and loss of the desire to rear children following ejection from their land, thought that the 'mere eleemosynary dole' was 'much the same, as if you were to rob a man of a hundred pounds and to give him a shilling'.[134] However, he recommended the resumption of the issue since it produced 'very great rejoicing and contentedness of mind' among the Aborigines at Stradbroke Island where the Passionist Fathers had established their mission in 1843. From his conversation with 'Boni', the old 'chief' of the Wollombi tribe, David Dunlop concluded that the annual gift

> was considered as a recognised tie between the ruler and the ruled . . . The Governor sold their ground to people who cut down the trees where the opossum dwelt, which had always furnished food for themselves, and warmth for their sleeping place, and for their women, and that in lieu thereof he gave blankets, which they accepted from want, but always spoke of as no recompense . . .[135]

Other contemporaries, however, felt that Polding and Dunlop were 'assuming too much in supposing that they could have such feelings'.[136] What the Aborigines really thought is impossible to say but Dunlop provided a hint by quoting the Wollombi 'chief's' complaint about Gipps' economizing measures:

> What we do, bail (no) not fight like New Zealand fellow, no. I gave

---

132 Ibid., p. 972.
133 Ibid., p. 981.
134 Ibid., p. 948.
135 Ibid., p. 972.
136 Question directed to Polding by Dr Charles Nicholson, ibid., p. 948.

land, and very hunger. No, did no bad, we get no blanket. What for?[137]

Dr Charles Nicholson's address of June 1844 for information on discontinuation of the blanket issue was intended to reveal the miserliness of Gipps' administration, as well as the hypocrisy of the official policy which he enforced. At the same time, Richard Windeyer asked for the production of correspondence relating to 'Jemmy Nyrang', an Aboriginal boy who had been admitted to Bathurst hospital suffering from a chronic scalp infection and a seriously diseased knee. The Colonial Secretary's Office had refused to authorize payment for medical attention and, like Oldrey, the Carcoar magistrates were obliged to meet the boy's expenses from their own pockets.[138] *The Sydney Morning Herald* very rightly took it up as an example of the administrative miserliness which underlay the colonial government's nominal philanthropy towards the Aborigines:

> The Colonists, even in defense of their cattle and sheep, and of their own lives, shall not treat the blacks ill; but neither the Magistrates nor the Colonial Surgeons shall expend a farthing of public money, or an ounce of public medicine, in treating them well, when bodily disease invokes compassion. Such is the practical tender-heartedness of our official Samaritans![139]

In the following year Windeyer moved for the appointment of a committee to investigate the possibility of improving the condition of the Aborigines, stating that the failure of all previous schemes made it all the more important to examine the problem more closely. Although he could not offer a practical solution, he felt that any plan should be tested against the opinions of Herman Merivale, professor of political economy at Oxford, whose *Lectures on Colonization* had recently been published. Given the failure of the Protectorate and the resentment aroused by its direct link with the Colonial Office, there was one passage in Merivale which must have caught Windeyer's eye:

> I cannot but regard the suggestion of establishing in the same colony 'responsible' government for the settlers, and a separate administration

[137] Ibid., p. 972.
[138] For the correspondence produced as a return to this address, see *V&P*, 1844, Vol. I, pp. 721-3.
[139] 10 October 1844.

for native affairs under the Home authorities, as unpractical. There cannot be two governments in the same community; certainly not unless some mode can be devised of having two public purses.[140]

Windeyer's original intention was to interview Aborigines as well as whites from each district of the colony, but his failing health cut short the Committee's hearings and no recommendations were made to the government.[141] His work, together with that of Thomson and Nicholson, indicates that there were some members of the squatting interest who were genuinely interested in the welfare of Aborigines once they had been 'pacified'. However, it was assumed that 'no plan for their welfare could have any chance of success, which did not premise their intermixture with the colonists.'[142]

Decline in the Aboriginal population of the towns and settled districts was so marked that it seemed pointless to talk any more about Christianization and civilization. In 1837 Threlkeld's analysis of population statistics based on blanket distribution had revealed a fifteen per cent decline of females over two years[143] and William Thomas estimated in November 1839 that in the Westernport district over the previous four years there had been seven deaths for every birth, amounting to a decline of more than thirty per cent.[144] Most people would have agreed with Alexander Thomson that 'but a small prophetic inspiration was needed to predicate the rapid and total extinction of the race'.[145]

It is likely that with the failure of the Protectorate, the defeat of his Aboriginal Evidence Bill in 1843 and the impossibility of solving racial conflicts by bringing Aborigines and whites to justice, Gipps despaired of doing anything constructive about the Aborigines. Besides, controversy over his 1844 squatting regulations and the whole question of land tenure were absorbing most of his flagging energies. In a despatch to Stanley of April 1846 enclosing

---

[140] *Lectures on Colonization and Colonies . . .* , London 1842, 2nd edn, 1861, p. 521.
[141] However, the Minutes of Evidence and replies from a number of correspondents to a comprehensive circular were published in *V&P*, 1845, pp. 937-1001.
[142] *The Sydney Morning Herald*, 20 August 1845.
[143] See Appendix III.
[144] Quoted by Howitt, *Impressions of Australia Felix*, p. 203. Another analysis made by Thomas for the period 1 September 1842 to 1 March 1843 revealed a similar ratio of deaths to births. *V&P*, 1843, p. 539.
[145] *The Australian*, 30 August 1843.

reports of the Crown Lands Commissioners on the Aborigines for 1845, he could only repeat the tired and hopeless phrases of earlier years: 'I very much regret that it is not in my power to notice in them any favourable alteration in the general condition of the Aborigines'.[146]

By this time the blanket issue and all assistance to the missions had been discontinued, while the Protectorate was receiving a mere pittance. However, the Native Police force, which had been revived at Port Phillip in 1842 by Henry Pulteney Dana,[147] had begun taking over the work of the Mounted Police and Border Police in 'pacifying' Aborigines in the still troublesome parts of the District. The Aboriginal troopers proved to be extremely skilful in tracking down and 'dispersing' Aborigines accused by squatters of sheep or cattle stealing and their bloodthirsty zeal in settling old tribal scores was applauded by their white officers as strong evidence that Aborigines could, after all, be civilized and usefully employed.[148] While he may not have been aware of the terrible slaughter perpetrated by the Native Police, Gipps' economical mind must have been impressed by the fact that their pay of three pence a day compared very favourably with the five shillings paid to white troopers engaged in similar work.

When Gipps left the colony in July 1846, the wheel had turned full circle. Arbitrary force in the form of the Native Police, soon to be stationed by Gipps' successor Sir Charles Fitzroy on the northern edge of the Liverpool Plains as well, constituted the colonial government's only real answer to the problem of racial strife in the squatting districts. During the brief period between 1838 and 1844 there had been a genuine, although ill-informed, attempt to bring Aboriginal-white relations under the framework of the law and to improve the spiritual, if not the material, welfare of the Aborigines. Now the situation reverted to what had been normal since the foundation of the colony. Racial conflicts resulting from the expansion of white settlement were settled by force of arms, the colonial government lending assistance to squatters and their servants in 'pacifying' Aborigines who refused to move off stations formed on their tribal territory and who believed that they had as

---

[146] Gipps to Stanley, 1 April 1846, *HRA*, XXV, p. 1.
[147] Foxcroft, *Australian Native Policy*, pp. 87-90.
[148] For descriptions of how the Native Police operated in the Port Phillip district, see Howitt, *Impressions of Australia Felix*, pp. 196-7.

much right to kill sheep and cattle as the whites had to kill kangaroos. This was the pattern which was to continue with little interruption during the pastoral settlement of Queensland and the Northern Territory and into the twentieth century.

APPENDIX I

CONFLICTS BETWEEN ABORIGINES AND WHITES, 1832-45

(i) *List of Europeans Killed by the Aborigines on the Liverpool Plains 1832-8*[1]

1832 Mr Surveyor Finch, had two men killed at the Big River, while on duty with Major Mitchell.

1835 About the end of this year a servant of Sir John Jamison was murdered on the Namoi River.

1836 In April two men of Mr Hall's were attacked (on the Big River) while splitting timber: one man was killed and the other escaped with a spear in his leg. The natives then attacked the hut and Mr Thomas Hall received a spear in the head.

1837 September. Mr George Bowman's hut (situated between the Namoi and Big Rivers) was attacked while the storekeepers were out, and two hutkeepers were killed.

1837 November. Two shepherds in the employ of Mr Cobb, on the Big River, were murdered while attending their sheep in the bush.

1838 January. Two men belonging to Messrs J. and Francis Allman were murdered at New England, and their sheep driven away.

1838 March. Mr Surveyor Finch had two men murdered, while in charge of a tent and some stores, at New England. Mr Cobban apprehended these Blacks with Mr Finch's property in their possession.

1838 March. Mr Cruikshank, at New England, had a shepherd murdered in the bush; and when the flock was found sixty or seventy sheep were missing.

1838 April. Mr Fitzgerald's hutkeeper on the Big River was killed, the hut stripped, and on the arrival home of the other men, they were also attacked but escaped, one having been speared through the leg, and another through the sleeve of his jacket.

   The sacrifice of property has been immense, and the attacks upon the persons of Europeans innumerable, but none are mentioned except where loss of life occurred. And it is to be remarked, that *not one* of the perpetrators of *any one* of these fifteen murders has been brought to justice, although they have been going on since 1832.

[1] *The Colonist*, 22 September 1838.

(ii) *1842 Petition from Squatters in the Port Fairy District*[2]

List of outrages recently committed by Natives in the neighbourhood of Port Fairy:

Man killed, 100 sheep taken, and hut robbed of everything it contained, including a double-barrelled gun, with ammunition.

300 sheep and 100 tons of potatoes.

5 horses taken, and 7 head of cattle killed, 56 calves, also 33 driven off, and two men wounded. The station has been attacked four times.

600 sheep taken, of which 130 were recovered.

Hut robbed, and two double-barrelled guns taken.

10 cows and 40 calves killed. Hut attacked several times, and men severely wounded.

Three flocks attacked simultaneously, one of which was taken away, and the shepherd desperately wounded: the major part was eventually recovered, one man taken but recovered.

200 sheep taken and men speared.

Shepherd fired at.

2 horses taken—station attacked and flock of sheep carried off, and shepherd dreadfully wounded.

2 horses killed—hut robbed, and men driven off the station.

Shepherd killed—found with a spear through his heart.

One horse taken.

30 sheep.

50 sheep.

250 sheep, and man wounded.

50 sheep.

260 sheep and man killed.

300 sheep.

700 sheep taken but mostly recovered.

180 sheep, station attacked and robbed, and hutkeeper severely wounded.

A very valuable bull killed, and a number of calves.

6 cows, 3 bullocks, 20 calves, man killed and cattle driven off.

200 ewes and 150 lambs.

These losses have principally occurred within the last two months.

(iii) *Conflicts in the Wellington District 1844-5*[3]

1. On the 13th October 1844, Mr Kinghorne's stockman was attacked and plundered by blacks of the Mole (Macquarie Marshes) whilst tailing his master's cattle on the run at Gerawhey.

2. 18th October 1844. The same blacks attacked the Gerawhey station, drove out the Superintendent and two men and took away a flock of sheep.

3. 21st October 1844. The sheep which had been recovered were again taken by the same blacks and everything in the huts destroyed. . .

[2] GD. ML. MS.A1228. pp. 256-8.

[3] Taken from the Annual Report of Commissioner W. H. Wright.

4. 27th December 1844. Two Border Policemen were at Gerawhey. At sunset a body of blacks advanced towards the hut and threw their 'Womerahs' at the Policemen and Mr Hay who were standing outside.
5. 26th January 1845. A black was shot by Mr Hay in self-defence.
6. July 1845. Mr Dalhunty's shepherd whilst following his flock at Mount Forster was surprised by a party of Aborigines, plundered of several small articles from his person and about forty of the sheep driven away by the blacks.
7. July 1845. The blacks burnt down the Gerawhey Station. . .
8. A large body of blacks attacked and plundered five stations on the Macquarie River.

(iv) Official list of all whites and Aborigines killed in the Port Phillip District, 1836-44.[a]

RETURN of Whites killed by the Aboriginal Natives in the District of Port Phillip, distinguishing the numbers East and West of the River Hopkins.

DATE	OCCURRENCE	LOCALITY	NUMBER IN EASTERN DIVISION	NUMBER IN WESTERN DIVISION	REMARKS
1836 July	Mr. Franks and Servants	Mount Cottrell	2	..	Murderers known, but could not be taken.
1838 April	Party with stock for Mr. Faithful, attacked by a large body of Natives	Near Swampy River, about 140 miles from Melbourne	10	..	Unsuccessful pursuit and enquiries; number killed not positively known.
May	Mr. Bowman's servant, Jones	60 miles from Melbourne	1	..	
December	Dr. Forster's servant, Mould	Goulburn River	1	..	Body disinterred and carried away by the Blacks.
1839 May	Mr. Hutton's shepherds, Bryan and Neill	Campaspe	2	..	
May	Mr. Macfarlane's servant	Upper Goulburn	1	..	
1840 January	Derwent Company's hutkeeper	Geelong District	1	..	
February	Hutkeeper Wilson	Near Portland Bay	..	1	
April	Mr. Anderson's servant	Near Portland Bay	..	1	
April	Mr. Chisholme's servant, Thompson	King River	1	..	Murderer tried and executed.
May	Mr. Codd, overseer	Mount Rouse	..	1	
May	Dr. Mackay's shepherd	Ovens' River	1	..	
May	Mr. Waugh's shepherds	Upper Goulburn	2	..	
June	Mr. Thompson's shepherd, Hayes	Kilambete	..	1	

Date	Name	Locality	In the Eastern Division	In the Western Division	Remarks
June	Messrs. Jennings and Playne's shepherd	Mount Campbell	1	..	
June	Watson and Hunter's shepherd	Upper Goulburn	1	..	
1841					
March	Mr. Oliphant's shepherd	Pyrenees	1	..	
May	Mr. Bennett's shepherd	Mount Alexander	1	..	
May	Mr. Morton and servant	Glenelg	..	2	
May	Mr. Gibson's shepherd	Glenelg	..	1	
May	Mr. Williams' hutkeeper	Mount William	..	1	
October	William Cook and another, by Van Diemen's Land Blacks	Mount William	..	..	Murderers tried and executed.
1842					
March	Mr. Allan	Loddon	1	..	
May	Mr. Ritchie's shepherd	Port Fairy	..	1	
May	Mr. Mackenzie's hutkeeper	Near Portland Bay	..	2	
1843					
August	Mr. Bassett, settler	Port Fairy	..	1	
1844					
April	Mr. Rickett's shepherd	Glenelg	..	1	
	TOTAL		27	13	In the Eastern Division; In the Western Division
	GRAND TOTAL....			40	In the District of Port Phillip

[4] *V&P*, 1844, I, 718-19. *Note:* Discrepancies in the figures follow original text.

RETURN of Aboriginal Natives killed by the Whites in the District of Port Phillip, distinguishing the numbers East and West of the River Hopkins.

DATE	OCCURRENCE	LOCALITY	NUMBER IN EASTERN DIVISION	NUMBER IN WESTERN DIVISION	REMARKS
1836 October	Curacoine shot		1	..	John Whitehead sent to Sydney for trial, but no witnesses attended.
1838 July	Mr. Bowman's sheep driven off; party attempting to retake them resisted by the Blacks		14	..	Number rests partly on statements made by the Aborigines.
July	Said to have been shot by two white men		2	..	Rests on statements made by the Aborigines.
1839 February	Shot by Mr. Bowman's servants	Pyrenees	2	..	Men tried for misdemeanor in burning the bodies and acquitted.
June	Shot by Mr. Hutton and the Police	Campaspe	6	..	
1840 January	Shot by Mr. Munro and party	River Colaband	3	..	Evidence insufficient for prosecution.
January	Said to have been shot by Mr. Hamilton	Western District	..	1	
February	Killed by Mr. Darlot's servants	Loddon	1	..	Tried and acquitted.
March	Killed attacking Mr. Winter's station		..	5	
March	Collisions with Messrs. Whyte	Wannon	..	30	Aggression by the Aborigines; number killed rests principally on their evidence.
June	Said to have been shot by Mr. Aylward and party		..	5	Aylward left the Colony; depends on statements of the Aborigines.
August	Collisions with Messrs. Wedge	Grampians	..	10	Depends partly on statements of Aborigines.
August	Said to have been shot by Mr. Dutton's servant	Loddon	1	..	Man charged absconded.
August	Shot by Mr. Francis in his sheepfold	Pyrenees	1	..	

Date	Particulars	Locality			Remarks
October	Shot by Police, in attempt to apprehend a party	near Melbourne	1		
October	Shot by Sentry, breaking out of Gaol	Melbourne	1		
December	Charged with felony; shot by Mr. Mackay	River Hume	1		
December	Shot by Mr. Francis	Pyrenees	5		
December	Said to have been shot by Mr. Henty's servants	Wannon		2	
1841					
February	Shot by Mr. Dutton's servants	Loddon	1		
March	Said to have been shot by a splitter	Mount Cole	1		
May	Found wounded, died in Melbourne Hospital	Mount Alexander	1		Supposed by Mr. Bennett's who was found murdered.
July	Reported to have been shot by Hall's men	Grampians		2	Rests on statements of Aborigines.
July	Reported to have been shot by three White men				Rests on statements of Aborigines.
August	Reported to have been shot by Captain Bunbury's stockkeeper	near Kirks, Purrumbeep	4		Rests on statements of Aborigines.
		near Mount William		1	Rests on statements of Aborigines.
1842					
March	Shot near Smith and Osbrey's station, three females and one child	Mount Rouse		4	Great investigations made; three persons tried for the murder and acquitted.
April	Killed in an affray with Dr. Mackay	Ovens' River	1		
September	Killed attacking Mr. Hunter's station			1	
1843					
November	Collision with Mr. Ricketts and others	near Portland Bay		3	
1844					
May	Shot by Police in endeavouring to recover stolen sheep	Pyrenees	1		
May	Shot in self-defence by Mr. Boyd's shepherd	Grampians		1	
		TOTAL	48		In the Eastern Division
		TOTAL		65	In the Western Division
		GRAND TOTAL....	113		In the District of Port Phillip

APPENDIX II

TRIALS OF ALL ABORIGINES 1824-43

*A List of All The Aboriginal Natives Tried and Convicted Before
the Supreme Court of New South Wales since...May 1824 to
February...1836.*[1]

NAME OF PRISONER	OFFENCE FOR WHICH TRIED	VERDICT	MONTH	YEAR	SENTENCE	ALTERATION OR COMMUTATION
Divil Divil	Violent Assault	Guilty	3 June	1825	Not sentenced	
Tommy alias Jacky Jacky	Murder	Guilty	24 Nov.	1827	Executed	
Broger	Murder	Guilty	20 Aug.	1830	Executed	
Little Dick		Not guilty				
Whip um up		Guilty				
Monkey		Guilty			Death recorded	Life to Van Diemen's Land
Charlie Muscle						
Little Freeman	Stealing in Dwelling House & putting in fear	Not Guilty	11 Feb.	1835		
Leggamy						
Major						
Currinbong Jemmy						
Tom Jones						
Legamy	Highway robbery	Guilty	12 Feb	1835	Death recorded	Life to Van Diemen's Land
Little Dick	Stealing in Dwelling House & putting in fear	Guilty of Larceny	12 Feb	1835	Transported for 7 years	To Van Diemen's Land
		Guilty			Death recorded	Life to Van Diemen's Land
Mickey Mickey and	Rape	Guilty	12 Feb.	1835	Death passed	Executed
Charlie Myrtle						
Toby	Stealing in Dwelling House & putting in fear	Guilty	12 Feb.	1835	Death recorded	Life to Van Diemen's Land
Little Freeman		Guilty	12 Feb.	1835	Death recorded	Life to Van Diemen's Land
		Guilty	12 Feb.	1835	Death recorded	
Hobby and	Stealing in Dwelling House & putting in fear	Guilty	5 Aug.	1835	Death recorded	
Maitland Paddy		Not guilty	22 Aug.	1835		
Charley	Murder	Guilty	22 Aug.	1835	Death passed	

[1] *BP*, No. 49.

(ii) *List of all Aborigines tried and convicted before the Supreme Court of New South Wales, 1837–43.* [2]

A RETURN of all trials of Aborigines, with the result arrived at, specifying those against whom initiatory steps have been taken and abandoned.

NO.	WHERE COMMITTED	DATE	NAME	OFFENCE	WHERE TRIED	GUILTY	NOT GUILTY	SENTENCE	BILL IGNORED	REMARKS
1	Port Macquarie	10th Feb., 1837	Jackey / Old Parker	Murder	Supreme Court		Not guilty			
2	Maitland	3rd ,, ,,	Charley	Stealing					Bill ignored	
3	Port Macquarie	15th March, ,,	Murphy							Discharged; no interpreter
4	Maitland	21st Feb., 1838	Wombarty / Lory Jack	Murder	Supreme Court	Guilty		Death		
5	Port Macquarie	6th April, ,,	Jackey Beramble	Murder	do.					Discharged by Proclamation
6	Bathurst	8th ,, ,,	Captain	Assault	do.					Discharged by Proclamation
7	Sydney	8th May, ,,	Big-nosed Jack	Murder						Escaped
8	Wellington	14th ,, ,,	Franky	Murder			Not guilty			Discharged
9	Melbourne	15th ,, ,,	Mooney Mooney / Bunia Logan / Mainga / Murrem Murrem Beel / Murry or Poen / Jack Sloe / Jin Jin	Killing sheep					Bill ignored	
10	Geelong	9th June, ,,	Hangmoon / Sandy	Murder	Supreme Court					Discharged by Proclamation
11	Muswellbrook and Namoi River	25th April, 1839	Billy / Jemmy / Cooper / King Jackey	Robbery	do.	Guilty		10 years transportation		
12	Wellington	4th June, ,,	Myall Tommy	Cattle stealing	Quarter Sessions		Not guilty			
13	Muswellbrook	21st ,, ,,	Mary Ann	Shooting with intent, &c.	Supreme Court		Not guilty			
14	Patrick's Plains	29th Aug., ,,		Horse stealing	do.		Not guilty			
15	Muswellbrook	16th Oct., ,,	Charley / Jimmy / Jackey / Billy	Stealing	Quarter Sessions					

No.	Place	Date	Name	Crime	Court	Verdict	Sentence	Remarks
16	Maitland	22nd ,,	Toby, Murphy	Robbery				
17	Cassilis	5th Feb., 1840	Talboy alias Jackey	Murder	Supreme Court	Guilty	Death	
18	Yass	4th March ,,	Blucher, Charley	Assault	Quarter Sessions			Discharged, being in a dying state
19	Bathurst	12th May, ,,	Gilderoy	Larceny	do.	Guilty	1 day's imprisonment and 50 lashes	
20	Yass	14th June, ,,	Billy alias Neville's Billy	Murder	Supreme Court	Guilty	Death	
21	Windsor	16th ,, ,,	Humpy George	Stabbing, &c.	Quarter Sessions	Guilty	Death	Escaped from Prison
22	Moreton Bay	Aug., ,,	Merridio, Nengavil, Bunmalleo, Dundoro	Murder	Supreme Court	Guilty	Death	Bunmalleo died in Hospital
23	Wellington	29th ,, ,,	Tommy Poker, Benjamin, Jemmy, Tommy Ban Ban	Spearing cattle	do.	Not guilty		
24	Melbourne	28th Sep., ,,	Weenaburnee, Konghomarnee	Murder	do.		Death	Tried at Port Phillip
25	Peel's River	23rd June, 1841	Sullivan	Spearing cattle				Bill ignored
26	Peel's River	18th Oct., ,,	Cumbo Jackey, Wellington	Spearing cattle	Circuit Court	Guilty	10 years transportation	
27	Bathurst	18th Nov., ,,	Joey alias Cudgenmolly, Jaco alias Currajomblay	Murder	do.			Discharged by Proclamation
28	Peel's River	10th Jan., 1842	Fryingpan	Spearing cattle	do.			Bill ignored
29	New England	9th May, ,,	Jerry	Murder	do.	Not guilty		
30	Paterson	13th Mar., 1843	Melville	Murder				Bill ignored; Supposed murder of an Aboriginal Black
31	Maitland	25th ,, ,,	Melville, Harry, Fowler	Murder; Assault with intent to kill	do.	Guilty	Death	
32	Port Macquarie	12th June, ,,	Sore thighed Jemmy, Jacky Jacky		do.	Guilty	Death	
33	Port Macquarie	24th July, ,,	Therramitchie	Murder	do.	Guilty	Death	

² V&P, 1843, p. 476.

APPENDIX III

STATISTICS SHOWING ABORIGINAL DEPOPULATION: 1835-7

An ABSTRACT from the Official General Returns of the Black Natives, taken at the Annual Distribution of the Government Donation of Blankets to each Tribe, within the four Divisions of the Colony, for the years 1835, 1836, 1837.[1]

	Men, Women, and Children
1. South and South-western District, from Sydney to Twofold Bay inclusive, 5 returns	422
2. Western District, Bathurst, Wellington Valley, 1 Return	127
3. North and North-western District, from Sydney to Port Macquarie inclusive, 10 Returns	1220
4. Home District, Sydney and Windsor inclusive, 8 Returns	325
Sum-total of 24 Returns in 1835 Individuals	2094

				Men	Women	Boys	Girls	Total
1835—Description of Persons, from 24 Returns				904	681	291	217	2094
1836—Ditto	ditto	15	ditto	727	461	225	169	1528
1837—Ditto	ditto	16	ditto	735	454	195	147	1531

PROPORTION OF SEXES, INCLUDING CHILDREN

1835—Of 2094 Persons, there were 75 Females to 100 Males.
1836—Of 1582   ditto   66 ditto 100
1837—Of 1531   ditto   64 ditto 100

Decrease of Females in two years, 15 per cent.!

	Men	Women	Boys	Girls	Total
*From 11 Returns of the most populous Districts, there were, in 1835	535	405	196	136	1272
From the same 11 Districts, in 1837	538	343	154	120	1155
Decrease in two years		62	42	16	117

NUMBER OF ADULT MALES, OF THE SUPPOSED AGES,
(the Women's are not returned.)

	10 years to 20	20 to 30	30 to 40	40 to 50	50 to 60	60 to 70	70 to 80
1835—of 850 Adult Males, from 24 Returns, there were	99	318	249	100	63	21	—
1836—Of 632 ditto, 15 returns,	74	261	211	86	39	11	—
1837—Of 702 ditto, 16 returns,	129	253	193	65	49	10	3

*The Returns not being complete sets, only eleven were found to correspond for the years 1835 and 1837.

December 30, 1837

L. E. THRELKELD

[1] 'Report of the Mission to the Aborigines at Lake Macquarie . . .', *V&P*, 1838.

APPENDIX IV

GOVERNMENT EXPENDITURE ON ABORIGINES 1821-42.[1]

NEW SOUTH WALES (ABORIGINES)

Return to an Address:—Dr. Thomson, 29th August, 1843:—Laid upon the Table 12th October, 1843

No. 1.

RETURN of the Expense defrayed from the Colonial Treasury of New South Wales, of every Mission to the Aborigines within the Colony, and of the Protectorate, and the Total Expense of the Protectorate, from their commencement to 31st December 1842; shewing the amount paid for each Mission, the expense of the Protectorate, and the Total Expense of the Aborigines, for each year.

EXPENSE OF EACH MISSION

YEAR	Aboriginal Native Institution			Mission of enquiry into the state and number of the Aboriginal population under Lieut. R. Sadleir			Mission under the Rev. L. E. Threlkeld, at Lake Macquarie			Mission under the Church Missionary Society, at Wellington Valley			German Mission at Moreton Bay			Wesleyan Mission at Port Phillip			Total expense of the several Missions in each year			Expense of the Protectorate, at Port Philip			Cost of Blankets and other expenses, not included in any previous column			Total expense of the Aborigines in each year		
	£	s.	d.	£	s.	d.	£	s.	d.	£	s.	d.	£	s.	d.	£	s.	d.	£	s.	d.	£	s.	d.	£	s.	d.	£	s.	d.
1821	185	0	11¾																185	0	11¾							185	0	11¾
1822	539	1	0½																539	1	0½				13	2	1¼	552	3	2
1823	962	0	0																962	0	0							962	0	0
1824	212	11	0																212	11	0							212	11	0
1825	66	6	0																66	6	0							66	6	0
1826	225	18	9	186	9	10													412	8	7							412	8	7
1827	315	1	9½	201	14	6	12	15	6										529	11	9½							529	11	9

1828	286 8 7	..	..	..	..	..	286 8 7	..	..	286 8 7
1829	165 3 2	..	..	..	..	..	165 3 2	..	..	165 3 2
1830	168 3 7	..	86 10 4	..	..	..	254 13 11	..	..	254 13 11
1831	132 10 0	..	186 0 0	..	..	..	318 10 0	..	14 0 0	332 10 0
1832	100 0 0	..	186 0 0	726 0 6	..	..	1012 0 6	..	412 1 8¾	1424 2 2¾
1833	6 5 0	..	186 0 0	433 6 8	..	..	625 11 8	..	340 13 1	966 4 9
1834	..	..	186 0 0	500 0 0	..	..	686 0 0	..	442 0 6	1128 0 6
1835	..	..	186 0 0	500 0 0	..	..	686 0 0	..	825 17 9½	1511 17 9½
1836	..	..	186 0 0	500 0 0	..	221 11 6	907 11 6	..	904 10 0	1812 1 6
1837	..	..	186 0 0	650 0 0	..	664 11 9¼	1500 11 9¼	..	851 19 10¾	2352 11 8
1838	..	..	186 0 0	500 0 0	310 19 2	1460 11 7¾	2457 10 9¾	990 7 6	1190 4 7	4638 2 10¾
1839	..	..	186 0 0	530 3 0	159 7 6	631 18 6	1507 9 0	3004 6 0	1330 7 6	5842 2 6
1840	..	..	186 0 0	500 0 0	321 5 10	795 0 5	1802 6 3	5611 12 6	961 4 0	8375 2 9
1841	..	..	186 0 0	500 0 0	494 1 4	449 14 10	1629 16 2	7618 3 3½	847 13 6	10095 12 11½
1842	..	..	..	500 0 0	231 0 4	315 0 1	1046 0 5	7967 5 1	689 10 0	9702 15 6
TOTALS..£	3364 9 10¾	388 4 4	2145 5 10	5839 10 2	1516 14 2	4538 8 9	17792 13 1¾	25191 14 4½	8823 4 8½	51807 12 2¾

REMARKS

The sums, which, in the Annual Statements for the Council, were brought to account under the Head Aborigines as arrears of previous years, have, in this Return, been posted to the Expenditure of the year for which they were incurred, in order that the actual expense of each year may, as nearly as practicable, be shewn.

Exclusively of the sums specified in this Return, one-half of the expense of the Border Police, is usually considered to be incurred on account of the Aborigines.

The half of this expense was,

in	1839	£5174 13 0
	1840	7512 8 9
	1841	8215 12 0
	1842	6813 15 0
	TOTAL	£27716 8 9

Audit Office, Sydney, New South Wales,
2nd September, 1843

WILLIAM LITHGOW,
Auditor General

[1] *V&P*, 1843, p. 475.

SELECT BIBLIOGRAPHY

1. Bibliographies and indexes
2. Official sources   (i) manuscript
                            (ii) printed
3. Other manuscript sources
4. Other printed sources
5. Newspapers
6. Contemporary books, pamphlets and memoirs
7. Later works   (i) Anthropology, sociology and Aboriginal white relations
                     (ii) Official policy towards Aborigines
                     (iii) Other works
                     (iv) Works for comparison

1. BIBLIOGRAPHIES AND INDEXES

Ferguson, J. A., *Bibliography of Australia*, Vols I-IV, Sydney 1941-55.

Greenway, J., *Bibliography of the Australian Aborigines and the Native Peoples of Torres Strait to 1959*, Sydney 1963.

—, *Bibliography of Unpublished References to Aborigines and Torres Strait Islanders*, 3 sections, unpublished MS, Australian National University Library.

Institute of Aboriginal Studies, Canberra, Card index of published references to Aborigines.

2. OFFICIAL SOURCES

(i) *Manuscript*

a. MITCHELL LIBRARY

Despatches to and from the Governor of New South Wales, 1838-46.

Enclosures to despatches, 1838-46.

Transcripts of missing despatches, 1838-46.

Public Record Office copies of despatches to and from the Governor of New South Wales, 1838-46. Microfilmed by the joint copying project of the Mitchell and Australian National University Libraries.

Aborigines Papers. ML, MS.A611. This volume contains Captain Grey's Report and Russell's and Gipps' comments on it, together with the replies to the circular letter on the employment of Aborigines distributed by the 1841 Committee on Immigration.

b. ARCHIVES OFFICE OF NEW SOUTH WALES

New South Wales Executive Council Records.
  Minute Books.
  Appendices to Minutes.
Governor's Minutes.
Colonial Secretary's Correspondence: In Letters (special bundles).
  Re Aborigines 1833-5, Box No. 4/6666.3.
  Distribution of blankets to Aborigines 1838-43, Box No. 4/1133.3.
  Re Aborigines and Native Police 1835-44, Box No. 4/1135.1.
Crown Land Commissioners' Correspondence, 1838-50.
Supreme Court Records.
  Muswellbrook Benchbook 1838-43, Box No. 4/5601. This contains
    depositions taken by E. D. Day during his investigation of the Myall
    Creek massacre.
  Proceedings of the Supreme Court, Vol. 156, 1838-9, Box No. 2/3341.
    This contains Judge James Dowling's notes on the first trial of the
    Myall Creek men.
  Notes of Criminal Cases in the Supreme Court, New South Wales, Tried
    Before W. W. Burton, Vol. 39 (1838), Box No. 2/2439. Contains
    Burton's notes on the second trial of the Myall Creek men.
  Papers relating to the Aborigines, 1796-1839, Box No. 1161. This
    important collection of official, semi-official and private documents
    was assembled by Judge W. W. Burton in 1838, presumably at the
    time when he was working on draft legislation for the protection of
    Aborigines. An itemised list of the contents can be found in the
    description of documents transferred from the Supreme Court to the
    Archives Office, ML reference book B1678.

c. LA TROBE LIBRARY

Gipps-La Trobe Private Correspondence. Indexed by G. Morrissey.
(ii) Printed

British House of Commons, Sessional Papers.
1831. *Van Diemen's Land. Return to an Address . . . dated 19th July*
    1831 for Copies of all Correspondence between Lieutenant-Governor
    Arthur and His Majesty's Secretary of State for the Colonies, on the
    Subject of the Military Operations lately carried on against the
    Aboriginal Inhabitants of Van Diemen's Land. PP, 1831, XIX, No.
    259, 86 pp.
1831. *New South Wales. Return to an Address . . . dated 19th July*
    1831 for Copies of Instructions given by His Majesty's Secretary of
    State for the Colonies, for promoting the Moral and Religious In-
    struction of the Aboriginal Inhabitants of New Holland or Van
    Diemen's Land. PP, 1831, XIX, No. 261, 19 pp.
1834. *Aboriginal Tribes (North America, New South Wales, Van Die-*
    men's Land and British Guiana.) Returns to several Addresses dated
    19th March 1834 . . . PP, 1834, XLIV, No. 617, 229 pp. The section
    dealing with the Australian colonies comprises:

1. Despatches and replies relating to the religious education of Aborigines of New South Wales.
2. Expenditure on such education.
3. Despatches and replies relating to the Aborigines of Van Diemen's Land not already published.
4. Expenditure on religious education of the Aborigines of Van Diemen's Land.

1836. *Report from the Select Committee on Aborigines (British Settlements;) together with the Minutes of Evidence, Appendix and Index. PP, 1836, VII, No. 538, 841 pp.*

1837. *Report from the Select Committee on Aborigines (British Settlements;) with the Minutes of Evidence, Appendix and Index. PP, 1837, VII, No. 425, 212 pp.*

1839. *Australian Aborigines. Return to an Address . . . dated 19th July 1839 for Copies or Extracts of Despatches relative to the Massacre of various Aborigines of Australia, in the Year 1838, and respecting the Trial of their Murderers. PP, 1839, XXXIV, No. 526, 56 pp.*

1844. *Aborigines (Australian Colonies). Return to an Address . . . dated 5th August 1844 for Copies or Extracts from the Despatches of the Governors of the Australian Colonies, with the Reports of the Protectors of Aborigines, and any other Correspondence to illustrate the Condition of the Aboriginal Population of the said Colonies, from the Date of the last Papers laid before Parliament on the subject. (Papers ordered . . . to be printed, 12th August, 1839, No. 526.) PP, 1844, XXXIV, No. 627, 437 pp.*

New South Wales Legislative Council, *Votes and Proceedings.*

1838. *Report from the Committee on the Aborigines Question, with the Minutes of Evidence. V&P, 1838, 60 pp.*

1839. *Report from the Committee on the Crown Lands Bill, with the Minutes of Evidence. V&P, 1839, I, 43 pp.*

1839. *Report of the Committee on Police and Gaols, with the Minutes of Evidence and Appendix. V&P, 1839, II, 346 pp.*

1841. *Report from the Committee on Immigration, with the Appendix, Minutes of Evidence, and Replies to a Circular Letter on the Aborigines. V&P, 1841, 50 pp.*

1843. *New South Wales. (Aborigines.)* (Return to an address made by Dr. Alexander Thomson on 29th August 1843, comprising details of government expenditure on Aborigines 1823-43, the results of all trials of Aborigines 1837-43, and a large collection of correspondence relating to the Protectorate and the missions.) *V&P, 1843, pp. 475-542.*

1844. *New South Wales. (Aborigines.)* (Return to an address of 26th July 1844, comprising correspondence relating to the medical treatment of Aborigines.) *V&P, 1844, Vol. I, pp. 711-5.*

1844. *New South Wales. (Aborigines.)* (Return to an address made by Sir Thomas Mitchell on 13th June 1844 for numbers of whites and

Aborigines killed in conflicts since the settlement of the Port Phillip
district.) *V&P*, 1844, Vol. I, pp. 717-9.

1844. *New South Wales. (Jemmy Nyrang—An Aboriginal Native.)*
(Return to an address from Richard Windeyer on 13th June 1844,
comprising correspondence relating to the medical treatment of an
Aboriginal boy at Bathurst hospital.) *V&P*, 1844, Vol. I, pp. 721-3.

1844. *Report from the Select Committee on Crown Lands Grievances
with Appendix, Minutes of Evidence and Replies to Circular
Letters. V&P*, 1844, Vol. II, pp. 117-358.

1845. *Report from the Select Committee on the Condition of the Aborigines, with Appendix, Minutes of Evidence and Replies to a Circular Letter. V&P*, 1845, pp. 977-1001.

1849. *New South Wales. Aboriginal Natives' Evidence.* (Return to an
address of 30th May 1849, comprising despatches relating to the
admissibility of Aboriginal evidence, 1839-49.) *V&P*, 1849, Vol. I,
pp. 985-90.

1849. *Report from the Select Committee on the Aborigines and Protectorate, with Appendix, Minutes of Evidence and Replies to a
Circular Letter. V&P*, 1849, Vol. II, pp. 417-75.

New South Wales Government Gazette, 1830-50.

Victoria

1859. *Report of the Select Committee of the Legislative Council on the
Aborigines. Victorian Legislative Council Papers*, Melbourne 1859,
105 pp.

1877-8. *Fourteenth Report, Victorian Legislative Assembly, Votes and
Proceedings*, Vol. II, 1877-8.

Queensland

1861. *Select Committee on the Native Police and the Condition of the
Aborigines Generally, Queensland Legislative Assembly, Votes and
Proceedings*, 1861, pp. 389-578.

3. OTHER MANUSCRIPT SOURCES

a. MITCHELL LIBRARY, SYDNEY

Aborigines Papers. ML, MS.A610. The contents are too diverse to list,
although much of the material consists of notes made by Protector
William Thomas.

Anon., *Aborigines of Australia*, ML, MS.B244.

Calvert, John, *Mineral and Topographical Survey of the Five Northern
Districts. New South Wales . . . 1845*, ML, MS.A3951. The first
part of this manuscript is the work of William Gardner, q.v.

Dunlop, Eliza Hamilton, *The Vase: Comprising Songs for Music and
Poems by Eliza Hamilton Dunlop*, ML, MS.B1541.

Dunlop, J., *Incomplete Account of the psychology and some of the customs of the aborigines of N.S.W.*, ML, MS. Document 468.

Eyre, Edward John, *Autobiographical Narrative of Residence and Exploration in Australia, 1832-39*, ML, MS.A1806.

Gardner, William, *Productions and Resources of the Northern Districts of New South Wales*, 2 vols, 1842-54, ML, MSS.A176.1 and A176.2.

Günther, Rev. James, *Correspondence 1826-78 and Notes on N.S.W. Aborigines*, ML, MS.A1450.

—, *Journal 1836-65*, ML, MS.B504.

—, *Lecture on the aborigines of Australia*, C.1838, ML, MS.B505.

Gurner Manuscripts, ML, MS.A1493. Includes letters by Bourke and Burton on the treatment of the Aborigines at Port Phillip.

Harpur, Charles, *Miscellaneous Poems*, ML, MS.A97.

Hobler, George, *Journal 1825-71*, ML, MSS.C422-39.

Lang, Rev. J. D., *Papers*, Vol. XX. ML, MS.A2240.

Le Souef, A. A. C., *Personal Recollections of Early Victoria*, Typescript, ML, MS.A2762.

Milson, Mrs., *Kamilaroi vocabulary and aboriginal songs; with Eng. trans. and notes by Mrs. Milson*, ML, MS.A1668. Mrs. Milson's authorship of the whole of this manuscript is doubtful and part is almost certainly the work of her mother, Eliza Dunlop, q.v.

Morey, E., *Papers*, Typescript, ML, MS.A883.

Riley, W. E., *Papers*, ML, MS.A109.

Sadleir, *Papers*, ML, MS.A1631.

Saunders, Rev. John, *Letterbook 1834-5, sermons, etc.*, ML, MS.B1106.

Thomas, William, *Papers*, ML, MSS.A7070-7078.

Threlkeld, Rev. L. E., *Papers*, ML, MS.A382.

Tindal Family Letter Book, ML, MS.A2068.

Watson, Rev. William, *Diary*, etc., ML, uncatalogued MSS, set 331.

Windeyer, Richard, *On the Rights of the Aborigines of Australia*, [c. 1844]. ML, MS.A1400.

Wren, Henry, *Journal*, ML, MS.A763.

b. ARCHDIOCESAN OFFICE, SYDNEY

Broughton, Bishop William Grant, *Letters*.

4. OTHER PRINTED SOURCES

Bride, T. F. (ed.), *Letters from Victorian Pioneers: Being a series of papers on the early occupation of the colony, the aborigines, etc. . . .*, Melbourne 1898.

British and Foreign Aborigines' Protection Society, *Annual Reports, 1838-46.* (Mitchell Library.)

—, *Extracts from the Papers and Proceedings*, 1839-46.

—, *Report of the Parliamentary Select Committee on Aboriginal Tribes. (British Settlements)*, Reprinted, with comments . . . , London 1837.

—, *Report from the Sub Committee on Australia with Notes*, London 1838.

—, *Outline of a System of Legislation, for Securing Protection to the Aboriginal Inhabitants of all Countries Colonized by Great Britain*, London 1840.

—, *England and Her Colonies, Considered in Relation to the Aborigines, with a proposal for Affording them Medical Relief*, London 1841.

Gunson, Niel, *Australian Reminiscences and Papers of L. E. Threlkeld, Missionary to the Aborigines, 1824-1859*, Australian Aboriginal Studies No. 40, Australian Institute of Aboriginal Studies, 2 vols, Canberra 1974. This collection includes: part of Threlkeld's 'Reminiscences' first published in *The Christian Herald, and Records of Missionary Intelligence*, Sydney 26 February 1853-28 April 1855; 'Memoranda Selected from Twenty Four Years of Missionary Engagements in the South Sea Islands and Australia . . . 1838', compiled for Judge W. W. Burton and now located in Supreme Court Papers, *NSWA*, Box No. 1123; Lake Macquarie Mission reports, 1838-1841; and selected correspondence, 1824-59.

Historial Records of Australia, Series I.

Plomley, N. J. B. (ed.) *Friendly Mission: The Tasmanian Journals of George Augustus Robinson*, Hobart 1966.

5. NEWSPAPERS

Sydney Gazette
The South-Asian Register
The Sydney Herald (after 31 July 1842. *The Sydney Morning Herald*)
The Australian
The Colonist
Commercial Journal and Advertiser
The Monitor
The Morning Chronicle
The Weekly Register of Politics, Facts and General Literature
Port Phillip Gazette
Port Phillip Herald

6. CONTEMPORARY BOOKS, PAMPHLETS AND MEMOIRS

Anon., *Aboriginal Claims Discussed in a Letter to a Colonist in Western Australia*, London 1838.

—, *Aborigines of Australia: Extract from a letter dated Perth . . . July 17 1836.*

—, 'A Few Words on the Aborigines of Australia'. *The New South Wales Magazine: or Journal of General Politics, Literature, Science, and the Arts*. I. No. 2, February 1843, PP, 49-62.

—, *Australia. A full and particular account of the Trial of Eleven Men, for the most horrible and cold-blooded Murder, and afterwards Burning: of twenty-eight individuals, men, women and children, without any provocation; being one of the blackest stains that ever disgraced the pages of British history . . .* Glasgow 1839.

—, *Australia. An Appeal to the World on behalf of the Younger Branch of the Family of Shem.* Sydney 1839.

—, *Narrative of the Capture, Sufferings, and Miraculous Escape of Mrs. Eliza Fraser*, New York 1837.

—, 'The Aborigines, and their Treatment Considered', *Australian and New Zealand Monthly Magazine*, 1842, pp. 290-5.

—, 'The Moral Character of the Natives of Australia', *The Visitor, or Monthly Instructor*, 1841, pp. 99-101; 149-52.

Arden, G., 'Civilisation of the Aborigines', *Arden's Sydney Magazine*, October 1843, pp. 65-82.

Backhouse, J., *Extracts from the Letters of James Backhouse . . .* , London 1838-41.

Balfour, J. O., *A Sketch of New South Wales*, London 1845.

Bannister, S., *Statements and Documents relating to proceedings in New South Wales in 1824, 1825 and 1826 . . .* , Cape Town 1827.

—, *Humane Policy or Justice to the Aborigines of New Settlements . . .* , London 1830.

—, *British Colonization and Coloured Tribes*, London 1838.

Bennett, Dr. G., *Wanderings in New South Wales . . .* , 2 vols, London 1834.

Boldrewood, R., *Old Melbourne Memories*, Melbourne 1884.

Breton, Lt. W. H., *Excursions in New South Wales, Western Australia and Van Diemen's Land . . .* , London 1835.

Buxton, C., *Memoirs of Sir Thomas Fowell Buxton . . .* , 6th edn., London 1855.

Byrne, J. C., *Twelve Years' Wanderings in the British Colonies . . .* , 2 vols, London 1848.

Coates, D. *et al.*, *Christianity the means of civilisation: shown in the evidence given before a committee of the House of Commons on Aborigines*, London 1837.

Cunningham, P., *Two Years in New South Wales*, 2 vols, London 1834.

Curr, E. M, *Recollections of Squatting in Victoria . . .* , Melbourne 1883.

Curtis, J., *Shipwreck of the Stirling Castle . . . to which is added the Narrative of the Wreck of the Charles Eaton*, London 1838.

Darwin, C., *Journal of Researches into the natural history and geology of the countries visited during the voyage of H.M.S. Beagle round the world*, 7th edn., London 1890.

Dawson, R., *The Present State of Australia; . . .* , London 1830.

Dredge, J., *Brief Notices of the Aborigines of New South Wales . . .* , Geelong 1845.

Eipper, C., *Statement of the Origin, Condition, and Prospects of the German Mission to the Aborigines at Moreton Bay . . .* , Sydney 1841.

Field, B., *Geographical Memoirs on New South Wales*, London 1825.

Hamilton, Rev. W., 'The Obligation of the Scottish Presbyterian Church of New South Wales to use Means for the Salvation of the Aborigines of the Territory' in his *Practical Discourses Intended for Circulation in the Interior of New South Wales*, Sydney 1843.

Harris, A., *Settlers and Convicts or Recollections of Sixteen Years' Labour in the Australian Backwoods by an Emigrant Mechanic*, with a Foreword by C. M. H. Clark, Melbourne 1953. (First published London 1847.)
—, 'Religio Christi' in A. A. Chisholm (ed.), *The Secrets of Alexander Harris*, Sydney 1961.
Haydon, G. H., *Five Years' Experience in Australia Felix* . . . , London 1846.
Haygarth, H. W., *Recollections of Bush-life in Australia* . . . , London 1848.
Henderson, J., *Excursions and Adventures in New South Wales* . . . , 2 vols, London 1851.
Hodgkinson, C., *Australia, from Port Macquarie to Moreton Bay*; . . . , London 1845.
Howitt, R., *Australia: Historical, Descriptive, And Statistic*; . . . , London 1845.
Howitt, W., *Colonization and Christianity: a popular history of the treatment of the natives by the Europeans in all their colonies*, London 1838.
—, *Land, Labour and Gold: Or Two Years in Victoria*, 2 vols, London 1855, reprinted facsimile Sydney 1972.
Hull, W., *Remarks on the Probable Origin and Antiquity of the Aboriginal Natives of New South Wales*, Melbourne 1846.
Irby, E. and L., *Memoirs of Edward and Leonard Irby*, Sydney 1908.
Kirby, J., *Old Times in the Bush of Australia: Trials and Experiences of Early Bush Life in Victoria during the Forties*, Melbourne 1895.
Lang, Rev. J. D., *An Historical and Statistical Account of New South Wales*, 2 vols, London 1834.
—, *National Sins the Causes and Precursors of National Judgements* . . . , Sydney 1838.
—, *Appeal . . . on behalf of the German Mission*, Sydney 1839.
Lang, G. S., *Aborigines of Australia: in their original condition and in their relations with white men*, Melbourne 1865.
Lloyd, E., *A Visit to the Antipodes* . . . , London 1846.
Lloyd, G. T., *Thirty-Three Years in Tasmania and Victoria* . . . , London 1862.
Loveless, G., *Narrative of the Sufferings of James Loveless, James Brine, and Thomas and John Standfield* . . . , London 1838.
Macarthur, J., *New South Wales: Its Present State and Future Prospects*, London 1837.
Maclehose, J., *The Picture of Sydney and Stranger's Guide in New South Wales for 1838*, Sydney 1838.
Mackaness, G., (ed.), *The Correspondence of John Cotton, Victorian Pioneer 1842-1849*, 3 Pts., Sydney 1953.
McCombie, T., *Australian Sketches*, Melbourne 1847.
—, *The Colonist in Australia; Or The Adventures of Godfrey Arabin*, London 1850.

R

McKenzie, Rev. D., *The Emigrant's Guide: or Ten Years' Practical Experience in Australia*, London 1845.

Merivale, H., *Lectures on Colonization and Colonies . . .* , 2nd edn, London 1861.

Meyrick, P. J. (ed.), *Life in the Bush (1840-1847): a memoir of Henry Howard Meyrick*, London 1939.

Miles, W. A., *Remarks upon the Language, Customs and Physical Character of the Aborigines of Australia*, Sydney n.d.

Mitchell, Sir T. L., *Three Expeditions into the Interior of Eastern Australia . . .* , 2 vols, London 1838.

—, *Journal of an Expedition into the Interior of Tropical Australia . . .* , London 1848.

Morgan, J., *The Life and Adventures of William Buckley*, Hobart 1852.

Mundy, Lt. Colonel G. C., *Our Antipodes or Residence and Rambles in the Australasian Colonies . . .* , 3 vols., London 1855.

Nathan, I., *The Southern Euphrosyne and Australian Miscellany, Containing Moral Tales, Original Anecdote, Poetry, and Music, an Historical Sketch, with Examples of the Native Aboriginal Melodies . . .* , London 1848.

O'Connell, J. F., *A Residence of Eleven Years in New Holland and the Caroline Islands . . .* , Boston 1836.

Parker, E. S., *The Aborigines of Australia: A Lecture Delivered in the Mechanics' Hall, Melbourne . . . May 10th, 1854*, Melbourne 1854.

Robinson, G. A., 'A Report of an Expedition to the Aboriginal Tribes of the Western Interior . . . 1841 . . .', *The Victorian Historical Magazine*, XII, No. 3, March 1928, pp. 138-70

Sturt, Captain C., *Two Expeditions into the Interior of Southern Australia . . .* , 2 vols., London 1833.

Strzelecki, P. E. de, *Physical Description of New South Wales and Van Dieman's Land*, London 1845.

Tompson, C., *Wild Notes from the Lyre of a Native Minstrel*, Sydney 1826, reprinted facsimile Sydney 1973.

Townsend, J. P., *Rambles and Observations In New South Wales . . .* , London 1849.

Westgarth, W., *A Report on the Condition, Capabilities, and Prospects of the Australian Aborigines*, Melbourne 1846.

Wheeler, D., *Effects of the Introduction of Ardent Spirits and Implements of War amongst the Natives of some of the South Sea Islands and New South Wales*, London 1839.

Young, Mrs. S. B., 'Reminiscences of Mrs. Susan Bundarra Young . . .', *JRAHS*, VIII, 1923, pp. 394-407.

7. LATER WORKS

(i) *Anthropology, sociology and Aboriginal-white relations*

Barzun, J., *Race: A Study in Modern Superstition*, London 1938.

Berndt, R. M., 'Influence of European Culture on Australian Aborigines', *Oceania*, XXI, No. 3, 1952, pp 229-35.

Berndt, R. M. and C. H., *From Black to White in South Australia*, Melbourne 1951.

Calley, M. J. C., 'Race Relations on the North coast of New South Wales', *Oceania*, XXVII, No. 3, 1957, pp. 190-209.

Corris, P. R., *Aborigines and Europeans in Western Victoria*, Australian Institute of Aboriginal Studies, Occasional Paper in Aboriginal Studies No. 12, Canberra 1968.

Curr, E. M., *The Australian Race . . .*, 4 vols, Melbourne 1886-7.

Davidson, D. S., 'An Ethnic Map of Australia', *Proceedings of the American Philosophical Society*, LXXVII, No. 4, November 1938, pp. 649-79 and map.

Elkin, A. P., *Aboriginal Men of High Degree*, Sydney 1954.

—, 'Reaction and Interaction: A Food Gathering People and European Settlement in Australia', *American Anthropologist*, LIII, 1951, pp. 164-86.

—, *The Australian Aborigines: How to Understand Them*, 3rd edn, Sydney 1954.

—, 'Australian Aboriginal and White Relations: A Personal Record', *JRAHS*, XLVIII, 1962, pp. 208-30.

Flanagan, R., *The Aborigines of Australia*, Sydney 1888.

Hartwig, M. C., *The Progress of White Settlement in the Alice Springs District and its Effects upon the Aboriginal Inhabitants, 1860-1894*, PhD thesis, University of Adelaide, 1965.

Hassell, K., *The Relations Between the Settlers and Aborigines in South Australia, 1836-1860*, Adelaide 1966.

Hiatt, L. R., 'Aborigines in the Australian Community' in A. F. Davies and S. Encel (eds), *Australian Society: A Sociological Introduction*, Melbourne 1965, pp. 274-95.

Hogbin, I. and L. R. Hiatt, *Readings in Australian and Pacific Anthropology*, Melbourne 1966.

Howitt, A. W. and L. Fison, *Kamilaroi and Kurnai*, Melbourne 1880.

Lippmann, L., *Words or Blows: Racial Attitudes in Australia*, Melbourne 1973.

Locke, A. (ed.), *When Peoples Meet: A Study in Race and Culture Contact*, New York 1942.

MacRae, Donald G. (ed.), *Man, Race and Darwin*, London 1960.

Mannoni, O., *Prospero and Caliban: The Psychology of Colonization*, 2nd edn, New York 1964.

Meggitt, M. J., *Desert People: A Study of the Walbiri of Central Australia*, Sydney 1962.

Mulvaney, D. J., 'The Australian Aborigines 1606-1929: Opinion and Fieldwork', *Historical Studies*, VIII, No. 30, May 1958, pp. 131-51; No. 31, November 1958, pp. 279-314.

—, 'Aborigines of Victoria', *Victorian Year Book*, No. 79, 1965.

Penniman, T. K., *A Hundred Years of Anthropology*, London 1935.

Radcliffe-Brown, A. R., 'Former Numbers and Distribution of the Australian Aborigines', *Official Year Book of the Commonwealth of Australia*, No. 23, 1930.

Reay, M. (ed.), *Aborigines Now: New Perspectives in the Study of Aboriginal Communities*, Sydney 1964.

—, 'The Background of Alien Impact' in R. M. and C. H. Berndt, (eds), *Aboriginal Man in Australia: Essays in Honour of Emeritus Professor A. P. Elkin*, Sydney 1965.

Ridley, W., *Kamilaroi and other Australian Languages*, 2nd edn, Sydney 1875.

Rowley, C. D., 'Aborigines and other Australians', *Oceania*, XXXII, No. 4, June 1962, pp. 247-66.

Sheils, H. (ed.), *Australian Aboriginal Studies*, A Symposium of Papers delivered at the research conference, Melbourne 1963.

Smyth, R. B., *The Aborigines of Victoria* . . . , 2 vols, Melbourne 1878.

Stanner, W. E. H., 'Durmugam, a Nangiomeri' in J. B. Casagrande (ed.), *In the Company of Man*, New York 1960, pp. 64-100.

—, *On Aboriginal Religion*, Oceania monograph No. 11, Sydney 1964.

Stevens, F. S. (ed.), *Racism: The Australian Experience*, 3 vols, Sydney 1971-2.

Tindale, N. B., 'Distribution of Australian Aboriginal Tribes: A Field Survey', *Transactions of the Royal Society of South Australia*, LXIV, 1940, pp. 140-231 and map.

—, *The Aboriginal Tribes of Australia* . . . , Berkeley 1974 (in press).

(ii) *Official policy towards Aborigines*

Barker, S. K., 'The Governorship of Sir George Gipps', *JRAHS*, XVI, 1930, pp. 251-9.

Beaglehole, J. C., 'The Colonial Office, 1782-1854', *Historical Studies*, I, No. 1, April 1941, pp. 170-89.

Bell, J., 'Official Policies Towards the Aborigines in New South Wales', *Mankind*, V, No. 8, November 1959, pp. 345-55.

Biskup, P., *Not Slaves Not Citizens: The Aboriginal Problem in Western Australia 1898-1954*, Brisbane 1973.

Bridges, B., *Aboriginal and White Relations in New South Wales 1788-1855*, MA thesis, University of Sydney, 1966.

—, 'Aboriginal Education in Eastern Australia (N.S.W.) 1788-1855', *The Australian Journal of Education*, Vol. 12, No. 3, October 1968, pp. 20-3.

—, 'The Extension of English Law to the Aborigines for Offences Committed *Inter Se*', *JRAHS*, 59, Pt 4, December 1973, pp. 264-9.

Carlyon, N. M., *G. A. Robinson—Chief Protector*, BA hons thesis, University of Melbourne, 1960.

Docker, E. G., *Simply Human Beings*, Brisbane 1964.

Duncan, A., *A Survey of the Education of Aborigines in New South Wales* . . . , MEd thesis, University of Sydney, 1969.

Foxcroft, E. J. B., *Australian Native Policy especially in Victoria*, Melbourne 1941.
Harrison, B. W., *The Myall Creek Massacre and its Significance in the Controversy over the Aborigines during Australia's Early Squatting Period*, BA hons thesis, University of New England, 1966.
Hasluck, P. M. C., *Black Australians: a survey of native policy in Western Australia, 1829-1897*, Melbourne 1942.
Howse, E. N., *Saints in Politics*, London 1960.
King, H., 'Some Aspects of Police Administration in New South Wales, 1825-1851', *JRAHS*, XLII, Pt 5, December 1956, pp. 205-30.
—, *Richard Bourke*, Melbourne 1971.
Knaplund, P., 'Sir James Stephen on a White Australia', *The Victorian Historical Magazine*, XII, No. 4, June 1928, pp. 240-2.
—, *James Stephen and the British Colonial System, 1813-1847*, Madison 1953.
McCulloch, S. C. (ed.), *British Humanitarianism*, Philadelphia 1950.
—, 'James Stephen and the Problems of New South Wales, 1838-1846', *Pacific Historical Review*, XXVI, 1957, pp. 355-64.
—, 'Sir George Gipps and Eastern Australia's Policy Towards the Aborigines', *Journal of Modern History*, XXXIII, 1961, pp. 261-9.
—, 'Unguarded Comments on the Administration of New South Wales, 1839-46: The Gipps-La Trobe Correspondence', *Historical Studies*, IX, No. 33, November 1959, pp. 30-45.
Macard, P., 'Early Victoria and the Aborigines', *Melbourne Historical Journal*, IV, 1964, pp. 23-9.
Mellor, G. R., *British Imperial Trusteeship 1783-1850*, London 1951.
Nelson, H. N., *Early Attempts to Civilize the Aborigines of the Port Phillip District*, MEd thesis, University of Melbourne, 1966.
Reece, R. H. W., 'Feasts and Blankets: The History of Some Early Attempts to Establish Relations with the Aborigines of New South Wales, 1814-1846', *Archaeology and Physical Anthropology in Oceania*, II, No. 3, October 1967, pp. 190-206.
Rowley, C. D., *The Destruction of Aboriginal Society*, Canberra 1970.
Sinclair, K., *The Aborigines Protection Society and New Zealand. A Study in 19th Century Opinion*, MA thesis, University of Auckland, 1946.
Spring, David, 'The Clapham Sect: Some Social and Political Aspects', *Victorian Studies*, V, No. 1, September 1961, pp. 35-48.
Turnbull, G., *Black War: The Extermination of the Tasmanian Aborigines*, Melbourne 1948.

(iii) *Other works*

Alexander, M., *Mrs. Fraser on The Fatal Shore*, New York 1971.
Bassett, M., *The Hentys: An Australian Colonial Tapestry*, London 1954.
Bates, Daisy M., *The Passing of the Aborigines: A lifetime spent among the natives of Australia*, London 1938.

Buckley, K., 'Gipps and the Graziers of New South Wales, 1841-1846', *Historical Studies: Selected Articles*, Melbourne 1964, pp. 57-102.

Campbell, J. F., *Squatting on Crown Lands in New South Wales*, edited and annotated by B. T. Dowd, Sydney 1968.

Champion, B. W., 'Lancelot Edward Threlkeld', *JRAHS*, XXV, 1939, pp. 279-329; 341-411.

Chomley, C. H., *Tales of Old Times: early Australian incident and adventure*, Melbourne 1903.

Cox, Ian C. (comp.), *Bennelong: First Notable Aboriginal*, Sydney 1973.

Elkin, A. P., *The Diocese of Newcastle* . . . , Newcastle 1955.

Finn, E., *The Chronicles of Early Melbourne 1835 to 1842*, 2 vols, Melbourne 1888.

Flanagan, R., *The History of New South Wales*, London 1862.

Gunn, D., *Links with the Past*, Brisbane 1937.

Gunson, W. M., 'The Nundah Missionaries', *Journal of the Royal Historical Society of Queensland*, VI, 1960-1, pp. 511-39.

Haydon, A. L., *The Trooper Police of Australia* . . . , London 1911.

Jervis, J., 'Exploration and Settlement of the North-Western Plains', *JRAHS*, XLVIII, Pt 5, December 1962, pp. 377-94.

Kiddle, M., *Men of Yesterday: A Social History of the Western District of Victoria 1834-1890*, Melbourne 1961.

Levy, M. C. I., *Governor George Arthur*, Melbourne 1953.

Molony, J. M., *An Architect of Freedom: John Hubert Plunkett in New South Wales 1832-1869*, Canberra 1973.

Nelson, H. N., 'The Missionaries and the Aborigines in the Port Phillip District', *Historical Studies*, XII, No. 45, October 1965, pp. 57-67.

Perry, T. M., *Australia's First Frontier: The Spread of Settlement in New South Wales 1788-1829*, Melbourne 1963.

Reynolds, H. (ed.), *Aborigines and Settlers*, Melbourne 1972.

Roberts, S. H., *History of Australian Land Settlement (1788-1920)*, Melbourne 1924.

—, *The Squatting Age in Australia*, 1835-1847, 2nd edn, Melbourne 1964.

Rowland, E. C., 'The Life and Times of Henry Dangar', *JRAHS*, XXXIX, 1953, pp. 1-23; 49-76.

Rusden, G. W., *History of Australia*, 2nd edn, 3 vols, Melbourne 1897.

Smith, B., *European Vision and the South Pacific*, Oxford 1960.

—, *Australian Painting 1788-1960*, London 1962.

Stevens, J. F., *The Runaway: The Life Story of Richard Craig*, duplicated typescript, North Tamborine 1962.

Thorpe, O., *First Catholic Mission to the Australian Aborigines*, Sydney 1950.

Vogan, A. J., *The Black Police. A Story of Modern Australia*, London 1890.

Walker, R. B., *Old New England*, Sydney 1966.

Woolmington, J. (ed.), *Aborigines in Colonial Society: 1788-1850*, Melbourne 1973.

(iv) *Works for comparison*

Bolt, Christine, *Victorian Attitudes to Race*, London 1971.

Boxer, C. R., *Race Relations in the Portuguese Colonial Empire 1415-1825*, Oxford 1965.

Davies, J. D., *Phrenology: Fad and Science, a 19th Century American Crusade*, New Haven 1955.

Fairchild, H. N., *The Noble Savage: A Study in Romantic Naturalism*, New York 1928.

Hanke, L., *The Spanish Struggle for Justice in the Conquest of America*, Philadelphia 1949.

Miller, J. O., *Early Victorian New Zealand. A Study of Racial Tension and Social Attitudes 1839-1852*, Oxford 1958.

Pearce, R. H., *The Savages of America: A Study of the Indian and the Idea of Civilization*, Baltimore 1953.

Price, A., *White Settlers and Native Peoples . . .*, Melbourne 1949.

Stanton, W., *The Leopard's Spots: Scientific Attitudes Towards Race in America 1815-59*, Chicago 1960.

Washburn, Wilcomb W., *Red Man's Land/White Man's Law: A Study of the Past and Present Status of the American Indian*, New York 1971.

—, 'The Moral and Legal Justifications for Dispossessing the Indians' in J. M. Smith (ed.), *Seventeenth Century America: Essays in Colonial History*, North Carolina 1959.

Weinberg, A. K., *Manifest Destiny: A Study of Nationalist Expansionism in American History*, Baltimore 1935.

INDEX

a' Beckett, William, 147, 151
Aboriginal customs and ceremonies
  disappearance of, 10
  sacred stones, 36, 41n, 55
  white attitudes, 55, 96-7, 96n, 109
Aboriginal evidence, admissibility of,
  134, 138, 160, 179-82, 188, 213
Aboriginal 'kings' and 'chiefs', 6, 47n,
  68, 109, 122, 211-12
Aboriginal labour see Employment of
  Aborigines; Wages, Aboriginal
Aboriginal land rights, 131, 166-73
Aboriginal population see Depopula-
  tion of Aborigines
Aboriginal reserves, 9, 16, 23, 110,
  117, 185, 201-2
Aboriginal trackers, 56, 125, 133
Aborigines, individuals
  Bennelong, 83
  Borijon, 194
  Bummery, George, 118-19
  Bungaree, 6, 7, 109
  Carnabyagal (Carnanbigal), 109,
    120
  Charley, 55
  Davey, 38, 39, 40, 41, 44, 156, 160
  Jabinguy, 118-19
  Jemmy Piper, 57
  Mahroot, 11-12
  Murral, Jack Congo, 118-19
  Musquito, 56
  Saturday, 111
  William Burd, 56
Aborigines, tribes
  Awakabal, 78
  Barrabool Hill tribe, 16
  Bangerang, 16
  Bogan River tribe, 51
  Botany tribe, 11
  Broken Bay tribe, 109
  Dutigallar, 122
  Goulburn tribe, 14
  Jajourong, 17
  Kamilaroi, 28
  Kwiambal, 34n
  Milmenrura, 101
  Mount Eeles tribe, 26
  Sydney tribe, 5

Watourong, 69n
Weraerai, 34n
Yarra tribe, 14, 69n
Aborigines in literature, 59-60, 87,
  164, 165
Aborigines brought up by whites, 11,
  12, 82
Aborigines' Protection Society see
  British and Foreign Abori-
  gines' Protection Society
Alcohol, 7, 8, 9, 10-11, 14, 20, 21,
  124, 188
Allman, Francis, 183
Amerindians, 99, 142, 170
Anderson, George, 36, 38, 40, 147-8
Appin, 109
Apsley mission, 72
Arden, George, 73, 83
Arndell, Thomas, 44
Arthur, Sir George, 10, 66, 71, 123
Asian labour, importation of, 139,
  189, 190
Atkins, Richard, 108
'Attachment', policy of, 66-70, 105,
  107, 110
Attacks on whites, Aboriginal, 23-5,
  27, 29-30, 38n, 47-8, 50, 99,
  101, 109, 216-18, 220-1. See
  also Cattle and sheep, theft
  and killing of by Aborigines
Australian, The, 10, 47, 144, 149, 157,
  166, 172, 180, 184, 200-1
Australian Aborigines' Protection So-
  ciety, 165, 172
Australian Agricultural Company, 19,
  28n, 35n, 79, 102, 179, 206
Australian and New Zealand Monthly
  Magazine, 167
Australian Philosophical Society, 84

Backhouse, James, 130, 204
Banks, Sir Joseph, 105
Bannister, Saxe, 86, 110, 112, 114-15,
  127, 130, 134
Barwon River, 48
Bateman's Bay, 65
Bathurst, 110-11, 112, 161
Bathurst, Lord, 110, 112-13, 115, 116

Batman, John, 10-11, 69n, 122-4, 168
Beecham, John, 130
Benalla, 24
Bennelong, 83
Bennet, George, 116
Bennett, Dr George, 98-9
Berry, Alexander, 87, 90
Big River, 29. See also Gwydir River
Bigge, J. T., 108
Bingara, 35n, 39n
Bingham, Henry, 53, 54, 126, 211
Black, Niel, 54-5
Blackstone, Sir William, 171, 173
Black Town, 63n, 64
Blake, John, 36n, 37, 38n, 39, 40n
Bland, Dr William, 87, 182
Blankets, 20, 71, 118, 124-6, 123n,
    125n, 209-12, 213, 214
Bligh, Richard, 61
Bligh, Sir William, 107-8
Blumenbach, Johann Friedrich, 84,
    94
Bogan River, 21-2, 51, 98, 187
Boldrewood, Rolf, 26, 197
Border Police, 21, 26, 51, 60, 176,
    179, 185-7, 192, 196
Borton, Edward, 159
Bourke, Sir Richard, 5, 20, 53, 68-70,
    118, 120, 121, 123, 124-7, 135,
    159, 206
Boyd, Benjamin, 21
Brady, Rev. John, 205
Brass plates, 47, 56
Breton, Lieut W. H., 81, 96, 98, 102
Brisbane, Sir Thomas, 63n, 110-11,
    116, 159
British and Foreign Aborigines' Pro-
    tection Society, 129-30, 134,
    138
British Association, 85n
Broken River, 24
Broughton, Bishop W. G., 65, 118,
    168, 205-6
Broulee, 210
Buccaneer Archipelago, 65-6
Buckley, William, 69
Bundin's Reef, 101
Bungaree, 6, 7, 109
Buntingdale mission, 73, 202, 204
Bunya pine, 183n
Burton, Judge, W. W., 44, 68, 119,
    141, 150, 153-6, 188

Buxton, Thomas Fowell, 127, 129-
    131
'Cannibalism', 97-9, 101, 102, 172
'Carnanbigal war', 109, 120
Cartwright, Rev. Robert, 63, 64
Cattle and sheep, theft and killing of
    by Aborigines, 26, 27, 30, 31,
    32, 47-8, 50, 54, 60, 96n, 107,
    110, 143, 195, 216-18
Charles Eaton, wreck of, 101
Chinese, Aboriginal attitude to, 58n
Church of England, 205-7
Church Missionary Society, 63n, 64,
    65, 72, 76, 116, 130, 184-5
'Clapham Sect', 127, 134, 135n
Clarence River, 25, 29n, 186, 192
Clarke, George ('The Barber'), 31n
Clarke, Rev. George, 63n, 76
Coates, Dandeson, 130
Collins, Colonel David, 10, 69n, 164
Colonial Literary Journal, The, 88
Colonial Office see Hay, Sir John;
    Horton, R. Wilmot; Huskisson,
    William; Rice, T. Spring, Sec-
    retary of State for Colonies
Colonist, The, 91, 93, 94, 161, 162,
    167, 168
Combe, George, 86, 90, 94
Commercial Journal, 148
Committee on Aborigines, British
    Settlements (1836-7), 130-3
Committee on Crown Lands Griev-
    ances (1844), 187
Committee on Immigration (1841),
    189-91
Committee on Police and Gaols
    (1841), 43
Committee on the Aborigines Ques-
    tion (1838), 9-10, 80, 91, 117n,
    199, 204
Committee on the Condition of the
    Aborigines (1845), 212-13
Committee on Transportation (1812,
    1838), 108, 150n, 189
Convicts
    access to firearms, 46
    attacks on Aborigines, 34-46, 48,
    57, 58, 105, 114
    cessation of supply, 189
    executed for killing Aborigines,
    108, 158
    from Van Diemen's Land, 55-6

living with Aborigines, 31, 69, 99
tracked by Aborigines, 56, 125, 133
Cotton, John, 169, 170-1
Cowper, Rev. William, 205-6
Craig, Richard, 192
Cranial capacity of Aborigines see Phrenology
Crawford, James Coutts, 26-7
Croke, James, 192
Crook, Rev. W. P., 77
Crown Lands Commissioners, 175-6, 187. See also Allman, Francis; Bligh, Richard; Fry, Oliver; Mayne, Edward; McDonald, C. J.; Oakes, Henry; Paterson, Alexander
Cunningham, Peter, 7, 56n, 98n
Cunningham, Richard, 98, 102, 121
Curr, E. M., 56, 59
Curtis, John, 100, 101

Dana, Henry Pulteney, 214
Dangar, Henry, 35, 38, 41, 145, 147, 153
Darling, Sir Ralph, 110n, 112-15, 116-17, 153
Darling River, 24, 57
Darwin, Charles, 20, 85n
Dawson, Robert, 79, 102, 115n
Day, E. D., 42, 46, 60, 146, 152, 153
'Degeneration', theories of, 73-5, 85n
Depopulation of Aborigines
  by area
    Geelong, 16
    Gippsland, 197
    Lake Macquarie, 18-19, 20
    Liverpool Plains, 45
    Nineteen Counties, 17
    Port Phillip District, 16, 23-4, 54
    Portland Bay, 16, 23-4
    Sydney, 5, 11
    Westernport, 213
  causes
    attacks by whites, 23-4, 45, 197
    disease, 8, 20-1, 54
    infanticide, 53, 191
    poisoning by whites, 48-9, 162
    sense of injustice, 211
  general statistics, 16, 213, 229
Disease see Epidemics; Venereal disease
Donkin, Sir Rufane, 130

Douglas, Thomas, 159
Dowling, Judge James, 119, 149, 194
Dredge, James, 202
Drought, effects of on Aborigines, 28, 50-2
Duncan, W. A., 166, 173-4, 180, 208-9
Dunlop, David, 210-12
Dunlop, Eliza, 164

Eaton, Andrew, 35
Education of Aborigines, 63-4, 66, 68-9, 132, 133. See also Wages, Aboriginal
Eipper, Christopher, 78
Elkin, A. P., 59
Ellis, William, 130
Employment of Aborigines, 6, 10, 11, 19-21, 36, 56, 72, 85, 90, 189-91, 214
Epidemics, 8, 20-1, 54
Eumeralla River, 23, 26
Evangelicals, 73-8, 116, 127-35, 162-4, 165-8, 198, 203
Exclusion of Aborigines
  from stations, 30, 31, 46-7, 48, 150-1, 183, 193
  from towns, 10, 13-16
Exeter Hall, 127, 131, 133, 134, 148, 198
Executive Council, New South Wales, 114-15, 120-1, 143, 157, 177, 178, 199
Extinction of Aborigines, belief in, 17, 19, 21, 75, 139, 213
Eyre, Edward, 57-8

Faithfull massacre, 24-5, 102, 143, 144, 177
Faithfull, William Pitt, 24-5
Fawkner, John Pascoe, 69n, 122n
Field, Barron, 6, 8, 84-7
Finn, Edmund, 12
Firearms
  use of by
    Aborigines, 13, 14, 188
    convicts, 30, 48, 55, 82
  ban on use of, 48, 188
Fitzroy, Sir Charles, 214
Fleming, John, 37, 38n, 39, 40
Flinders Island Aboriginal Establishment, 66, 83, 136, 199-200

Foot, Frederick, 41, 146
Forbes, Sir Francis, 115, 116, 153
Foster, Thomas, 37, 39, 41, 146
Foster, William, 147
Franklin, Sir John, 66, 136, 199
Fraser, Captain James, 99
Fraser, Mrs Eliza, 99-101
Fry, Oliver, 187, 192
Fyans, Foster, 16, 54

Gall, Franz, 86
Gardner, William, 29
Gawler, Sir George, 62, 141
Geelong, 123, 145
Geelong and Dutigalla Association
    see Port Phillip Association
Gellibrand, J. T., 102, 122n
'German mission', 52, 77, 78, 101, 204
Gipps, Sir George, 3, 136, 137, 138,
    139, 142, 158, 160-1, 171,
    213-14
  abolition of blanket issue, 209-10
  attempts to limit settlement, 183
  attitude towards
    Aborigines, 141, 189, 210
    squatters, 144-5, 176
  career and character, 140-1
  comments on Grey's Report, 188-9
  creation of Aboriginal reserves, 201
  determination to enforce law, 144,
    175-6, 182-3
  dismissal of Robert Scott, 160
  disputes with
    Australian Agricultural Com-
      pany, 178-9
    Bishop Polding, 206-8
  exasperation with Protectorate, 202
  fear of Evangelical influence, 198,
    203
  handling of Myall Creek case, 145,
    158-9, 160-1
  introduction of Border Police,
    175-6
  notice on legal status of Aborigines,
    176-7
  parsimonious administration, 209-12
  petitioned by squatting interest,
    143-5, 183
  termination of assistance to mis-
    sions, 204
  threatened by The Sydney Herald,
    156, 159
  unwillingness to enact special leg-
    islation, 175-6, 188
  use of Native Police, 214
Gippsland, 14, 28, 34n, 197
Glenelg, Lord, 120, 121, 123-4, 135-8,
    148, 158, 160, 175, 176, 198,
    199
Glennie, James, 30
Goderich, Lord, 118
Government expenditure on Abori-
    gines, 117-18, 125, 132, 138-9,
    169, 200, 208-12, 214, 230-1.
    See also Blankets; Native Ins-
    titution; Parramatta 'feast'
Government proclamations re Abori-
    gines, 107-8, 109-10, 112, 127,
    176-7, 178-9
Government Gazette (N.S.W.), 120,
    199
Grey, Captain George, 71-2, 141,
    188-9
Grey, Sir George, 130, 131
Günther, Rev. James, 72, 75, 78, 184,
    204
Gwydir River, 25, 29, 30, 33, 34, 35n,
    36, 47, 51, 59, 61, 82, 151

Half-castes see Part-Aborigines
Hall, E. S., 166
Hall, Rev. William, 63n
Hamilton, James, 88
Handt, Rev. J. C. S., 204
Harper, John, 65
Harpur, Charles, 59-60
Harris, Alexander, 27, 48, 81-2, 140,
    161-2, 174
Hawkesbury River, 105, 106n, 107,
    109
Hay, Sir John, 112
Henderson, George, 56
Henry, William, 75-6
Hesse, G. B., 102
Hobart, Lord, 106, 108
Hobbes, Thomas, 172
Hobbs, William, 36, 41, 42-3, 146,
    148, 153
Horton, R. Wilmot, 115
House of Commons
  addresses to, 118, 128-9
  Aborigines Committee, 130-4, 135,
    136
  Committee on Transportation, 108,
    189

Howitt, Richard, 79-80
Howitt, William, 133-4
Hunter, Sir George, 105-6, 107
Hunter River, 17, 28, 29, 112-14, 147
Hunter River Black Association, 147, 148n, 149
Hurst, Rev. Benjamin, 73
Huskisson, William, 115

Imlay, Alexander, 21, 173
Indians see Amerindians
Infanticide, 53, 98-9, 172, 191
Intermarriage, 53, 191, 205

Jeffcott, Judge William, 193
Jervis Bay, 11n

Keck, Henry, 158-9
'Kidnapping' of Aboriginal women, 52-5, 126-7, 178-9
Kilmaister, Charles, 35-6, 38, 39-41, 149, 152
Kinchela, John, 119
King, Philip Gidley, 106-7, 108
King, Philip Parker, 143-4, 150
'King' Bungaree, 6, 7, 109
Knight, William, 153, 159

La Trobe, Charles Joseph, 15, 23
Lake Macquarie mission, 17, 20, 83, 87, 116, 190, 203-4, 205
Lake Victoria, 25, 120, 121
Land Fund, 138, 139, 169, 174
Land rights see Aboriginal land rights
Lang, Rev. J. D., 62, 73-4, 87, 93, 101, 128, 129, 130, 163-4, 165, 167, 205, 208
Langhorne, George, 68, 206
Larnach, John, 147
Law and justice, administration of
    problems, 191-7
    prosecutions
        of Aborigines, 55, 118-19, 193, 194-5, 225-7
        of whites, 105-6, 110n, 114-16, 145-61, 191-4
    See also Aboriginal evidence, admissibility of; Legal status of Aborigines
Lee, William, 51, 102, 183-4
Lee case see Lee, William
Legal status of Aborigines
    British subjects, 34, 105, 108, 135, 142, 176-7

conquered people, 71
foreign nation, 110, 112-13, 135
offences inter se, 71-2, 118-19, 194
    See also Aboriginal land rights
Legislation relating to Aborigines
    Great Britain
        Enabling Act (1843), 180
    New South Wales
        Aboriginal Evidence Bill (1839), 180; (1844), 180-2; (1849), 182n; (1876), 182n
        Crown Lands Bill (1839), 175
        Firearms Bill (1839), 188
        Judge Burton's draft Bill (1838), 175
        Publicans' Act (1839), 188
    South Australia
        Aboriginal Evidence Bill (1844), 182n
    Western Australia
        Aboriginal Evidence Bill (1841), 180n
Legislative Council, New South Wales, 9-10, 175, 176, 180-2, 183, 194-5, 199, 204-5, 212-13
Leichhardt, Ludwig, 30n, 102
Lettsom, Major Samuel, 14-15
Licences, 'squatting', 28n
Liverpool Plains, 28-48, 50, 55, 58, 145, 147
Locke, John, 167, 171
London Missionary Society, 17n, 76, 116
Lonsdale, Captain William, 69
Lowe, Lieut Nathaniel, 112, 113-14, 115
Lowe, Robert, 181, 182

Macarthur, Hannibal, 187
Macarthur, James, 81, 83, 183-4
McCombie, Thomas, 12-13
McDonald, C. J., 186, 187
McGill, 19n, 20, 56
Macintyre River, 48, 51
Mackenzie, Rev. David, 90
Mackintosh, Sir James, 173
McLeay River, 56, 60, 186
Maconochie, Alexander, 66-8
Macquarie, Lachlan, 5n, 11, 63, 108-110, 124
'Macquarie City', 64n
'Major Nunn's campaign', 32-4, 45, 157, 165, 196-7

Manilla River, 31, 34
Maoris, 6, 11, 63n, 85, 97
Maria, wreck of, 101
Marsden, Rev. Samuel, 76, 150n, 208-9
Martial law, proclamation of, 110, 112
Massacres
  Appin, 109
  Bathurst, 111, 161
  Bluff Rock, 187
  Charles Eaton, 101
  Clarence River, 186
  'Deepwater' (New England), 187
  Faithfull massacre, 24-5, 102, 143, 177
  Gippsland, 34n, 197
  Gravesend, 43-4
  'Hornet Bank', 38n
  Lee case, 51, 187
  Liverpool Plains, 28-48, 61
  Major Mitchell's encounter, 57, 119-121
  'Major Nunn's campaign', 32-4, 196-7
  Maria, 101
  Myall Creek massacre, 34-42, 44
  'Port Macquarie murders', 45, 157, 165
  Rufus Creek, 25
  Slaughterhouse Creek, 33, 60
  Slaughterhouse Gully, 34n
  Stirling Castle, 99-101
  Vinegar Hill,
  Wannon River, 191-2
  Waterloo Plains, 29
  See also 26n
Mayne, Edward, 43, 46, 59, 186, 197
Medical treatment of Aborigines, 210, 212
Mendicancy, Aboriginal, 6-8, 12, 13, 14
Mercer, George, 123, 124
Merivale, Herman, 212-13
Merri Creek, 122
Meyrick, Henry, 27-8, 175, 197
Miles, W. A., 74, 75n
Miscegenation, 8, 19, 30, 52-5, 70, 90-1, 126-7, 178, 191, 205
Missions and missionaries, 17, 20, 52, 63n, 64-5, 68, 72, 74, 75, 76, 77, 78, 83, 87, 109, 116, 184-5, 190, 202, 203-5, 206-7, 208-9.

See also Church Missionary Society; Flinders Island Aboriginal Establishment; London Missionary Society; Society in Aid of the German Mission; Wesleyan Missionary Society
Mitchell, Sir Thomas, 17, 19, 21-3, 25, 28n, 31n, 32n, 51, 57, 87, 119-121, 135-6, 178, 181, 184
Mixed-bloods *see* Part-Aborigines
Monaro, 17, 21
Monitor, The, 49, 161, 166
Montagu, John, 199
Mooney River, 48
Moreton Bay, 52, 65, 78, 99, 183n, 101, 204
Morning Chronicle, The, 166, 173, 182, 208-9
Motte, Standish, 134, 180n
Mount Harris line, 183, 184
Mounted Police, 14-15, 26, 32-4, 111n, 112, 114
Murral case *see* Murral, Jack Congo
Murral, Jack Congo, 118-19, 194
Murray River, 50, 57, 58
Murrumbidgee River, 27, 50, 51, 57, 58
Myall Creek massacre, 34-42, 44. *See also* Myall Creek trials
Myall Creek station, 35-6, 37, 38, 39-40, 41-2, 145
Myall Creek trials, 145-161
  first trial, 147-9
  final judgment, 153-6
  Gipps' reactions, 158-9, 160-1, 199
  impact on
    enforcement of law, 162, 191-2
    Evangelicals, 162-6
    popular opinion, 149, 159, 199
    race relations, 161-2
  part played by
    Plunkett, 148, 150-1, 152-3, 156, 160-1
    the squatting interest, 147, 149-50
    The Sydney Herald, 147-8, 151, 152, 157
  release of four accused, 160-1
  second trial, 151-6

Namoi River, 29, 32, 47, 51, 177
Native Institution, 63, 64, 65, 84, 109, 124

Native Police, 26, 48, 67-8, 214
Negroes, 36n, 57, 58n, 122n, 140-1
Newcastle, 6, 20, 101, 112, 114, 203
New England, 25, 48, 186
New South Wales Corps, 33
New Zealand see Maoris
Nicholson, Dr Charles, 73
Normanby, Lord, 138
Nunn, Major J. W., 32-4, 45, 139, 177-8

Oakes, Henry, 186-7
Oldfield, Dr Roger, 5-8, 11
Oldrey, Captain William, 210, 212
Oral tradition see Payne, Len; Wall, Cecil
Orton, Rev. Joseph, 65, 76-7
Osbrey, T., 193
Overlanders, 24, 57-8
Oxley, John, 28

Parker, Edward, 16-17, 201
Parkes, Henry, 164-5
Parramatta 'feast', 5, 17, 111, 118, 124-5
Part-Aborigines, 8, 53, 90-1, 191
Passionist Fathers, 65, 207
Paterson, Alexander, 31, 178
Payne, Len, 35n, 38n, 39n, 43n, 44n, 146n
Phillip, Sir Arthur, 17, 104-5, 170
Phrenology, 85-93
Plunkett, J. H., 121n, 147, 148, 192, 203
Poisoning of Aborigines, 48-9, 162
Polding, Bishop J. B., 65, 73, 206-8, 211
Police, 9, 15. See also Border Police; Mounted Police; Native Police
Pomare, Queen, 209
Port Fairy, 26, 49, 50, 193
Port Macquarie, 56, 157
Port Phillip Aboriginal Protectorate, 3, 49-50, 136-8, 142, 166, 169, 185, 198-203, 201-2
Port Phillip Association, 69n, 70, 122
Port Phillip Gazette, 13, 14, 15, 179
Port Stephens, 19, 114-15
Portland, Duke of, 105-6
Portland Bay, 16, 23-4, 25, 54
Prichard, Dr James Cowles, 85n
Prostitution, 8, 52-5
Protection of Aborigines see Segregation, principle of

Protectorate see Port Phillip Aboriginal Protectorate
Protectors see Dredge, James; Parker, Edward; Robinson, G. A.; Sievewright, C. W.; Thomas, William
Punitive expeditions see Massacres

Quakers, 8-9, 130, 134, 180n, 204

'Reid's Mistake', 116
Rice, T. Spring, 118
Robinson, G. A., 13, 14, 136, 142, 165, 193, 198, 199, 200, 202, 203
Roman Catholic Church, 205-9
Rufus Creek, 25
Rusden, Thomas, 24-5
Russell, Lord John, 138, 139, 169, 185, 189, 191, 195
Russell, John, 36-9, 149

Sadleir, Richard, 63n, 117, 118
Saunders, Rev. John, 93, 165, 166, 208
Schmidt, Rev. Wilhelm, 52
Scott, Archdeacon T. H., 65, 117-18
Scott, Robert, 29, 30, 80, 81, 82, 147, 160
Secretary of State for Colonies see Bathurst, Lord; Glenelg, Lord; Hobart, Lord; Normanby, Lord; Portland, Duke of; Russell, Lord John; Stanley, Lord
Sectarianism, 205-9
Segregation, principle of, 63-70, 110 see also 'Attachment', policy of; Exclusion of Aborigines
Severn River, 48
Sewell, George, 153, 159
Shelley, Rev. William, 63n, 109
Shelley, Mrs, 63n, 91, 109
Sievewright, C. W., 50, 86n, 185, 192, 201, 202-3
Smith, F., 193
Snodgrass, Colonel Kenneth, 30, 32
Society for the Propagation of Christian Knowledge Among the Aborigines, 84
Society in Aid of the German Mission, 77, 166
South America, 163, 166, 205
South Australia, 135

Spurzheim, Gaspard, 86
Squatting interest
  agitation for Asian labour, 139, 189, 190
  attitudes to
    Aboriginal evidence, 160, 180-2
    Aboriginal labour, 189-90
    Aboriginal land rights, 169-174
    missions, 83, 185, 202
    Port Phillip Protectorate, 49-50, 201-2
  concern over squatting tenure, 169, 183-4
  petitions to government, 29, 48-9, 112, 143-5, 183
  reactions to Myall Creek, 48-9, 147, 151, 161-2
Stanley, Lord, 138-9, 194, 204, 213
Steele, Rev. Dr Robert, 207
Stephen, James, 134, 135, 139, 189
Stephen, Sidney, 118-19
Stirling Castle, wreck of, 99-101, 102
Stradbroke Island, 65, 207
Strzelecki, P. de, 51, 79-80, 91n
Sturt, Charles, 96, 97
Supreme Court, New South Wales, 118-19, 148-156, 183, 194
Sydney Gazette, 9, 38n, 45, 119, 156, 157, 159, 161
Sydney Herald, The, 93, 148, 150-1, 152, 156, 157-8, 159-60, 161, 165, 170, 179, 200, 201-2
Sydney Mechanics' School of Arts, 87, 88
Sydney Morning Herald, The, 47, 88, 212

Tasmania see Van Diemen's Land
Therry, Rev. J. J., 205
Thomas, William, 14n, 16, 189-90, 213
Thomson, Dr Alexander, 185, 194-5, 204-5
Thomson, Deas, 15, 56, 120, 192, 199-200, 203, 207
Threlkeld, Joseph, 44, 45
Threlkeld, Rev. L. E., 17, 41n, 43, 44-6, 52-3, 56, 60, 75, 78, 86-7, 92, 113, 114, 116, 118, 190, 199n, 203-4, 208, 213
Throsby, Captain Charles, 64
Treaties with Aborigines, 122-4, 132, 168

Tuckfield, Rev. Francis, 73
Twofold Bay, 21, 102
Tyerman, Rev. Daniel, 116

Ussher, Bishop, 74

Van Diemen's Land, 55-6, 65, 66, 127, 129, 130, 198, 199-200
Vattel, Emerich de, 171
Venereal disease, 21, 54-5, 78
Villiers, C. L. J. de, 68

Wages, Aboriginal, 21, 72, 190-1, 214. See also Employment of Aborigines
Walker, Rev. William, 64-5, 74
Wall, Cecil, 39n
Wallace, Dr F. L., 88, 91
Wannon River, 23, 191
Warialda, 48
Watson, Rev. William, 72, 126n, 184-5, 204
Wedge, J. H., 70-1, 122n
Weekly Register, The, 102-3, 166, 182
Wellington Valley mission, 20, 65, 72, 75, 77, 78, 83, 184-5, 204
Wentworth, W. C., 178-9
Wesleyan Missionary Society, 64, 65, 74, 116, 202
Western Australia, 180n
Westernport, 70, 83, 193, 213
Westgarth, William, 79
Wheeler, Daniel, 8-9
White Australia, 139
Whyte brothers, 191-2
Wild white men, 31n, 69
Willis, Judge W. W., 193, 194
Windeyer, Richard, 147, 172-3, 180-1, 212-13
Windsor, 105, 118, 164
Women, Aboriginal
  cohabitation with whites, 8, 30, 36, 52-5, 70, 90-1, 126-7, 178, 191, 205
  conflicts over, 24-5, 30, 53-5, 95-6
  depopulation, 213
  employment, 19-20
  'kidnapping', 52-4, 126-7
  massacres, 38-9, 44, 45, 61, 197
  status, 55
  white attitudes to, 90-1, 95-6
Wright, Judith, 58

Young, Rev. Peter, 206, 207